Articulate While Black

Articulate While Black

BARACK OBAMA, LANGUAGE, AND RACE IN THE U.S.

H. SAMY ALIM

and

GENEVA SMITHERMAN

FOREWORD BY MICHAEL ERIC DYSON

OXFORD
UNIVERSITY PRESS

OXFORD
UNIVERSITY PRESS

Oxford University Press is a department of the University of Oxford.
It furthers the University's objective of excellence in research, scholarship,
and education by publishing worldwide.

Oxford   New York
Auckland   Cape Town   Dar es Salaam   Hong Kong   Karachi
Kuala Lumpur   Madrid   Melbourne   Mexico City   Nairobi
New Delhi   Shanghai   Taipei   Toronto

With offices in
Argentina   Austria   Brazil   Chile   Czech Republic   France   Greece
Guatemala   Hungary   Italy   Japan   Poland   Portugal   Singapore
South Korea   Switzerland   Thailand   Turkey   Ukraine   Vietnam

Oxford is a registered trademark of Oxford University Press
in the UK and certain other countries.

Published in the United States of America by
Oxford University Press
198 Madison Avenue, New York, NY 10016

© Oxford University Press 2012

Library of Congress Cataloging-in-Publication Data
Alim, H. Samy.
Articulate while Black : Barack Obama, language, and race in the U.S. /
H. Samy Alim & Geneva Smitherman ; foreword by Michael Eric Dyson.
p. cm.
Includes bibliographical references and index.
ISBN 978-0-19-981296-7 (alk. paper) – ISBN 978-0-19-981298-1 (pbk. : alk. paper)
1.   Black English–United States.   2. Race awareness–United States.
3. Obama, Barack–Language.   4. Obama, Barack–Oratory.
5. African Americans–Languages.   6. English language–Social
aspects–United States. 7.   Language and education–United States.
8. Sociolinguistics–United States.   I. Smitherman, Geneva   II. Title.
PE3102.N42A43 2012
306.440973–dc23
2012010289

ISBN 978-0-19-981296-7
ISBN 978-0-19-981298-1

9 8 7 6 5 4 3 2 1
Printed in the United States of America
on acid-free paper

None of us—black, white, Latino, or Asian—is immune to the stereotypes that our culture continues to feed us, especially stereotypes about black criminality, black intelligence, or the black work ethic. In general, members of every minority group continue to be measured largely by the degree of our assimilation— how closely speech patterns, dress, or demeanor conform to the dominant white culture—and the more that a minority strays from these external markers, the more he or she is subject to negative assumptions.

—Barack Obama

Every conversation about black speech is a conversation about black intelligence and ultimately black humanity.

—Michael Eric Dyson

CONTENTS

Foreword: Orator-In-Chief

I chuckled in amusement in the Spring of 2012 as President Obama regaled the audience with his humor in what has to be one of the most enjoyable roles for the commander-in-chief: standup comedian at the annual dinner for the White House Correspondents' Association. Obama's pace and timing were a lot better than those of the professional comics charged with bringing down the house that night. Jimmy Kimmel rushed through his jokes a bit too nervously and even stepped on some of his lines. Obama, on the other hand, was smooth and effortless, confident that his zingers would find their mark. His swag quotient was also pretty high that night. He let it be known that his musical prowess consisted of more than a melodically accurate one-off rendition of a line from Al Green's R&B classic "Let's Stay Together," which he had delivered at an Apollo Theater fundraiser three months earlier. Obama's version of the soul legend's tune went viral in Black communities as a sign of the president's effortless embrace of Black Culture despite the criticism that he keeps Blackness at bay. At the Apollo fundraiser, after drawing huge applause from his largely Black audience, Obama addressed the Rev. Al Green, who, along with India Arie, had sung at the affair, by saying: "Don't worry Rev., I cannot sing like you, but I just wanted to show my appreciation." At the Correspondents' dinner, Obama showed his appreciation for Hip Hop and proved his Rap bona fides, and not just by citing the easy or apparent fare. To truly strut his stuff, he'd have to display an aficionado's grasp of Rap Culture's range and appeal and flash a little insider savvy.

The set-up for Obama's Hip Hop coolness was a perfect storm of conspiracy theory and Black cultural signification. "Now, if I do win a second term as president," Obama teased his audience, "let me just say something to all my conspiracy oriented friends on the right who think I'm planning to unleash some secret agenda." He paused for a few seconds, then hit them with the affirmation of the right's worst nightmare: "You're absolutely right!" Obama had a mischievous look on his face and lowered his voice in a faux ominous fashion to clinch the conspiratorial conceit. "So allow me to close with a quick preview of the secret agenda you can expect in a second Obama Administration. In my first term I sang Al Green," the president deadpanned in drawing a contrast between his unfinished first term and his hoped-for follow up. "In my second term, I'm goin' with Young Jeezy!" He accented the second syllable of Jeezy and stretched it out a bit in dialectal deference to Black street pronunciation, so that it sounded like Gee-zeeee. The audience roared its approval of his self-confident reference to his Harlem debut, as much out of the desire to be hip right along with him as to reward his surefooted grasp of Hip Hop Culture. To drive home his hipness even more, he ad libbed a line that garnered a nod of approval from his adoring wife, whose approval ratings, the president noted that night, are higher than his. To be sure, it was in part the politics of romance, but there was a deeper story to his playfulness. Turning to First Lady Michelle Obama as she smiled broadly and signaled her affirmation at the head table, Obama humorously exclaimed, "Michelle said, 'Yeahhh!'" After the laughter rippled across the room, Obama bragged, "I sing that to her sometime." Michelle Obama bent her head and blushed at the public confession of private affection. President Obama flashed his famous pearls for the crowd in the hotel and across the globe.

Obama's gesture dripped with meaning. It was more than a fetching moment of affection between him and his wife played out for the world to see, an inside joke inside the joke. (Let's not forget that not all such inside knowledge was gleefully accepted. During the '08 campaign, their infamous "fist-bump," a love-tap of camaraderie and an affectionate gesture of "We're in this thing together babe," made the cover of the well-heeled *New Yorker* magazine and earned the enmity of even the limousine liberal set as a sign of some kind of kinky Black—and for some terrorist—code). This may have been an even more veiled message to Hip Hop's constituency in the hood that America's first Black president, despite the claims otherwise, hadn't really forgotten about them or their needs. Even though he was joking, the first thing Obama suggested about his Administration's second term was an explicit embrace of Hip Hop by the commander in chief. The humor couldn't ultimately dim the spotlight Obama gave to the culture.

Obama's reference to Young Jeezy carried even more weight. Jeezy was not simply a protégé of Obama favorite Jay-Z, but he was the rapper who famously touted Black pride during unofficial Inauguration ceremonies with his anthem "My President is Black," a tune he originally recorded with rapper Nas six months before Obama's election. Given the racial lay of the land, Obama could hardly embrace all of Jeezy's sentiment without blowback and complication. (After the national tragedy of Trayvon Martin's death in 2012, Obama couldn't even say that if he had a son, he'd look like Martin, without the bellicose and belligerent rhetoric of the right wing bellowing forth). In a harmless context where even plausible deniability seemed unnecessary, Obama returned the favor to Jeezy. It was if to say, "Yeah, beyond narrow views of race and Blackness, and beyond the hate of the ignorant, your president *is* black." The president didn't have to *think* that for the president to *mean* that. Such is the nature of Black signifying, such is the nature of political speech, such is the nature of Black rhetoric—and such is the nature of the oral traditions of Blackness that often invisibly ramify in a culture where there's always a grammatical ram in the linguistic bush.

The beautiful thing about *Articulate While Black* is that it breaks down Obama's speech making and oral signifying, and his talkin and testifyin and a lot more besides with far greater skill, depth, and insight than I've shown here. This book is an erudite primer on the protocol and etiquette of Black rhetoric, its rules and regulations, its sites and sounds, its gloriously labyrinthine and infinitely interpretable practices, its complicated meanings, its bedazzling variety and undulating cadences, and its cerebral intensifications and interruptions along the borders of what's seen as linguistically "proper" and "standard." In the process, Alim and Smitherman leave little doubt about the cogency of their argument: that without being a past master of Black (American) rhetoric, Obama wouldn't be president of the United States of America.

To say that he spoke his way into office is not to reduce Obama's achievement to his ability to speak "proper" or "standard" English. It's a lot more complicated than that. Language is as big as politics, as large as the geography that encompasses the American populace and the demography that dots the national landscape. Obama's achievement, likewise, is bigger than adding up the parts of speech he uses. It's also about understanding the cultural traditions that feed and shape his linguistic appetites. It's about knowing the racial practices against which that speech is pitched. It's about engaging the racial environments in which speech is formed. It's about knowing how Black speech is always much more than about *what* things are said, but about *how* those things are said. And how those things are said involves, of course, the mechanics of grammar, the intonations, the pace, the cadence, and the flow of Black rhetoric, but it includes as well the political and social realities that weigh on the tongue as mightily as the local dialects and accents that mingle in the mouths of citizens.

How Black folk are heard makes a big difference in how Black folk are perceived. Beliefs about Black folk invariably get focused on what we're talking about, and how we're talking about it, and all of that is seen as an index of our intelligence and humanity, or our stupidity and savagery. Sure, language means that for other folk too, just not as intensely, or with as much weight as for Black folk, at least here in the United States. Our social horizons widen or narrow through words that flow from our mouths; our destinies are shaped by how those words are heard in the ears of those with the power to make decisions about our existence.

That's why Obama is unavoidably representative of Blackness beyond what he says about his, or our, Blackness. *How* he speaks is talking too, beyond the substance, or at least the content, of his speech. His style of speech is a substance of sorts too, perhaps not as independent of the political machinations into which it pours as some might hope or believe, but a substance that must be grappled with nonetheless. Too many folk make the mistake of believing that Black style is a substitute for substance, something set in opposition to substance, when in truth it's a vehicle for substance. Black style is a substantial indent on the national psyche that houses, and helps to form, its expression at any given time and place. Whether in Bahia or Brooklyn, or in Milan or Michigan, the accents of Black speech are about more than the accents of Black people; they're also about the accidents of identity and history and the particular marks that Black folk leave on language and culture. Our Blackness accents both sentences on the page and sentences in the pen – filled with black ink or Black flesh. The line between linguistic and political practice can't even be separated in how we might imagine our imprisonment in the words spoken of us or by us. Our Blackness is linguistic and political practice rolled into one.

The paradox is that even the most powerful (Black) man in the world can't escape how Black speech is heard and read. That signals the democracy of language when it refers to Black folk. Death may be the great equalizer, but language is a close second. No matter how high Obama ascends, he's brought back down to the inescapable fact of his Blackness and the way he speaks it fluently in contexts not used to hearing Blackness as much as they are used to exploiting it. No matter what folk think of Black Language and its rudiments and permutations, when they hear it spill from Obama's mouth, they hear it invade their televisions and radios; they also hear it filter through their politics, infiltrate their legislative bodies, and get fidgeted over and exasperatingly parsed by the Supreme Court. Obama's Black speech has now become America's way of speaking and being heard by the world. That's why there's such resistance to Obama's policies—those policies are rooted in Black speech. There's a lot of resistance to the uppity character of Black speech not knowing its linguistic place, no matter how it is shorn of "Negro dialect," as Senator Harry Reid memorably phrased it.

The Tea Party and the Birthers despise Obama so much that they want to banish him from Americanness. They want metaphoric sovereignty, well perhaps, they really want the sovereignty of metaphor, over Obama's body: they want to unbirth his existence, uproot him from American soil, foreclose against his house of American identity and offer him a sub-prime loan of American political capital. The big problem is that Obama has set the terms, symbolically, and sometimes literally, for how America behaves (mind you, that's not a small problem for progressives who accuse him of rubberstamping imperialist agendas), and thus they must challenge his legitimacy to act in such an authoritative fashion. But Obama has to bail *them* out – financially and linguistically! Despite the claim of the right wing that it's pro-life, it wants to retroactively abort Obama's existence, purge him from the record as unofficial and illegitimate, remove his legislation from the books and repeal "Obamacare," and wipe the slate clean of his political speech. Wiping away his political words also means wiping away his cultural and racial words, the way his body and mouth have left their marks all over America. Obama not only politically beat his opponents (and not a few of his ideological "allies"), but he beat them culturally. He not only licked his opponents with his politics, but he licked them with his tongue. The thought is just too ugly for most of them to abide.

Articulate While Black brilliantly dissects the politics of language as embedded in the politics of race, and the politics of race as tied to the politics of language. It helps us understand just what Obama is saying because the authors understand so well what Black folk are saying, and how we say it, and thus, they help the nation to put what Obama is saying in a broader, Blacker context. That Blackness is not limiting but freeing; not closed but open; not rigid but fluid. Obama fits along a continuum of Black expression, and depending on the circumstance or condition, slides easily from one end to the other, from vernacular to "proper" expression, from formal to informal, from high-tone to gutter-dense, from specifying to signifying in the blink of an "I." The authors show how that "I" is not the beginning of isolation, but the start of a new quest of identity joined to the long pilgrimage of identity that borrows from centuries of speaking and existing. In the process, a lot of switches are being flipped: codes, styles, media, frames, cultures, and races. In fact, Alim and Smitherman do a great deal of switching themselves, sliding from dense academic prose to streetwise vernacular at the drop of a hat, proving they are brilliant examples of the very practice they dissect.

Alim and Smitherman are supremely capable of explaining Black speech and Obama's place in the Black rhetorical and linguistic universe. Smitherman is a word warrior and ancestral diviner whose pioneering examination of Black discourse has helped us to understand and accept the Blackness of our speech without excuse or apology. Her vibrant prose has sung the story of our linguistic adventures into self-definition and self-knowledge for more than a generation, and her elegant depositions in the court of public reason as a witness to our struggle for self-expression on the front lines of linguistic battle are both legion and legendary. Alim has raised the stakes of ethnographic examinations of Black rhetoric. His critical work has shed valuable light on the rhetorical practices of young Black folk whose speech in urban cultural settings has yet to be honored for its immense contribution to American rhetoric. His brilliant reflections on Hip Hop Culture provide a powerful example of rigorous academic investigation linked to a savvy street-based understanding of the culture and its rhetorical innovations. His important examinations of linguistic profiling, and his valiant insistence that teachers fully grapple with Black speech in the classroom, are crucial resources for experts and laypeople alike.

Alim and Smitherman help us to comprehend the complexity of Black articulateness in both senses: they help us to unpack the adjectival character of the word, to be *articulate* while Black, and they help us to understand the word as a verb, to learn how we *articulate* while Black. *Articulate While Black* brings what Obama says, and how he says it, into sharper view and helps us to navigate the complexities of Black linguistic habits and the complications of Black rhetoric writ large.

And perhaps most pressing on the pop cultural front, they challenge seventies Scottish blue-eyed soul group Average White Band for the most creative use of the acronym AWB. The group's biggest hit single was 1974's "Pick Up the Pieces," and its B-side was "Work to Do." In these song titles, Alim and Smitherman's AWB, and the rest of us too, find powerful objectives: to pick up the pieces of Black linguistic practice and show how the shards of Black speech, and the fragments of Black rhetoric, are broken off from cultural traditions and racial practices to which they must be connected in order to be understood. And we all have work to do in understanding, explaining and enjoying the richness of Black Language as it flows not only from the mouth of our First Orator, but as it sings in the throats of millions of Black folk the world over who have little idea of the brilliance and beauty in their tongues. I'm glad to join their band and to play my part in amplifying their mighty music.

Michael Eric Dyson
University Professor of Sociology
Georgetown University
June 2012

Showin Love

Alim

I'll never forget the day that big care package came to me in the mail more than fifteen years ago. There I was, an undergraduate student at the University of Pennsylvania—being schooled by the likes of Farah Jasmine Griffin, Ira Harkavy, William Labov, James Peterson, and James Spady (both Jameses had introduced me to Docta G's classic *Talkin and Testifyin: The Language of Black America*)—sittin on the floor of my dorm room, tearin through that package as quickly as I could! I had sent Geneva Smitherman my senior honors thesis on Black Language, and she responded! I was blown away by her generosity of spirit—in that package were numerous articles and copies of her books, including her latest at the time, *Black Talk: Words and Phrases from the Hood to the Amen Corner* (hardcover too!). What I'll most remember about that package was the inscription: "Stay on the case. We need your work." It's difficult to describe all that those few words meant to me. The "we" made me feel like I could become a member of a strong community of scholars, and the fact that anyone would "need" scholarly work was a sign that academic scholarship can and should be marshaled for the purposes of social justice.

Over the last decade and a half—whenever I may have gotten weary of the academic enterprise—G's words stayed with me and kept me goin. Since then, we have worked together in multiple capacities and developed a strong, nurturing relationship. So, for me, the first person I gotta show love to is Docta G, a.k.a. Geneva Smitherman. G, I would tell you that the opportunity to coauthor this book with you is like a dream come true, but you already know.... Thanks for being my conscience and a true guiding light for more than two generations of scholars.... Much love and much respect, now and always.

Gracias también a toda mi familia de Nayarit. Les dedico este libro a ustedes con mucho amor, cariño y respeto. Muchísimas gracias a todos ustedes por su apoyo y por quererme sin condiciones. Un abrazo fuerte.

G

Much love and respect to you, too, L.T. (a.k.a. Alim), my brilliant, creative friend and coauthor, who was blessed with the vision for this work. Also gotta show some love to my Midwest Fam—Austin Jackson, Kyle Mays, Jeff Robinson, and AJ Rice. Thanks so much for the technical support, for sharing yall knowledge, and especially for all dem late night intellectual battles! Last, but mos def not least, sendin special love to my son, Tony Smitherman, and my grands, Anthony and Amber Smitherman for bein there when I need yall.

Alim and G

In writing this book, we also benefited from the work of a growing critical mass of language scholars working on race and ethnicity. We thank all of the scholars who participated in these two conferences: UCLA's "Race & Ethnicity in Language, Interaction & Culture," where we delivered the earliest ideas on Barack Obama, language, and race (co-organized by H. Samy Alim and Candy Goodwin with the Center for Language, Interaction & Culture in 2009) and Stanford's "Racing Language, Languaging Race" (co-organized by H. Samy Alim, John R. Rickford, and Arnetha F. Ball with the Center for Race, Ethnicity, and Language in 2012). Together, we are coming to a new understanding that language varieties are not just lists of features that belong to a given race; rather linguistic features can be employed by speakers as they shape their identities or, more accurately, engage in processes and projects of identification. President Barack Obama's use of Black Language, for example, is very much a conscious racial project or, at the very least, a result of secondary language socialization (becoming an adult in a Black community). In the same way that the President selected "Black" on the US Census to mark his racial identity, he also selects particular linguistic resources to be employed in the multifaceted racial project of "becoming Black." And as we show later in the book from Rush Limbaugh's harping on *ask* versus *aks*, his language is sometimes still racialized as "Black," even when he doesn't use features typically associated with Black Language.

We have also benefited from sociolinguistic and linguistic anthropological work on the relationships between race, ethnicity, and language—from folks like Mary Bucholtz, Elaine Chun, Jane Hill, Paul Kroskrity, Rosina Lippi-Green, Adrienne Lo, Norma Mendoza-Denton, Angela Reyes, Jonathan Rosa, Jennifer Roth-Gordon, Bonnie Urciuoli, and Ana Celia Zentella, among others. In particular, we also benefited from the brilliant insights and constant support of a whole crew of Black scholars of language, all of whom have taken the sociolinguistic analysis of Black Language to new heights: John Baugh, Renee Blake, Jennifer Bloomquist, Charles DeBose, Keith Gilyard, Lisa Green, Lanita Jacobs, Sonja Lanehart, Marcyliena Morgan, Django Paris, Elaine Richardson, and Arthur Spears, among others. And of course, a big shout out to our homie, John R. Rickford (Co-director of the Center for Race, Ethnicity, and Language at Stanford), whose work has long inspired us and who we thank in particular for his close reading of the manuscript. To all: We need yall work! Keep it comin...

In addition to the language folks, we've also leaned on the insights of another group of scholars—the whole cadre of new (and some not so new, hey now) Black intellectuals who are steadfast in their commitment to raise the level of the discourse on race in America: Ta-Nehisi Coates, William Jelani Cobb, Davey D, Michael Eric Dyson (special thanks for lacing us with that brilliant foreword!), dream hampton, Melissa Harris-Perry, Marc Lamont Hill, Jay-Z, Bakari Kitwana, Joan Morgan, Nas, Mark Anthony Neal, Imani Perry, James Peterson, Mark Sawyer, Tracy Denean Sharpley-Whiting, James Spady, and Cornel West, among many others. You have all, through your work and inspiration, impacted this book.

For Alim, many colleagues at Stanford University have been helpful during the writing of this book, especially those in African and African American Studies (AAAS), the Center for Comparative Studies of Race and Ethnicity (CCSRE), and the departments of Anthropology and Linguistics. And, of course, Alim is grateful for the support offered by Dean Claude Steele and colleagues in the School of Education, particularly those affiliated with the new Race, Inequality, and Language in Education (RILE) program. This work has also greatly benefited from many critical conversations with the homie and Executive Director of the Institute for Diversity in the Arts (IDA), Jeff Chang (Can't wait to read your next book, *Who We Be*!), Program Administrator Ellen Oh, the "IDA RIDAS," and all of da bomb students in "Race, Ethnicity, and Language," and "Hip Hop, Youth Identities, and the Politics of Language."

Lastly, there are two people who deserve stupid, phat shoutouts for their critical readings of early, in-progress drafts of this manuscript. First, Kate Geenberg, who suffered through many conversations with Alim and read very drafty chapters with the closeness and criticality matched only by a few senior scholars in this game. (We talkin on some Bucholtzian-type level of close reading!) Kate, despite the demands of your own research agenda, you somehow managed to be critical reader, editor, and research assistant all in one! Thanks for pushing us on so many levels. Second, to Dee, thanks for printing, reading, commenting, and discussing/dee-bating many critical points as these chapters were being written. And for always being there to lend a ear—and a heart—to every situation. Thank you for bein a frieeeeeend. Much love.

Lastly—forreal this time—in *Articulate While Black*, we've integrated three bodies of knowledge on language and identity, Black Language, and race in an effort to *language race*, to view the racial politics of the United States through the lens of language. We've taken Barack Obama as both our subject and our point of departure at this critical moment in American history. At the start, we were faced with many questions: How does the language use of a very public figure—the POTUS—impact our understandings of Black Language, race, and ethnicity in the United States? Given Black Language's marginalized status in dominant culture, what are the social and cultural implications of the United States having its first Black Language–speaking president (not to mention one that can get that dirt off his shoulder like Jay-Z, give his wife a Pound, and croon like the oh-so-smooth Al Green)? How would looking at the language of Barack Obama help us understand why major debates about language, race, and education erupt into moments of racial crisis in America—from the *Martin Luther King Junior Elementary School Children v. Ann Arbor School District Board* (the "Black English" case) to the Oakland "Ebonics" controversy, to racial gaffes and blunders (from many Republicans *and* Democrats), to even well-intentioned compliments about President Obama's "articulateness"? Rather than being in constant crisis mode, how can we think differently—more critically—about the relationships between language, race, and power in American society?

President Obama's race, together with his use of language, often evokes a volatile mixture of emotions, inciting an enormous amount of media discourse. But as we roll into the 2012 elections, we need more than a quantitative increase in our "race talk." We need clarity. It is our view that linguists are uniquely positioned to push and to problematize how we think and talk about race. On that measure, we hope we have achieved some modicum of success.

P.E.A.C.E.

Alim & G

1

"Nah, We Straight"

Black Language and
America's First Black President

[Barack Obama] speaks with no Negro dialect, unless he
wants to have one.[1]
—Harry Reid

You go to the cafeteria...and the black kids are sitting
here, white kids are sitting there, and you've got to make
some choices. For me, basically I could run with anybody.
Luckily for me, largely because of growing up in Hawai'i,
there wasn't that sense of sharp divisions. Now, by the
time I was negotiating environments where there were
those kinds of sharp divisions, I was already confident
enough to make my own decisions. It became a matter of
being able to speak different dialects. That's not unique
to me. Any black person in America who's successful has
to be able to speak several different forms of the same
language....It's not unlike a person shifting between
Spanish and English.[2]
—Barack Obama

I still get goose bumps thinking about it. It was that moving of an experience. I remember being in Miami on Memorial Day weekend in 2008, six
months before America elected its first Black president. It was hot, and for
anyone who's ever been to Miami, yeah, it was humid. The kind of humidity
that made you feel like you was swimmin instead of walkin. Some folks had
taken like three different buses just to get there. When the last bus finally
pulled up to the stadium, madd people rushed out. We waited for hours,
but it didn't matter. The air had that electrified feelin to it. Then, outta
nowhere, the afternoon thunder rolled in and dropped buckets of water on
thousands of people who had already been waitin outside for hours. Instead
of complainin, folks huddled under umbrellas with strangers, engaged in
political conversation, and broke out into chants of "Yes we can! Yes we

can!" Couldn't nu'in break our stride that day. Not even the rain. We were here to see Barack Obama for ourselves. We'd seen him on TV, heard him in interviews, and now it was our turn. As the doors to the stadium swung open, thousands of people packed the house, runnin for they seats like it was a Rick Ross concert or something!

Anyone who's ever been to an Obama rally remembers that excitement well. The energy of the 20,000 racially diverse folks gathered that day, screaming in a frenzy as Barack Obama was introduced, was unforgettable. He stood there at the podium for a good five minutes, unable to speak over the roar of the booming crowd. He just looked out and smiled—and folks went wild! He slowly moved to pick up the mic but couldn't find it. He searched the podium, as if deliberately building up the suspense, and the crowd went even wilder. Then Barack leaned back like he was Hip Hop artist Fat Joe ("lean back, lean back") and tilted his head all calm and cool-like into the podium to take a look. Finally, he picked up the mic, looked back out into the crowd, laughing, "But I ain't even say anything yet!" As the crowd went bananas, Barack worked the predominantly Black section in front. "Oh, the hardcore is over here in the front, huh?" [Crowd roars! Barack moves to the side] "Oh, no wait, the *real* hardcore is over here!" [Crowd is outta control by now, and it lasted for several minutes!] Caught up in the frenzy of the jam-packed arena, I thought to myself, "This guy is a legend in his own time...and *will* be our next president."

As a linguist, of course, I couldn't help but think about how Barack was using Black Language to connect with this racially diverse crowd. It struck me that, for the first time, despite all the hootin and hollerin about Bill Clinton being our first "Black" president, America may have its first Black Language–speaking president. As the campaign marched on, folks from across the political spectrum began commenting on Barack's language, from linguist John McWhorter's playful use of "Blaccent" to Hip Hop icon Snoop Dogg's observation that Obama had "the right conversation." And as it was later revealed, Harry Reid's racialized comments about Barack Obama's language— that he "speaks no Negro dialect, unless he wants to have one"—gave us all pause. What *exactly* did that mean? As we (me and Geneva) talked about the many language-related moments of the campaign, the idea for this book was conceived. It occurred to us that, despite this being some Americans' most poignant "postracial" moment, there was much work to be done.

Languaging Race: Viewing Race through the Lens of Language

While numerous books on President Obama have focused on the racial politics of his presidency, none has examined these issues from a critical linguistic perspective. Notable works, such as William Jelani Cobb's *The Substance of Hope: Barack Obama and the Paradox of Progress* (2010) and Randall Kennedy's *The Persistence of the Color Line: The Racial Politics of the Obama Presidency* (2011), provide insightful historical and political analyses yet make only passing mention of language. In *Articulate While Black*, we complement these insights by viewing language as central to racial politics in the United States. This is especially important to us since, despite the constant monitoring and mocking of Black Language, we maintain that Barack Obama's mastery of Black cultural modes of discourse was crucial to his being elected America's forty-fourth president. For some obvious and not so obvious reasons, we argue that the "brotha with the funny name" (as some Black folks called him) wouldn't have gotten elected if he couldn't kick it in a way that was "familiarly Black."

In this book, we provide a much-needed contribution to discussions on race and Barack Obama by *languaging race*, that is, by examining the politics of race through the lens of language. Though language remains relatively unexamined by scholars of race and ethnicity, it plays a crucial role in the construction of racial and ethnic identities. As University of California, Santa Barbara professor of linguistics Mary Bucholtz notes in her *White Kids: Language, Race and Styles of Youth Identity*, "Language is often overlooked as an analytic concern in research on race, yet it is nonetheless central to how race is culturally understood."[3]

The same holds true for the nonacademic world. We have a far more developed conversation on race than on language. For example, whether we agreed or disagreed with Attorney General Eric Holder when he famously said that we are "a nation of cowards when it comes to race,"[4] we were able to engage the dialogue. But when was the last time you heard anyone say that we are a nation of cowards when it comes to language? Unlike race, we have no national public dialogue on language that recognizes it as a site of cultural struggle. In American public discourse, language is often overlooked as one of *the* most important cultural tools that we have for distinguishing ourselves from others. Language, no doubt, is a significant form of "symbolic power."[5] Yet its central role in positioning each of us and the groups that we belong to along the social hierarchy lies largely beneath the average American's consciousness.

Viewing race through the lens of language, *Articulate While Black: Barack Obama, Language, and Race in the U.S.* provides new insights about the relationships between language and racial politics in the Obama era. Throughout this book, we analyze several racially loaded cultural-linguistic controversies involving Barack Obama. In the process, we reveal and challenge American ideas about language, race, education, and power in order to help take the national dialogue on race to the next level. In much the same sense that Black philosopher and Union Theological Seminary professor Cornel West wrote that (and about) "race matters" nearly two decades ago, this book does the same for language.[6] By theorizing language and race together, we show how "language matters" to the national conversation on race.

Since language is one of the most salient yet least understood means we have for creating our identities, we open up with an exploration of the way Barack Obama uses language in his speeches, interviews, and everyday interactions. More than just providing a sociolinguistic perspective on Barack Obama's language use, though, we provide a sociolinguistic perspective on Black Language more generally. The linguistic perspective on Black Language varies drastically from the general public's perspective—just about everything you thought you knew (or "thought you thought," as the brothas out East useta say) about Black Language couldn't be further from the linguistic facts.[7]

"The Most Powerful Speaker of Our Age": The Obama Generation on Obama

Throughout our conversations with and surveys of Americans of the Obama generation (mostly 18–24, with a few in their early thirties), it became clear that he was extremely highly regarded as a speaker and communicator. As one respondent put it, Barack Obama is "the most powerful speaker of our age." The word used most frequently to describe Barack Obama's language and language use was *eloquent*. Folks also often remarked that he spoke "with conviction" and regularly used words like *confident* to describe his language. Beyond his eloquence and confidence, Barack came off as "poised," "composed," and "always in control of the situation." He struck listeners as being "highly educated" but "not in a way that patronizes his audience." To many, despite the Republican framing of him as "elite" and "too professorial," he was "able to communicate complicated ideas in a straightforward manner." He was often described as "clear," "direct," "down to earth" and also as "careful," "measured," and "deliberate." More than that, he was "inspiring," "empowering," and "motivating," and while using language to "build up a sense of community," he also managed to "speak as if speaking to individuals (as if he was speaking to me)."

Barack Obama struck a chord with this generation like no other presidential candidate. As one White respondent commented:

> Dignified yet humble, assertive yet calm/collected, stern yet compassionate, and formal while authentic, President Obama's language transcends the typical blandness of modern politicians (at least the old, white, male variety) and I believe that he is truly able to inspire hope and confidence through his speeches.

As compared with previous presidents, his language was described as "dynamic," "captivating," "intoxicating," and "rhythmic almost to the point of hypnosis." His speeches were seen as "vibrant, charismatic" and "replete with imagery," as "prose that flirts with the boundary of poetry." In short, Barack Obama was viewed as one helluva gifted orator, quite possibly the most effective and powerful that this generation has witnessed.

"Nah, We Straight": Styleshifting from Ben's Chili Bowl to Ray's Hell Burger

Our conversations and surveys further revealed that, in Barack Obama, America heard a speaker who was "strategic" and "hyperaware" of his audience. While being cognizant of your audience may come with the territory as far as politics go, what distinguished Obama was his successful stylistic performance. It's one thing to know that you gotta say "the right things" in terms of *content* but quite another to be able to say "the right things" in the right way in terms of *style*. Barack was seen as someone who could speak directly and comfortably with folks across regions, generations, socioeconomic divisions, racial and ethnic groups, and political and religious views.

Barack Obama's global family history, diverse life experiences, and socialization within multiple cultures within and beyond the United States, along with his biracial background, surely helped him hone his styleshifting skills.[8] At the beginning of this chapter, we quoted Obama's description of his experience as a young man of Color growing up in American schools as one where you had "to make some choices." In an American context, in which sharp racial divisions in friendship groups are still the order of the day, Barack had to learn to speak "several different forms of the same language." In much the same way that many bilingual/bicultural Americans *codeswitch* between two languages (English and Spanish, for example), many bilingual/bicultural Americans *styleshift*—move in and out of linguistic styles—between varieties of the same language (Puerto Rican English and White Mainstream English, for example).[9]

While Barack Obama's ability to styleshift is one of his most compelling and remarkable linguistic abilities, it is also par for the course for many Black Americans who travel in and out of Black and White social worlds and work environments. In fact, Black Americans in our conversations and surveys were more likely than Whites and others to note Obama's styleshifting abilities. Further, although many Americans clearly noted his linguistic flexibility, only non-Black Americans described Barack's language as static, or as "simply White English." One White respondent, speaking for all Americans, went so far as to say, "His language is seen as white across racial lines." Along the same lines, a self-described "Latina with Mexican immigrant parents" offered these observations:

> When Obama addresses other groups, specifically communities of color such as African-Americans, we would expect…the use of more casual language and a different pronunciation of words to be shown. Instead, he uses the same language style for this group as well. This is due to the fact that…he cannot code-switch between the dominant white-american language variety and the African-American one.

Another respondent, a self-identified "Hispanic & Caucasian Chicana," commented, "I've never heard him deviate from normative English."

Compare these observations to this Black woman's response from Philly, "President Obama's language is ever changing as a reflection of his environment and the racial or political composition of his audience." Black Americans, more than any other group, were most sensitive to Barack's styleshifting and offered more complex and layered descriptions of his linguistic steez (style). Black Americans not only noted the range and ability of Obama's styleshifting, many also distinguished between his language (grammatical structure) and his style (language use).[10] Or as one Chi-Town brotha put it: "Barack Obama may not sound 'black' in a transcription of his speeches, but he definitely sounds black over audio recordings." Let him explain:

> I think that I would describe President Obama's language and speech as Standard American English. Based off of my observations, there is nothing particular about the language that he uses that would separate him from the Standard American English model. However, I do feel that the *way* that he speaks is particularly African American. This refers more to his rhetoric, intonation, and style. However, his speech or the extent to which he plays up his Black manner of speaking varies depending on his setting. I feel that he possesses a good balance and mix between the two manners of speaking, and pulls it off successfully, where it doesn't seem unnatural for him. [emphasis in original]

A Black woman echoes these observations:

> If I had to describe Barack Obama's language in one word, I'd describe it as interesting.…He's able to tiptoe the line between Standard English and a semi-African American type of dialect. It's

not really African American in terms of the way he uses grammar (he doesn't use "be"...), but his mannerisms and his style of speech—the way he draws certain vowels out and some of the slang terms he uses—is somewhat characteristic of Black speech.

While these two respondents differed in terms of their view of the degree to which Barack Obama sounded "Black," both made critical distinctions between his language and his style. Both also noted that his grammar, for the most part, was pretty much "standard." By contrast, a sista from Cali makes observations about instances of Barack Obama using Black Language style as well as syntax. Noting both the range of Barack's styleshifting and distinguishing between his language and style, she notes that he reserves "the nonstandard grammatical structure" of Black Language for "settings that are primarily Black." She then offered an example of Barack's language from his visit to Ben's Chili Bowl, which she described as "a racially mixed, very informal location in the heart of D.C."

This now famous example was captured on YouTube.[11] In the clip, Barack Obama is seen interacting with a Black cashier. When offered his change, he declined with the statement, "Nah, we straight." While this may seem like a simple phrase, in these three words we have three different linguistic features that are aspects of Black Language.

(1) Barack Obama says "nah" rather than "no." This is a big deal for linguists for a number of reasons. Whereas the vowel in "no" is a diphthong, the vowel in "nah" is a low monophthong. In other words, the vowel sound in "no" is like the one in "note," whereas the vowel sound in "nah" is like the one in "not" (which is not to be confused with the way some White speakers may pronounce "nah" like the vowel sound in "gnat," or the way some southern speakers pronounce "naw" like the vowel sound in "gnaw"). All of this work on vowel sounds has actually led most linguists to consider "nah" a lexical variant of "no," meaning that it is a different way of saying the same thing but which might mark social difference. In this case, although "nah" is used to some extent by speakers throughout the United States, it is more often than not associated with the speech of Black folks.

Varying between lexical variants and different pronunciations are linguistic hallmarks of Barack Obama's styleshifting. For instance, in a South Carolina speech with a racially mixed audience, which we analyze later in this chapter, Barack says "wit mah Bahble" for "with my Bible." In this case, the diphthong in *my* and *Bible* was rendered as *ah*. (This phonological process is known as the monophthongization of diphthongs—say that shit five times fast).

(2) Despite some hilarious misinterpretations of the word *straight* (nah, he wasn't talkin bout his sexual orientation!), Barack Obama used the word in its Black, now-crossover youthful sense to mean he was "OK," "fine," "alright" with not getting his change back. Many observers have noted Barack Obama's use of Black slang in relation to Hip Hop Culture, using such words as *flow* or *tight*.[12] Other than its ever-evolving slang, the lexicon of Black Language is not as widely known outside the Black community. Barack Obama also uses words and phrases from this less widely known dimension of the Black Lexicon, which have survived for generations in the Black community, such as "trifling," "high-yella," "Tom/Uncle Tom," and "house nigger."[13]

(3) In addition to words, phrases, and pronunciation, the third Black linguistic feature in Barack's "Nah, we straight" is known as copula absence. The copula refers to *is* and *are* and other forms of the verb *to be*. Now, while this might be TMLI (too much linguistic information), this feature is actually one of the most important and frequently studied features of Black Language. Leading sociolinguist and Stanford University professor John R. Rickford once described the *copula* as Black Language's "showcase variable," because it is a feature that gives Black Language its distinctiveness, setting it apart from other varieties of American English.[14] In the twenty-first century, the Black Language copula has blown up all over the Black Twitterverse in TTs (trending topics) and hashtags such as #uknowuugly. While this has actually confused many non-Black tweeps, it can be rendered simply as: "You know you are ugly."[15] Non-Black tweeps sometimes call out this use of copula absence as a sign of "Black people's ignorant ways" or "their lazy, ungrammatical speech." Black tweeps, on the other hand, respond by noting that Twitter is all about being concise. Rather than "deficient," one could argue that copula absence is "efficient." (You only get 140 characters to say what you need to say!) Yet when Barack and other Black speakers use this form, it's actually rarely about efficiency and most definitely not about Black people's "lazy, ungrammatical speech." Contrary to popular opinion, Black Language actually has a more complex verbal system than any other White American variety of English. This is due mostly to its origins as a Creolized form of African and European language varieties.[16] Now, before explaining further, we warn you it's about to get real linguistic up in here. But, yo, these next five points are necessary, though, if we're gonna understand why breakin down Barack's linguistic steez is so important. Aight, here we go...

The first point is that while speakers of White American varieties of English only have two ways of representing the copula, speakers of Black Language have three. In Black Language, you can say all three of these, depending on the situation: (1) "We are straight," (2) "We're straight," or

(3) "We Ø straight." In White varieties of English, you are restricted to the first two forms. Black folks can shift between these three variants, all of which have the same literal meaning but differ in social meaning.

Speakers of Black Language don't just be leavin the copula out whenever they feel like it, though. The second point is that copula absence follows a very well-documented set of linguistic constraints. That means that you can't just decide to always use the zero copula form (as in "We Ø straight"). Take this example from a Black minister in San Francisco: "The Black Man Ø on the rise, and the White man, he Ø runnin scared now, because we Ø wide awake today and he know we Ø not just gon lay down and accept things as they are." While the copula can be absent before prepositional phrases and locatives ("The Black Man Ø on the rise"), progressive verbs ("he Ø runnin scared"), adjectives ("we Ø wide awake"), negatives, and the future marker *gon* ("we Ø not just gon lay down"), it cannot be absent when it is in sentence-final position ("as they are"). The copula can't be absent in the first-person singular form either. Like, if Barack had said something like, "Nah, I straight," that'd be a bad look cuz it's ungrammatical in the Black Language system.

Now if that wasn't complicated enough, the third point is that these linguistic constraints on copula use are also ordered such that the copula is more likely to be absent in decreasing order before *gon* ("She Ø gon do it"), a verb + *ing* ("She Ø doin it"), locatives ("She Ø at the bus stop"), adjectives ("She Ø happy"), and noun phrases ("She Ø the boss"). Fourth, copula absence also depends on phonological (pronunciation) constraints, such as if there's a vowel or a consonant before or after its use. Lastly, as shown in great detail in Alim's *You Know My Steez: An Ethnographic and Sociolinguistic Study of Styleshifting in a Black American Speech Community*, Black folks also shift their use of the copula in regularly patterned ways depending on the race, gender, and cultural knowledge of the person they're speaking to. For example, on the one hand, Black youth display high levels of copula absence in their peer groups and when talking with Black male Hip Hop heads. On the other, they are much more likely to use the copula (*is* or *are*) when speaking to White women who know nothing about Hip Hop. All of this is what linguistic experts mean when they say that Black Language is "rule-governed" and "systematic" like any other language variety (told y'all it wasn't nu'in simple about Barack's use of "Nah, we straight").

Now, if we compare Barack's language use in Ben's Chili Bowl with his language use in Ray's Hell Burger, we can get a really good sense of how Obama shifts styles. One of Obama's favorite spots, Ray's Hell Burger is located in Arlington, Virginia, and has a predominantly White clientele. In the nearly eight-minute clip of his appearance there, Obama's language is informal ("How're you doin, man?" "We'll check that out"), but he does not use features of Black Language.[17] Obama is seen, however, interacting briefly with a Latina employee, whom he winks at and says, "Hola," in a form better than el español típico de la mayoría de los gringos. His Spanish greeting was taken up by the employee who responded right away, "Hola!"

Revisiting Barack's Ben's Chili Bowl experience, we have generally the same speech situation (lunchtime at an informal restaurant), speech event (a service encounter between customer and employee), and speech act (ordering food).[18] We see Barack Obama in a crowded restaurant with a multiracial crowd in Washington, D.C. The interaction went down like this:

> BARACK: [Handing over his money to the cashier] You just keep that. Where's my ticket. You got my ticket?
> CASHIER: [Offers Barack his change]
> BARACK: Nah, we straight. [Reaching over to take his soda]
> CUSTOMER: You got cheese fries, too?
> BARACK: Nah, nah, that's you, man...
> [Video cuts away and returns after Barack receives his chili dog]
> BARACK: Now, do y'all have some Pepto Bismol in this place?
> ALL PRESENT: [Laughter]
> BARACK: [Walking back up to the counter, addressing cashier again] Hey, how come he's got some cheddar cheese on his and I don't have any on mine?
> ALL PRESENT: [Laughter] Woahhh!
> CASHIER: Whatever you like, sir.
> BARACK: We got some cheese, you can sprinkle on it? [Gesturing the sprinkling of cheese, then *signifyin*] Not, not, not, not the Velveeta but the...
> CUSTOMERS: [Laughter]
> CUSTOMER: The cheddar cheese!
> BARACK: The *cheddar* cheese.

In addition to the three main features we discussed in "Nah, we straight," we can see here that Barack's language is generally informal with phrases like "You got my ticket?" and "Nah, nah, that's you, man." We also see his use of other features of Black Language (and southern varieties of English), which folks often use in more casual environments. Barack's use of *y'all* ("Do y'all have some Pepto Bismol in this place?"), for example, is the preferred way to mark the second-person plural on such occasions.

In addition to Barack's language (grammatical structure), we can also look at his style (language use). The Pepto Bismol joke shows Barack's use of humor, which flows into a type of banter that many African Americans know well. In this case, Obama expresses his discontent about not getting cheese on his chili dog in a lighthearted and humorous example of signifyin.[19] "Not, not, not, not the Velveeta" is characteristic of a sometimes subtle mode of discourse in Black communication that includes acts such as snappin, bustin, crackin, playin the dozens or dissin someone through wit and humor. Here, the president of the United States wanted some real cheese, not that fake Velveeta stuff!

"As for Your Greasy-Mouthed Self": The Art of Signifyin and Talkin Trash

Other examples of Barack's signifyin abilities include his "roast" of Donald Trump at the White House correspondent's dinner in 2011. The roast included some classic signifyin that, although lighthearted and entertaining, was incredibly witty and cutting. In the weeks before the dinner, Donald Trump was all over the media championing the Birther Movement, insinuating that he'd make a run for president, and directing some pretty pointed questions at the president. Well, the president had some answers:

> Donald Trump is here tonight. Now I know that he's taken some flack lately, but no one is happier, no one is prouder to put this birth certificate matter to rest than Donald. And that's because he can [letting out a laugh under his breath] finally get back to focusing on the issues that matter, like, did we fake the moon-landing? [Crowd laughter] What really happened in Roswell? [Crowd Laughter] And where are Biggie and Tupac? [Big laughter and applause] All kidding aside, obviously we all know about [gesturing out towards Trump] your credentials and breadth of experience [Crowd laughter]...um, for example, um...[Donald Trump is shown uncomfortably scratching the side of his neck with his index finger]....No, seriously, just recently in an episode of *Celebrity Apprentice* [Crowd laughter], at the Steakhouse, the men's cooking team did not impress the judges from Omaha Steaks, and there was a lotta blame to go around, but you, Mr. Trump, recognized that the real problem was a lack of leadership. And so ultimately you didn't blame Lil Jon or Meatloaf [Crowd laughter], you fired Gary Busey! [Crowd laughter] [Then matter-of-factly, Barack adds] And these are the kinds of decisions that would keep me up at night. [Uproarious crowd laughter and applause]

First, Barack Obama made out the conspiracy theory that somehow the president of the United States is not a citizen of his own country to be completely foolish. Second, he framed Trump as inane and inept for being preoccupied with making calls for the president to "prove" his citizenship instead of focusing on more serious issues. Third, the president cut deeper into Trump's rump by highlighting his lack of legitimate political experience. He framed him as nothing more than a reality show star, busy makin "serious" decisions like who was to blame for "the failure of the men's cooking team." Then in a one-two punch, he "praised" Trump for firing the right chef on his show and quickly followed with, "And these are the kinds of decisions that would keep me up at night." With this one-liner, he underscored the enormous difference between him and Trump in terms of their political experience and capacity to govern. Stay in your lane, son.

Another example of Barack's siggin was when he and Hip Hop mogul P. Diddy got into it. Four years before Barack's election as President, Diddy described an exchange he had with him in these terms: "I had the privilege to meet Barack Obama, interview him...and also joke around with him, have some, you know, we had some funny banter back and forth. We was really like snappin on each other."[20] In the clip, Obama, after wiping the sweat off of his forehead repeatedly throughout the interview, is urging young people to vote (for John Kerry, at the time, instead of George W. Bush):

> BARACK: Well, some people just gotta remember what happened in Florida, you know, when George Bush won the Presidency, he thinks, based on just a tiny [pronounced "tahny," there goes the monophthongization of diphthongs again] margin of votes....And like I said, don't let people overpromise what you can do through politics. It's not gonna solve the problems of the entire world, but it makes a little bit of difference....You get registered, you vote—that takes about 15 minutes. And if you can't spend 15 minutes on deciding what your community's gonna look like and what your country's gonna look like, then you don't have any cause to complain.
>
> DIDDY: He makin sense [No copula needed]. That's what we need. We need people to make sense. We applaud you. [Then the *signifyin* begins]...And I wanna apologize for not sweatin, but I do this so much...
>
> BARACK: [Begins to protest and takes off his suit jacket] [Unseen staff start laughing]

DIDDY:...I'm so *cool*. I just want y'all to see. Everybody I'm interviewing is sweatin. I'm not even touchin my brow. [Laughter
from staff continues]. I'm so cool. [Barack still wiping sweat off
his face] And I wanna apologize. [Then he really begins *clownin*]
I ain't tryna make you look bad or nu'in like that but I'm just
so cool. Um, we, we...

BARACK: [Talking to the camera, pointing at Diddy] He, he wearin
a T-shirt...[No copula needed]

DIDDY: [Bent over laughing]

BARACK:...I tell ya, if he was wearin one of those fancy designer
clothes he's designin, he'd be sweatin just like me.

DIDDY: The guy's good. The guy's good y'all. Let's give it up for
him.

BARACK: [Slapping Diddy on the back, smiling] I appreciate you
guys, thank you.

DIDDY: Peace, peace, thank you.

Barack has proved himself to be a pretty skilled signifier but Diddy was
a fool wit that one! Layin it on Barack. And hammin it up for the
camera too.

Now, there are two things of interest here in terms of styleshifting. One,
of course, is how Barack was able to engage the Black cultural mode of
discourse known as signifyin. The other is how he accommodated his linguistic style closer to the style of P. Diddy throughout the interview. What
began as extremely formal and reserved, with mostly "standard" English
responses, ended with several examples of Black phonological and grammatical features. Diddy, generously using copula absence throughout the
interview, finally gets one back from Barack ("He Ø wearin a T-shirt"), as
Barack shifts his linguistic steez structurally to match the Black discourse
genre. That right there—shifting between discourse modes and linguistic
forms in the same interaction—is a prime example of styleshifting.

These few examples (and there are many others) show that Barack
Obama can hold his own when it comes to the art of signifyin and talkin
trash. Obama talks about learning these skills in high school while playing
on the university basketball courts "where a handful of black men...would
teach [him] an attitude that didn't just have to do with the sport. That
respect came from what you did and not who your daddy was. That you
could talk stuff to rattle an opponent, but that you should shut the hell up
if you couldn't back it up."[21] Further, in his high school years, Barack writes
about an illustrative exchange between him and his homie Ray, who introduced him to "the black parties that were happening on the army bases."[22]
Ray and other Black friends "eased [Barack's] passage through unfamiliar

terrain" in the process of his *becoming Black* or becoming well versed with Black American cultural signs, symbols, tropes, practices, and worldviews.[23] Language use was central to the cultural socialization process.

The following signifyin exchange between him and Ray provides a glimpse into the ways that Barack became socialized into Black linguistic ways of speaking:

> [Ray talking] "I mean it this time," he was saying to me now. "These girls are A-1, USDA-certified racists. All of 'em. White girls. Asian girls—shoot, these Asians worse than the whites. [You should recognize that as copula absence now, "these Asians Ø worse"] Think we got a disease or something."
>
> "Maybe they're lookin at that big butt of yours. Man, I thought you were in training."
>
> "Get your hands out of my fries. You ain't my bitch, nigger...buy your own damn fries. Now what was I talking about?"
>
> [The exchange continues with Ray claiming racism across dating and sports practices and Barack denying that it's always racism]
>
> ...[Ray talking] "Tell me we wouldn't be treated different if we was white. Or Japanese. Or Hawaiian. Or fucking Eskimo."
>
> "That's not what I'm saying."
>
> "So what are you saying?"
>
> ...[Barack signifies on Ray, claiming that his poor diet and training, rather than racism, are more likely the reasons why he wasn't starting on the football team] "As for your greasy-mouthed self," I added, reaching for the last of his fries, "I'm saying the coaches may not like you 'cause you're a smart-assed black man, but it might help if you stopped eating all them fries you eat, making you look six months pregnant. That's what I'm saying."[24]

"Y'all Know about Okey-Doke, Right?" Black Sermonizing—Barack Obama's Communicative M.O.

Despite his ability to flex Black Language across many contexts and signify with the best of em, Americans in our survey most often described Barack Obama's speech as "mirroring" that of a Baptist preacher. In fact, one could say that "the Black preacher style" was seen as Barack's communicative M.O. Black Americans, in particular, were not only more likely to frame Barack as a Black preacher, but they also usually provided more nuanced and descriptive readings of his "preacher style." Collectively, Black folks touched on Barack's cadence, timing, effective use of pauses, metaphors, rhythm and repetition, as well as Black discourse modes of signifyin and storytelling. They described Barack's "preacher-like" speech as

—having a slow and pointed cadence...words intermittently separated with pauses pregnant with meaning

—he uses the passion and rousing speech tools of preachers in Black churches...such as signifyin', using words that have double meaning that blacks pick up

—he uses repetition...altering pitch and stress

—he adopts a more Pastoral African-American vernacular and references more Biblical verses

—bringing...citizens along with storytelling and narration...his storytelling ability usually wraps around to connect to a larger theme

—often he uses metaphors and stories....His ability to tell stories is one of his greatest strengths...through persuasive storytelling, he taps into the unconscious mind where we make decisions, making it that much easier for him to influence the audience through his language

—he consciously uses sophisticated code-switching and rhythmic patterns

Generally, White Americans didn't go into as much detail, but almost all of those who noted his preacher style linked him to iconic Black preachers and ministers, such as Martin Luther King Jr. or Malcolm X. Having presumably less experience worshiping in Black churches, some White folks went way out and described Obama as "singing" in his speeches. While Black folks often refer to a "sing-song" quality in Black speech, the Black survey respondents did not describe Barack this way, probably due to the relative flatness of his speech when compared to the best Black preachers. One White male respondent compared Barack Obama's style to that of a "preacher" and then immediately made the direct link to "MLK's...singing" or "chanting": "At his best, he has the deliberate and enthusiastic pace of a talented preacher. It's almost as if he's singing or chanting as opposed to talking. This, of course, is not unlike how other talented orators, like MLK, sound." The next example is the most detailed description of Barack Obama's preacher style provided by the survey's White respondents:

Obama's composure always remains cool and collected with a strong sense of inner peace—he never lets emotional intensity

take over his speeches. At the same time, he is also the 21st century echo of African-American preacher style characterized by
such strong orators as MLK....Additionally, his speech is effective because his delivery is not boring or monotonous, but rather
like a song. The way Obama alters his pace, tone, and rhythm is
similar to the way a preacher speaks, which is essentially close to
singing. The intonation, emphasis, and pauses and silences that
characterize his speaking style are churchy and religious.

Obama is indeed particularly well versed in a mode that draws on Black
preacher style. No doubt his time at Trinity was a firsthand language
immersion experience in the Black Church's ways with words. In his "A
More Perfect Union" speech (a.k.a. "The Race Speech"), for example, Obama
painted a vivid picture of Reverend Wright's Trinity services and connected
with many Black churchgoers and others who recognize the Black Church
as an important cultural institution: "Like other black churches, Trinity's
services are full of raucous laughter and sometimes bawdy humor. They are
full of dancing and clapping and screaming and shouting."[25]

Obama learned a mode of Black sermonizing. While not attempting to
duplicate it to the letter in the political sphere, he readily engaged in a
"stylistic sampling" of the Black Church's Oral Tradition, as one respondent
put it. In his "More Perfect Union," for example, Obama began his speech-
sermon by framing slavery as America's "original sin." Opening with this
religious frame primed the audience for the most important moment of the
speech, which to us, sounded like the climax of a sermon. From approximately the last eight minutes of his speech, Obama uses a number of
Black preacher–style rhetorical devices. He cites Scripture; offers the flock
("Americans") a choice between good and evil, right and wrong; and then,
through the effective use of timing, repetition, and narrativizing, offers
us a way to perfect our character (ourselves and the Union). The only way
to truly witness the man's skillz is to examine the lengthy excerpt below,
which is notated to highlight his multilayered use of repetition[26] and which
includes a truncated sample of his storytelling:

> In the end, then, what is called for is nothing more, and noth-
> ing less, than what all the world's great religions demand—that
> we do unto others as we would have them do unto us. Let us
> be our brother's keeper, Scripture tells us. Let us be our sister's
> keeper....
>
> For we have a choice in this country. **We can** accept a politics
> that breeds division, and conflict, and cynicism. **We can** tackle

race only as a spectacle...**We can** play Reverend Wright's sermons on every channel, every day and talk about them from now until the election....**We can** pounce on some gaffe by a Hillary supporter as evidence that she's playing the race card, or **we can** speculate on whether white men will all flock to John McCain in the general election regardless of his policies.

We can do that. [He repeats "We can" and articulates the entire phrase in a lower, breathy voice to give it the sound of genuine feeling. Pausing to add rhetorical effect]

But if we do, I can tell you that in the next election, we'll be talking about some other distraction. And then another one. And then another one. And nothing will change.

That is one option. Or, at this moment, in this election, **we can** come together and say, "Not this time." *This time we want to talk about* the crumbling schools that are stealing the future of black children and white children and Asian children and Hispanic children and Native American children. *This time we want* to reject the cynicism that tells us that these kids can't learn....They are our kids, and we will not let them fall behind in a 21st century economy. Not this time.

This time we want to talk about how the lines in the Emergency Room are filled with whites and blacks and Hispanics who do not have health care....

This time we want to talk about the shuttered mills that once provided a decent life for men and women of every race, and the homes for sale that once belonged to Americans from every religion, every region, every walk of life. *This time we want to talk about* the fact that the real problem is not that someone who doesn't look like you might take your job; it's that the corporation you work for will ship it overseas for nothing more than a profit.

This time we want to talk about the men and women of every color and creed who serve together, and fight together, and bleed together under the same proud flag. *We want to talk about* how to bring them home from a war that never should've been authorized and never should've been waged, and *we want to talk about* how we'll show our patriotism by caring for them, and their families, and giving them the benefits they have earned....

There is one story in particular that I'd like to leave you with today—a story I told when I had the great honor of speaking on Dr. King's birthday at his home church, Ebenezer Baptist, in Atlanta.

There is a young, twenty-three year old woman, a white woman, named Ashley Baia who organized for our campaign in Florence, South Carolina. She had been working to organize a mostly African American community since the beginning of the campaign.... Now Ashley might have made a different choice. Perhaps somebody told her along the way that the source of her mother's problems were blacks who were on welfare and too lazy to work, or Hispanics who were coming into the country illegally. But she didn't. She sought out allies in her fight against injustice.

Anyway, Ashley finishes her story and then goes around the room and asks everyone else why they're supporting the campaign.... And finally they come to this elderly black man who's been sitting there quietly the entire time. And Ashley asks him why he's there. And he does not bring up a specific issue.... He simply says to everyone in the room, "**I am here because of Ashley**."

"**I'm here because of Ashley**." By itself, that single moment of recognition between that young white girl and that old black man is not enough.... But it is where we start...

In the eight-minute excerpt, Barack repeats "we can" seven times in succession (and emphasizes it once for rhetorical effect) before moving listeners to "we want," shifting the focus from our failures to our collective goals for action. He then effectively uses a combination of the phrases "Not this time," "this time," and "this time we want to talk about" to begin 10 different successive ideas.[27] All the while, he presents us with the choice between "division...conflict, and cynicism" and coming together to say, "Not this time." Finally, he humanizes that choice with the story of young White Ashley and an older Black man and suggests that together we can work to perfect the union.

In this "A More Perfect Union" speech, Barack was addressing a national audience made up of folks across the racial and linguistic spectrum. In majority Black contexts, however, where Black linguistic norms prevail, Barack Obama's been known to take his Black church stizzy to the next level. Specifically, he can shift into a deep Black style of *call and response*, a communicative strategy that breaks down conventional divisions between "audience" and "speaker."[28] Shot through with action and interaction, call and response is concentric in quality, with the audience becoming both observers and participants in the speech event. The audience's verbal and nonverbal responses co-sign the power of the speaker's call. Barack

Obama's speech in front of a predominantly Black crowd in South Carolina provides a quintessential example. He fired folks up to the point where they was damn near testifyin. Walkin across the stage, he looked out into the crowd:

BARACK'S CALL: They're tryna bamboozle you. [Pause]

CROWD'S RESPONSE: [Black woman seen waving her sign like a fan, Black men shaking their heads in recognition; crowd laughter] Yes!

BARACK'S CALL: It's the same old okey-doke. [Pause]

CROWD'S RESPONSE: [Laughter, agreement] That's right!

BARACK'S CALL: [Looking out to audience with a half smile] Y'all know about okey-doke, right? [Pause]

CROWD'S RESPONSE: Yeahhh! Yes! [Laughter]

BARACK'S CALL: It's the same old stuff!

CROWD'S RESPONSE: Yeahhh!

BARACK'S CALL: Just like if anybody starts gettin one of these emails sayin, "Obama is a *Muzlim*." [Pause]

CROWD'S RESPONSE: Yes! They do it!

BARACK'S CALL: I've, I've been a member of the same church for almost twenty years. [Pause]

CROWD'S RESPONSE: C'mon now! Alright!

BARACK'S CALL: Prayin to Jesus!

CROWD'S RESPONSE: [Hits a climax with uproarious shouts and applause]

BARACK'S CALL: Wit mah—wit mah Bible [pronounced *Bahble*]. [Pause]

CROWD'S RESPONSE: Amen! [Continued applause]

BARACK'S CALL: Don't *LET* people turn you around [continued applause] because they're just makin stuff up!

CROWD'S RESPONSE: Yes, they are!

BARACK'S CALL: That's what they do!

CROWD'S RESPONSE: Yes, they do!

BARACK'S CALL: They try to bamboozle you!

CROWDS RESPONSE: [Laughter] Hoodwink you!

BARACK'S CALL [now a response to "Hoodwink you!"]: Hoodwink you! [Laughter]

Barack Obama's masterful use of the call-and-response mode of Black Communication transformed this venue in South Carolina into a Baptist church lit with the spirit. Well, at least for the Black folks that were present. *Weellll*...While Black folks were shoutin, hollerin "Amen!" and goin back and forth with Barack in a culturally familiar verbal dance—until the lines between caller and responder were blurred—most White folks on the scene were either looking on blankly or smiling quietly. It's quite possible that White folks knew that something else was going on but couldn't quite figure out what it was. Of course, Blacks in the audience and most reading this now recognized that Barack was also recalling famous lines associated with Malcolm X (ironically, a Muslim) about White people trying to "bamboozle" and "hoodwink" Black folks. Like a coded verbal game of catch, Barack threw it out, the Black audience caught it, and then threw it back for him to catch. It wasn't that White audience members didn't approve of what was being said; it was that they were simply unable to play the game.[29]

Familiarly White, Familiarly Black, Familiarly American, Familiarly Christian: The Syntax and Style of Barack's Language

All of Barack's flexible linguistic abilities that we have described thus far were critically important to his being elected. This was perhaps the single most consistent finding in our survey: Barack Obama's mastery of White mainstream English ways of speaking, or "standard" English, particularly in terms of syntax, combined with his mastery of Black Culture's modes of discourse, in terms of style, was an absolutely necessary combination for him to be elected America's first Black president. One respondent in particular articulated this sentiment perfectly. When asked about Barack Obama's language and language use, she explained:

> When Obama was on the campaign trail, his speeches mirrored that of a Baptist preacher. The way certain words were stressed and the rise and fall in his speech were very reminiscent of the church. Sprinkled with imagery, metaphors and historical references, coupled with an underlying theme and you had speeches that captivated not only Americans, but the world....I feel like Obama has been able to balance his multi-racial identity and his Black experiences. His speeches are a great example of that balance. Obama has the ability to use Standard English in a "Black" context by using the "preacher" format to develop his speeches and then delivering them in Standard English. By combining these two experiences, Obama was able to appeal to a larger

audience of people. Whites did not feel alienated by his language, and Blacks felt a sense of familiarity with his speech pattern.

Of course, mastery of so-called "standard English" is mandated in American politics, but it was Barack's ability to combine this variety with Black ways of speaking that was ultimately crucial. His linguistic style mattered in at least three ways. First, Barack Obama's mastery of White mainstream ways of speaking allowed White Americans to feel more comfortable with him. He used a language variety that was familiarly White, which rightly or wrongly, did not "alienate" Whites in the way that Black Language sometimes does. Relatedly, his style of speaking was seen as "transcending" Blackness, with many describing him as "exceptionally articulate," making (unintentional) racist links between "articulateness," "Whiteness," and "intelligence."[30] Though some Americans noted that White, male mainstream ways of speaking English are problematically mapped onto "the language of politics" and "the language of success," Black Americans highly regarded Barack's proficiency in this style as well. Using positive terms, many respondents across racial lines described Barack's ability to use "standard English," "typical American English," "normative English," "standard American English," "polished standard English"—and our personal favorite, "a language literally born of the American educational system's upper echelon."

Second, not only did Whites feel that Barack spoke familiarly White, many Black folks felt that he spoke familiarly Black. While some Black women respondents noted that his "sounding Black" had to do with his "manly (deep) voice" or his "baritone," more often Blacks described Obama's speech style in terms of "a Baptist preacher" or in the "tradition of the Black Church." So, while responding positively to Barack's command of "standard" English syntax, the real clincher for Black folks was that Barack could kick it in a style that was recognizable to the community as "something we do." Rightly or wrongly, to many Black folks, anything less than that mighta made the brotha suspect. This is because, sociolinguistically speaking, the way we use language often hints at our politics, indexing our (dis)alignment with particular groups or causes. We read into people's words for clues, signs, anything that might help us figure out where they stand. In the case of Barack Obama, accurately or not, many Black folks read his use of Black modes of discourse as indexing a political alignment with the Black community.

Thirdly, Barack's ability to bring together "White syntax" with "Black style" and to speak familiarly Black was not only important for the Black community, it was also critically important for the White community for at least two reasons. One, Whites have always dug Black preacher style, so long as it didn't come at them too hard in that caustic, biting, damn-you-to-hell kinda way. (There *is* a reason why many Black folks refer to Martin

Luther King Jr. as "White America's favorite 'Negro'" and why, after hearing Reverend Jeremiah Wright's sermons, for instance, White Americans
don't know whether to shit or go blind!)

The second and most critical reason why speaking familiarly Black
was important for Whites is this: It made Barack both "American" and
"Christian." Not only are White Americans more familiar with a Black
Christian identity, but due to the contentious history of the Nation of
Islam and contemporary tensions with immigrant Muslims in post-9/11
America, many Whites also fear "(Black) Muslims." Speaking familiarly
Black made Barack familiarly American and familiarly Christian. To bor-
row from one Asian American respondent who wrote about forever feeling like a "foreigner" in the United States, "Barack needed to not only
be American; he needed to be 110 percent American." After all, who can
forget the lunacy of some White folks at the McCain-Palin rallies ("I, I,
I don't trust him—he's A-A-Arab!")? And the never-ending and overwhelmingly White Birther Movement, which even includes the likes of your boy
Donald Trump? Growing up in Hawai'i and Indonesia with a Kenyan father
and Muslim family roots was apparently too much for White folks to handle. Now, let's not kid ourselves here—it ain't like White folks got a lock
on xenophobia and anti-Muslim bias. Sounding familiarly Black, and thus
familiarly American and familiarly Christian, also won over those in the
Black community who questioned Obama's heritage ("He ain't Black—he
from Kenya!" or "Ain't he a Mooozlim?") or weren't down with what they
saw as his appropriation of the Black American struggle ("He's probably
one of those Africans who doesn't like us, but will use the label 'African
American' to take advantage of affirmative action programs").[31]

In sum, Barack's styles of speaking clinched his victory because he put
most Americans at ease. Here was a Black candidate for president whom
Black folks could trust because "he sounds White, but not *too* White" and
White folks could trust because "he sounds Black, but not *too* Black." Of
course, it would be too simple to leave it there. The reality is that Whites,
too, were happy with a Black man who "sounded White, but not *too* White."
His familiarly Black style Americanized and Christianized him, helping
them get over their irrational fears of a "foreign Muslim" or a "socialist
African." Blacks, too, were likely happy with a Black man who "sounds
Black, but not *too* Black." Quiet as it's kept, because of Black Language's
marginalized status in broader American society, some Black folks suffer
a linguistic shame that hypercriticizes any speech that sounds "too Black."
The stories of people "cringing" every time they hear Magic Johnson speak,
for example, are all too common. In a similar way that Barack Obama's
familiarly Black style helped some White folks get over irrational fears of
a "foreign/Black Muslim" or a "socialist African," his familiarly White style

helped some Black folks get beyond irrational insecurities that "the whole race" would be deemed "ignorant" because of one Black person's speech.

Caught between discriminatory discourses of language, citizenship, religion, and race, Barack Obama's language use hit that ever-so-small "sweet spot" that appealed to the majority of Americans. It didn't matter how many times he repeated that he wasn't a Muslim or how many times he presented his birth certificate; what mattered more to most Americans, even if subconsciously, was not what he said but how he said it. More than any other cultural symbol, Barack Obama's multifaceted language use allowed Americans to create linguistic links between him and famous African American male historical figures. These links served to simultaneously "Whiten," "Blacken," "Americanize," and "Christianize" Barack in the eyes and ears of both Black and White Americans.

With No *White* Dialect, Unless He Wants to Have One: Language, Race, Power

To be sure, hittin that small sweet spot ain't easy. While styleshifting may often appear simple, humorous, or lighthearted, it is also loaded with complex issues of identity and power. From a critical linguistic perspective, styleshifting, and language in general, is anything but a neutral practice. Returning to our survey, some Americans recognized that not everyone can shift like Barack Obama, in part, because not everyone has access to both White and Black ways of speaking. What troubled a few Americans, in particular, was the fact that while no one would ever expect White candidates to have to sound "Black," "Latino", or "Native American," for example, to be taken seriously, Barack Obama *needed* to "sound White." As one White American bluntly put it: "In order for Obama to sound 'knowledgeable' to the majority he must speak like a white man, enunciate clearly, say r's, etc." Another noted that "Obama *has* to speak that way," further explaining: "For an African American to become president of a country that is governed dominantly by white men, he had to publicly lose all traces of 'blackness.'" The White woman who noted that Obama's language "is seen as white across racial lines" also had this to say:

> In many ways, he *has* to speak the way he does. We have never had a 'black' president before. It's an idea that many voters had to get comfortable with, and one that others may never be comfortable with. He has to comfort all those that are skeptical by modeling himself closer to the presidents [the 43 White men] that have come before.

These responses demonstrate that language is loaded with power. Which languages are preferred in which contexts? By whom? Which groups are included—or excluded—by these decisions? Who benefits? Can we imagine a context, for example, in which Harry Reid based a White man's electability on the fact that he speaks with no White dialect unless he wants to have one? Simply put, why must Black Americans shift toward styles considered White in order to be "successful"? These questions show that the way we talk can either grant or deny us access to social, political, and economic opportunities (think jobs, schools, etc.). Barack certainly knew this when he said that Black people who want to be "successful" have to be able to "speak several different forms of the same language."

All of these issues rushed to the front of Black minds when Senate majority leader Harry Reid (Democrat from Nevada) famously distinguished Obama from previous Black candidates for president like Al Sharpton and Jesse Jackson. He claimed that (White) Americans might actually vote for Obama, in part, because he was "light-skinned" and spoke "with no Negro dialect, unless he wanted to have one." The messed up color-coded comment and outdated terminology aside, Reid's assessment of Barack Obama's style-shifting was pretty much on point. It's worth restating, though, that rather than a peculiar exception to the rule, Barack Obama's linguistic practices mirror those of many Black Americans who negotiate Black and White social worlds on the regular. As Barack Obama said, "That's not unique to me."

What is unique to Obama, though, is that he was not your average run-of-the-mill-type brotha—he was a senator running for president of the United States of America. Reid's comments sadly implied what our White respondents made explicit, that if a Black man wanted to be elected president he'd better keep his language in check, less any "hints" or "traces" of his "Negro-ness" leak out into the public eye/ear. Given that intense amount of social scrutiny, we can assume that Barack's linguistic flexibility is not merely a function of his diverse life experiences. It is also a creative response to the awareness—one shared by many Black Americans—that White America continues to have a love-hate relationship with Black America and its language. Despite the fact that Black Language stays on White people's minds and in their mouths, White America continues to interpret Black linguistic forms as signs of Black intellectual inferiority and moral failings.

Reid's comments make it clear that White America rewards Black Americans who don't sound "too Black," particularly in contexts that matter—from classrooms to courtrooms to corporate boardrooms. Syracuse University professor of finance and political analyst Boyce Watkins got right to the heart of the matter when he reflected on the broader social implications of Reid's linguistic description of President Obama:

What is saddest about [Harry] Reid's commentary, however, is that it reminds many African-Americans across the country that if our speech patterns or appearance are "too black" (whatever that means) or too different from what some consider acceptable, we are going to be deemed inferior. It seems that looking, sounding and behaving like a white man is the only way I might be considered to be as good as a white man. That is White Supremacy 101.[32]

It is precisely this White cultural hegemony—captured concisely by the Black folk idiom, "if it ain't White, it ain't right"—that we hope to disrupt in this book in terms of language. Because, as Americans, whether we like it or not, we not only see race but we hear it too.

NOTES

1. See: http://politicalticker.blogs.cnn.com/2010/01/09/reid-apology-for-negro-dialect-comment/. Last accessed: 09-01-2011.
2. One of Barack Obama's most insightful interviewers was none other than "Sir Charles"—NBA legend Charles Barkley, that is. His book, *Who's Afraid of a Large Black Man?* (New York: Penguin Press, 2006) features interviews on race in America with Barack Obama, Bill Clinton, Jesse Jackson, Tiger Woods, Morgan Freeman, George Lopez, and Ice Cube, among others. Obama's quote is from page 25.
3. In Mary Bucholtz's *White Kids: Language, Race, and Styles of Youth Identity* (Cambridge, UK: Cambridge University Press, 2011, 5). Not only is language often overlooked in popular discussions of race, but White people are often missing too. Bucholtz's book is the first to use the tools of linguistics to examine the construction of diverse White identities in the United States.
4. US Attorney General Eric Holder made these comments at the Department of Justice African American History Month Program on February 18, 2009. According to Holder, "One cannot truly understand America without understanding the historical experience of black people in this nation. Simply put, to get to the heart of this country one must examine its racial soul. Though this nation has proudly thought of itself as an ethnic melting pot, in things racial we have always been and continue to be, in too many ways, essentially a nation of cowards." The full transcript can be found at: http://www.justice.gov/ag/speeches/2009/ag-speech-090218.html. Last accessed: 09-01-2011.
5. See Pierre Bourdieu's *Language and Symbolic Power* (Cambridge, MA: Harvard University Press, 1991).
6. See Cornel West's *Race Matters* (Boston: Beacon Press, 1993), a groundbreaking classic on race in America. According to West, "The fundamental litmus test for American democracy—its economy, government, criminal justice system, education, mass media, and culture—remains: how broad and intense are the arbitrary powers used and deployed against black people" (vii). From this perspective, West continues to be the most vocal Black critic of Barack Obama.
7. The sociolinguistic research on Black Language—also known as African American English, African American Vernacular English, African American Language, Black English, Ebonics and still, by Harry Reid anyway, "Negro dialect"—can be found in numerous

volumes in research institutions across the country. It's the most oft-studied variety in the United States. See the work of linguists Guy Bailey, John Baugh, Lisa Green, William Labov, Sonja Lanehart, Marcyliena Morgan, John R. Rickford, Arthur Spears, Donald Winford, and others.

8. While shifting between Black and White varieties may be par for the course for many Black Americans in contact with Whites, Barack's a global, multilingual brotha. He's been known to flex his Spanish skills from time to time. In his most recent visit to Puerto Rico (2011), for example, he got quite a response for using the word *Boricua* to describe Puerto Rican culture. In *Dreams from My Father*, Barack explains that he learned enough Spanish in Harlem to "exchange pleasantries" with his Puerto Rican neighbors. Barack's linguistic flexibility is most likely due to the fact that as a young child he had a remarkable range of linguistic experiences. He not only noted his father's British accent, he also learned some Hawai'i Creole from his grandfather and others in Hawai'i (25), and it took him "less than six months to learn Indonesia's language, its customs, and its legends" (36). Though he has probably lost some of his knowledge of Indonesian, YouTube videos show him greeting Indonesians in their language. Later in life, Barack wrote about greeting some of his Kenyan relatives in Luo, demonstrating that he's the kind of person to make every effort to communicate with others (374). More recently on March 21, 2012, Fahima Haque wrote in *The Washington Post* about Barack Obama's interaction with a deaf community college student, demonstrating his impressive sign language skills (http://www.washingtonpost.com/blogs/therootdc/post/president-obama-impresses-with-his-sign-language/2012/03/21/gIQAXG37RS_blog.html. Last accessed: 04-19-12). So, in addition to his socialization into Black Language and White mainstream ways of speaking, Barack's communicative flexibility spans a broad range of experiences and is a testament to the idea that language socialization occurs across the life span. In other words, we don't speak only the language of our family or hometown. If we are sufficiently motivated and have a broad range of experiences, we pick up ways of speaking throughout our lifetime. Peep the new volume by Alessandro Duranti, Elinor Ochs, and Bambi Schieffelin, eds., *The Handbook of Language Socialization* (Boston: Wiley-Blackwell, 2011) for more on the language socialization process from top linguistic anthropologists in the game.

9. *Styleshifting* is a technical linguistic term used to describe the way speakers shift in and out of particular linguistic styles. It might be helpful to think of your voice box as a gearbox. A steep incline calls for a low gear. However, when the road flattens out again, you may wanna kick it into a higher gear, and so on. Most of us adapt to the changing contexts of our communicative encounters in much the same way drivers adapt to the changing conditions of the road. The difference is that most speakers shift styles quite unconsciously as they move throughout their day-to-day lives. As an incredibly successful politician, Barack Obama must be conscious of his speech in ways that the average American's probably not required to be. Just as driving skills increase with varied experiences, so does one's ability to styleshift. Barack Obama, then, if we carry our analogy a bit further, is more like a NASCAR driver than your average run-of-the-mill motorist. Of course, this analogy also points to issues of social inequality. We ain't all pushin Maybach's on nicely paved streets, nahmean? For recent scholarly work on Black American styleshifting, check out H. Samy Alim's *You Know My Steez: An Ethnographic and Sociolinguistic Study of Styleshifting in a Black American Speech Community* (Durham: Duke University Press, 2004). For White styleshifting, check out Mary Bucholtz's *White Kids: Language, Race, and Styles of Youth Identity* (Cambridge, UK: Cambridge University Press, 2011). And for Puerto Rican styleshifting and codeswitching, check Ana Celia Zentella's now classic, *Growing Up Bilingual* (Malden, MA: Blackwell, 1997). For an excellent edited volume with chapters by leading experts, check out Penny Eckert and John Rickford's (eds.) *Style and Sociolinguistic Variation* (Cambridge, UK: Cambridge University Press, 2001).

10. Geneva Smitherman made this distinction in her pioneering book on Black Language, *Talkin & Testifyin: The Language of Black America* (Boston: Houghton Mifflin, 1977; republished, Detroit: Wayne State University Press, 1986).

11. Fastest way to find it is to search for "Barack Obama Real Cool": (http://www.youtube.com/watch?v=30-lYueJivk). Last accessed: 09-01-2011.

12. One Black respondent went beyond Barack's ability to speak across different racial groups (Blacks and Whites) and described his ability to speak across different segments within the same racial group ("very high intellectuals" and "street kids that love hip-hop"): "One time, Obama was able to fit a rap song into his speech perfectly, based on the way he spoke his previous statements. He mentioned how he had been receiving criticism, and instructed himself, and anyone else who has 'haters' to brush that dirt off of their shoulders (reference to Jay-Z song). This shows how Obama can reach everyone in the audience when he speaks, from the very high intellectuals to the street kids that love hip-hop."

13. Barack Obama uses all of these lexical items in *Dreams from My Father*. In Geneva Smitherman's *Black Talk: Words and Phrases from the Hood to the Amen Corner* (Boston/New York: Houghton Mifflin, 1994, 2000), *trifling* "describes a person who fails to do something that he/she is capable of doing; irresponsible; inadequate" (285). Barack uses *trifling* in exactly this sense on page 226 in *Dreams*: "'We're trifling. That's what we are. Trifling. Here we are, with a chance to show the mayor that we're real players in the city, a group he needs to take seriously. So what do we do? We act like a bunch of starstruck children, that's what.'" Smitherman defines *yella/high yella* as a term used to describe "a very light-complexioned African American; praised in some quarters, damned in others. Community ambivalence stems from *high yellas*' close physical approximation to European Americans." (303). In *Dreams*, Barack writes about becoming "familiar with the lexicon on color consciousness" (193) in the Black community and uses the term *high-yella* on page 273 in *Dreams*: "the high-yella congregations that sat stiff as cadets as they sang from their stern hymnals." *Tom/Uncle Tom* is described by Smitherman as "a negative label for a Black person, suggesting that he/she is a sell-out, not down with the Black cause. *Tom* comes from the character Uncle Tom in Harriet Beecher Stowe's nineteenth century novel, *Uncle Tom's Cabin*, who put his master's wishes and life before his own." (284). Barack uses these terms to describe his puerile attempt to belittle another Black classmate in college: "Tim was not a conscious brother. Tim wore argyle sweaters and pressed jeans and talked like Beaver Cleaver....His white girlfriend was probably waiting for him up in his room, listening to country music....'Tim's a trip, ain't he,' I said, shaking my head. 'Should change his name from Tim to Tom.'" (101–102). *House nigger*, Smitherman explains, historically referred to "an enslaved African who worked in Ole Massa's house," rather than in the field (*field nigga*), and "was viewed as loyal to Massa." (130). Malcolm X updated this term in the 1960s to refer to the working-class Blacks as *field niggas* and middle-class Blacks as *house niggas*. *House niggas* were "more likely to deny the existence of racism or make excuses for it, to identify with whites and the system, and thus unlikely to engage in protest or rebellion." This is precisely how Barack Obama used the term when he realized that his Muslim grandfather, whom he always imagined to be "an independent man, a man of his people, opposed to white rule" in Kenya, turned out to be anything but that. "What Granny had told us scrambled that image completely, causing ugly words to flash across my mind. Uncle Tom. Collaborator. House nigger." (406).

14. Rickford, J. R., Ball, A., & Blake, R. (1991). "Rappin on the Copula Coffin: Theoretical and Methodological Issues in the Analysis of Copula Variation in African American Vernacular English." *Language Variation and Change*, 3, 103–132. For Rickford's most extensive paper on the copula, check out "The Creole Origins of African American Vernacular English: Evidence from Copula Absence," available at www.johnrickford.com.

15. Yo, just had to share a few. The first one is a retweet from @djtaylor12: "#uknowuugly when you look in the mirror with the lights off." This next one is from @Doyinakalyrical:

"#uknowuugly when your twitpic is still the twitter default egg." LOL! It ain't all jokes, though. Some folks provide more critical commentary, like this one: "#uknowuugly when u preach about GOD all the time, yet u have the most stank, ugly, negative, un-GODLY attitude there is! YEAH I SAID IT." Chuuuch! Catch Alim on @hsamyalim.

16. The copula is just one example of BL's complex verbal system and the Africanization of American English. According to John R. Rickford, copula absence "provides one of the strongest arguments for possible Creole and African influences on the grammar" of Black Language. Many Caribbrean Creoles and West African languages do not have the copula in some grammatical environments, and patterns of its absence in Black Language mirror that of its absence in Creoles (See Alim's *You Know My Steez*, 141–160, for strong evidence of this from Black youth in the San Francisco Bay Area in Cali). Rickford also notes that "the very presence of certain aspect categories in [Black Language]—particularly the completive (marked by *done*) and the present durative, or habitual (marked by *be*)—may be attributed to their prevalence in West African languages, which is well documented in the work of William Welmer and others. Even the existence of a category of remote past (marked by *BEEN*) may go back to distinctions in languages like LuGanda and KiKongo. Moreover, the tendency of [Black Language] to encode its most important tense-aspect distinctions through a series of preverbal markers (*be, bin, done, BIN, fitna, had*, and so on) rather than through verbal affixes strikingly parallels the pattern in Caribbean Creoles." (from John R. Rickford and Russell Rickford's *Spoken Soul: The Story of Black English*, New York: John Wiley & Sons, 2000, 154).

17. Check it: http://www.youtube.com/watch?v=TDy9I9C1xUM&feature=related. Last accessed: 09-01-2011.

18. Linguistic anthropologists will recognize these terms. They refer to an approach to the scientific study of a culture and their communication patterns known as "the ethnography of communication." A *speech situation*, the largest level of the three levels of analysis, describes the social occasion in which speech may occur (in our example, lunchtime at an informal restaurant). You will hear many *speech events* inside of a *speech situation* (in our example, a service encounter between customer and employee). A *speech act* refers to each action of speech inside of a *speech event* (in our example, ordering food). Check John Gumperz and Dell Hymes's edited volume for an early classic, *Directions in Sociolinguistics: The Ethnography of Communication* (New York: Holt, Rinehart & Winston, 1972).

19. *Signifyin* has been described as a means to encode messages or meanings in conversation, usually involving an element of indirection. According to Claudia Mitchell-Kernan: "The black concept of *signifying* incorporates essentially a folk notion that dictionary entries for words are not always sufficient for interpreting meanings or messages, or that meaning goes beyond such interpretations. Complimentary remarks may be delivered in a left-handed fashion. A particular utterance may be an insult in one context and not in another. What pretends to be informative may intend to be persuasive. Superficially, self-abasing remarks are frequently self-praise." Check out her classic article, "Signifying and Marking: Two Afro-American Speech Acts" in John J. Gumperz and Dell Hymes, eds., *Directions in Sociolinguistics* (New York: Holt, Rinehart & Winston, 1972, 82).

20. This interview was taped for www.diddy.com. You can catch it at: http://www.youtube.com/watch?v=Ne_87Kw35pE. Last accessed: 09-01-2011.

21. From Barack Obama's *Dreams from My Father: A Story of Race and Inheritance* (New York: Crown Publishers, 1995, 79).

22. Ibid. 72.

23. In many ways, *Dreams from My Father* details Barack Obama's search for "a Black identity." He writes, "Away from my mother, away from my grandparents, I was engaged in a fitful interior struggle. I was trying to raise myself to be a black man in America, and beyond the given of my appearance, no one around me seemed to know exactly what that meant." (76). Barack Obama, to use Awad Ibrahim's terms, was in the pro-

cess of *becoming Black*. Many Black Americans, particularly those on the margins of what most Americans see as a normative Black identity (sons and daughters of African immigrants, for example), know this process well. Awad Ibrahim, Sudanese professor of education at the University of Ottawa, describes the process like this: "To become Black is to become an ethnographer who translates and searches around in an effort to understand what it means to be black in North America, for example." It is a process of "entering already pronounced regimes of Blackness." (from "Whassup, Homeboy? Joining the African Diaspora: Black English as a Symbolic Site of Identification and Language Learning" in *Black Linguistics: Language, Society, and Politics in Africa and the Americas*, eds., Sinfree Makoni, Geneva Smitherman, Arnetha Ball, and Arthur Spears (New York: Routledge, 2003, 181–183). Black feminist cultural critic Joan Morgan, who is Jamaican, described the process of becoming Black in America in these terms: "As a matter of both acclimation and survival, we learn [African American] history. We absorb the culture. Some of us even acquire the accent." (See her essay, "Black Like Barack" in T. Denean Sharpley-Whiting, ed., *The Speech: Race and Barack Obama's "A More Perfect Union,"* New York: Bloomsbury, 2009, 63). For both of these scholars two things are central to the cultural socialization process of becoming Black in the United States: (1) being positioned as "Black" by others in society and experiencing anti-Black racism, and (2) positioning yourself as "Black" by acquiring "Black" ways of speaking. That dialectic of positionality is what Obama navigates throughout *Dreams from My Father*.

24. From Barack Obama's *Dreams from My Father: A Story of Race and Inheritance* (73–74). Years later, Obama would take these skills with him on the campaign trail as an adult. As William Jelani Cobb writes in *Barack Obama and the Paradox of Progress* (New York: Walker, 2010): "[Obama] showed up in a Marion, South Carolina barbershop and immediately commenced trash-talking a patron's alligator shoes. It was a risky move, but his underlying point was to illustrate that he understood [Black] barbershop protocol. The campaign printed up posters of him sitting in that barbershop and distributed the DVD of his visit." (72).

25. For a full transcript of the speech, see T. Denean Sharpley-Whiting, ed., *The Speech: Race and Barack Obama's "A More Perfect Union,"* (New York: Bloomsbury, 2009, 237–251). It was delivered on March 18, 2008, in Philadelphia and is known as "The Race Speech" or just "The Speech." You can also catch it on YouTube: http://www.youtube.com/watch?v=zrp-v2tHaDo. Last accessed: 09-01-2011.

26. This excerpt is notated to demonstrate the multilayered use of repetition. For example, the phrase "we can" is marked in bold. Each instance of "this time" is underlined. Each use of "we want to talk about" or "we want" is in italics. Overlapping repeated phrases like "*This time we want to talk about*," are marked with "This time" underlined and in italics. Whole phrases such as "**I am here because of Ashley**" are marked in bold and underlined.

27. Georgetown University professor Michael Eric Dyson also notes Obama's use of "anaphora," which is repetition of the "same word or phrase at the beginning of successive sentences." What's interesting here is that Obama layers his repetition of multiple words and phrases, creating an advanced use of this strategy, one that is common in the Black preacher tradition. See Dyson's full comments and other examples of Obama's use of this rhetorical device at: http://www.smh.com.au/news/opinion/a-presidentpreacher-from-anaphora-to-epistrophe/2009/01/18/1232213445525.html. Last accessed: 09-02-11.

28. For great examples of Obama's rendering of *call and response* in text, check *Dreams from My Father*, pages 293–295. You can also hear this portion of Barack's South Carolina speech here: http://www.politico.com/news/stories/0309/19538_Page2.html. Last accessed: 09-01-11.

29. Writing about Black music, Imani Perry discusses another level of call and response. "To make something good...means in part to effectively employ the call-response trope on several levels, and, just as important, to know what is good requires a sophis-

ticated...understanding of the symbolic references and cultural history from which the music derives." (*Prophets of the Hood: Politics and Poetics in Hip Hop*, Durham, NC: Duke University Press, 36). Relating this to Barack's speech in South Carolina, Barack put out the encoded Malcolm X call, and his Black audience responded. While there is some scholarly debate about whether or not Malcolm X used those exact words, the important point is that Barack Obama tapped into the symbolism and cultural history of Malcolm. He was also employing another level of signifyin, one that is central to the Black literary tradition. According to Henry Louis Gates, Jr.'s *The Signifyin(g) Monkey; A Theory of African-American Literary Criticism* (New York/London: Oxford University Press, 1989), signification relies on one's knowledge of previous texts and the author's (speaker's) ability to reinterpret them in new ways. Certainly, signifyin on a Muslim minister's words to ensure that he was seen as anything but a Muslim qualifies. Barack done did it again.

30. The phrase "exceptionally articulate" was actually used by one White American and "articulate" was used overwhelmingly by White respondents more than any other group. This led us to develop the idea of "articulate as an exceptionalizing discourse." But, yo, check the next chapter for more on this problematic "articulate" business.

31. Or as one 58-year-old African American barber put it: "When you think of a president, you think of an American.... We've been taught that a president should come from right here, born, raised, bred, fed in America. To go outside and bring somebody in from another nationality, now that doesn't feel right to some people." Quoted in William Jelani Cobb's *Barack Obama and the Paradox of Progress* (Walker, 2010, 69). White folks in particular continue to struggle with Obama's nationality and religion. Just recently, during the Republican primaries leading up to the 2012 presidential race, a poll showed that about half of Republican voters in Alabama and Mississippi still believe that Barack Obama is a Muslim. And even scarier is the fact that about a quarter believe that his parents' interracial marriage should have been illegal (http://articles.latimes.com/2012/mar/12/news/la-pn-poll-obamas-a-muslim-to-many-gop-voters-in-alabama-mississippi-20120312. Last accessed: 04-19-12). If that's not wild enough, how about recent comments in April 2012 from rock star and Romney-endorser Ted Nugent? In addition to calling the president a "criminal" and his administration "vile," "evil," and "America-hating"—not to mention using extremely dangerous and violent language—he also claimed that the United States would turn into a "suburb of Indonesia" under Obama's second term (http://abcnews.go.com/Politics/OTUS/secret-service-ted-nugent-violent-anti-obama-message/story?id=16159549#. T5IFxRzwHn0. Last accessed: 04-19-12).

32. Check the full article at: http://www.thegrio.com/opinion/reids-negro-dialect-remark-politically-incorrect-but-totally-right.php. Last accessed: 09-01-2011.

2

A.W.B. (Articulate While Black)

Language and Racial Politics in the United States

He's the first mainstream African American
who is articulate and bright and clean and
a nice-looking guy.[1]
—Joseph Biden

I didn't take Sen. Biden's comments personally,
but obviously they were historically inaccurate.
African-American presidential candidates like
Jesse Jackson, Shirley Chisholm, Carol Moseley
Braun and Al Sharpton gave a voice to many
important issues through their campaigns,
and no one would call them inarticulate.[2]
—Barack Obama

Let's paint the picture. We're at the Takoma Theatre in Washington, DC. Packed house. A predominantly Black crowd with a token White person or two in the front rows (you KNOW they gon get called out!). Well-known Black comedian Chris Rock struts across the stage wearin black pants, black belt, black shirt, and a shiny black leather jacket. "Lotta stuff goin on this year. Everything racial this year. What's the big thing this year? Election." Movin his hand across the stage from right to left in that crazy-expressive Chris Rock way, he imitates White Americans' belief in a potential Black candidate for president, "He should ruuun, he could wiiin." [Laughter from the crowd]. Rock responds to the suggestion, "He can't wiiin. [He] can't win! [He] got a better chance of winnin the bronze in female gymnastics [Big laugh from the crowd]...than being the President of the United States. Get the fuck out! White people ain't votin for [him]." [Laughter]. "Say they are. They. Are. NOT!" [Laughter and applause]. "Okay! Just gon soup his head up, make him run, he'll get kilt tryna run. Shhhit..." Rock continues with his side-splittin performance, suggesting that White people say they're gonna vote for this

31

Black candidate "cuz it seem like the right thing to say," just like answering "yes" to the social pressure of being asked to be an organ donor.

Rock continues, "[He] can't be pres-i-*DENT*. Get the hell outta here. You know how I could tell [he] can't be President? Whenever [he] on the news, White people always give him the same compliments, *always* the same compliments." Imitating White folks again, performing the wide-eyed White supporter with even more exaggerated gestures, "He speaks so *well*." [Laughter]. "He's so well-spoken. He speaks so *well*. I mean, he really speaks *well*. He speaks so well!" [Laughter]. Then, in his inimitable style, he begins to break it down, "Like that's a compliment. 'Speaks so well' is not a compliment, okay? 'Speaks so well' is some shit you say about retarded people that can talk!" [Laughter]. "What do you mean he speaks well? What'd he have a stroke the other day?! He's a fuckin educated man! How the *fuck* you expect him to sound, you dirty muthafuckas, what are you talkin about?!" [Extended laughter and applause]. Leaving no doubt about his point, he *really* brings down the house with this one, "What voice were you lookin to come outta his mouth?! What the *fuck* did you expect him to sound like?!" [Imitating an exaggerated style of self-deprecating slave speech, with a big wide grin showing his teeth] " 'I'ma drop me a bomb today. I be pres-o-dent.' " [Laughter and applause]. Rock struts back to the other side of the stage, "Get the fuck outta here!"

Chris Rock's hilarious skit was not about Barack Obama. In fact, it was about Colin Powell and was first performed by Rock over 15 years ago.[3] Like much of Rock's comedy, the skit is loaded with insightful folk social and linguistic analyses of race in America, touching on issues that played out again and again during the last two election cycles with Barack Obama. As is the case with most perceptive folk analyses, Rock's routine articulated the heretofore unarticulated—putting words to a feeling that Black folks have long felt but not expressed.

We present a metalinguistic analysis of Barack Obama's language—that is, we're gonna talk about *the talk about* the way Barack Obama talks. We consider the racially coded meanings of *articulate* and how they function to reproduce racist ideologies and, importantly, racial inequalities. The "articulate" question is not just cultural and symbolic but also linked to real-life consequences for those on the linguistic margins of American society.

Racism 2.0: Articulateness as a Function of "Enlightened Exceptionalism"

In the run-up to the 2008 presidential campaign, most Americans were taken by surprise by the young, charismatic Black candidate Barack Obama.

As a relative unknown, he seemed to have gripped the nation's imagination in a way that few presidential candidates had before him. Many White folks, in particular, given their extreme isolation from Black communities and other communities of Color, didn't know how to respond to Barack Obama and searched for some kind of interpretive frame with which to understand this incredibly successful Black politician-professor. We know his academic credentials well: a graduate of two Ivy League institutions (Columbia University and Harvard Law School), first African American editor of the *Harvard Law Review*, and a law professor at the University of Chicago. This highly educated Black man also became the Senate's sole African American. This, along with his multiracial background, his global family biography, and his meteoric rise to the top of American politics, threw many Americans off. What do we call this guy? Is he "Black"? Is he "too Black"? Is he a "Mooozlim"? Is he even "American"? The questions about Obama's race—arguably America's greatest obsession—went on and on and on.

Given our narrow definition of *Black* in the United States, Barack Obama (the candidate with "the funny name") seemed like an anomaly. This narrow perspective, combined with the pervasive stereotypes about Black men in American society—"stereotypes about black criminality, black intelligence, or the black work ethic,"[4] as noted by Obama himself—worked to induce many White folks to make sense of Barack through a theory of exceptionalism. Because he's not like "those other Blacks," he must be the exception to the rule that frames all Black people as lazy, dumb, and/or criminal. Thus, according to this thinking, because of his difference, he should be rewarded—even elected—for being "better" than most of his people. As race theorist Tim Wise has written in *Between Barack and a Hard Place: Racism and White Denial in the Age of Obama*, this is not your mom and pop racism, the kind that has plagued the history of this country since its inception, leading to genocide, slavery, incarceration, and so on. "Consider this, for lack of a better term, Racism 2.0, or enlightened exceptionalism," Wise writes. It is a "form of racism that allows for and even celebrates the achievements of individual persons of color, but only because those individuals generally are seen as different from a less appealing, even pathological black or brown rule."[5] To Wise and others, the fact that candidates such as Barack Obama are called upon to "transcend" their race not only proves that America is far from being postracial, but it also "confirms the salience of race and the machinations of white hegemony."[6] Whereas no one would even think of describing a White candidate as having to transcend race, in a hyperracial America, a Black man can't win without doing just that. (Many will recognize the parallel here to gender, where women, in a field dominated by men, are often asked to transcend gender if they are to "appeal" to male voters—just ask your girl, Hillary. And then tell us, what is a Black woman to do?).

Wise may have overargued the case that this kind of "enlightened exceptionalism" got Barack elected. For one thing, the majority of White people did not vote for Barack Obama. Second, as Tulane University political science professor Melissa Harris-Perry reminds us, while social science research shows that White people unconsciously prefer White faces over Black and even lighter-skinned Black faces over darker-skinned ones, these effects are "negligible in determining election outcomes."[7] According to Harris-Perry, partisan identification, issue positions, and previous elected office have far greater effects. Still, there is "a there *there*" when it comes to a theory of exceptionalism. Wise's theory of enlightened exceptionalism captures a longstanding Black folk theory of articulateness, where, as Chris Rock argued above, Black folks are praised and rewarded as being "exceptional" for something that they believe is hardly exceptional at all.

Five White Guys and a "Magic Negro": The Policing of Black Language

Using the case of Barack Obama as an example, we have noted a particular fascination, obsession if you will, with his language and communicative behavior, which have been the subject of extreme scrutiny. The intense scrutiny is a type of social monitoring that highlights the fact that his language, and Black Language more generally, are constantly policed by White and other Americans in the public sphere. Further, this type of language policing also throws into relief the complex and inextricably linked relationship between language and race in America. Take, for example, the various media crisis moments that surrounded Barack Obama over the last five years in regard to the word *articulate*. A review of the last five years of the biography of the word shows how one person's seemingly harmless compliment can be another's glaringly offensive insult.

While *articulate* has a long history, the story begins for now in early 2007 when then Democratic presidential hopeful Senator Joseph Biden described Barack Obama as the "first mainstream African American who is articulate and bright and clean and a nice-looking guy."[8] That same week, in an unrelated incident, former president George W. Bush got in on the action and answered a reporter's question about Barack Obama by saying, "He's an attractive guy. He's articulate."[9] These two comments created an uproar in the Black community, as the racialized and classed meanings of the word *articulate* began to enter the already troubling racializing discourses of the 2008 presidential campaign. As many Blacks noted, these remarks by two extremely high profile White politicians merely echoed the numerous comments from many average, ordinary, run-of-the-mill White folks. Why was everybody and they mama callin Barack Obama "articulate"?

Of all the adjectives Biden used to describe Obama, *articulate* stood out for being "so pervasive" and for being used so "differently by blacks and whites" that Lynette Clemetson called for a "national chat, perhaps a national therapy session." Writing in *The New York Times* on "The Racial Politics of Speaking Well"[10]—or what some Black folks refer to as "Articulate While Black"[11]—Clemetson argued that, in attempting to explain his remarks, Joe Biden just dug his hole deeper and cast Barack Obama as completely out of the ordinary, describing him as "incredible" and "a phenomenon." The core of the issue for Clemetson is this: "When whites use the word in reference to blacks, it often carries a subtext of amazement, even bewilderment....Such a subtext is inherently offensive because it suggests that the recipient of the 'compliment' is notably different from other black people." As Georgetown University professor Michael Eric Dyson added, "Historically, it was meant to signal the exceptional Negro....The implication is that most black people do not have the capacity to engage in articulate speech, when white people are automatically assumed to be articulate."[12]

In his characteristic way, Obama brushed Biden's dirt off his shoulder in interviews, but he released a written statement that pointed out the racialized meanings contained within the subtext of the "compliment." "I didn't take Senator Biden's comments personally, but obviously they were historically inaccurate. African-American presidential candidates like Jesse Jackson, Shirley Chisholm, Carol Moseley Braun and Al Sharpton gave a voice to many important issues through their campaigns, and no one would call them inarticulate."[13] Obama's statement demonstrates his refusal to be White America's "exceptional Negro," one willing to accept "praise" at the expense of other Black politicians and Black people in general. His comments also highlight the fact that "compliments" like "articulate" and "speaks so well" are too often racially coded to mean "articulate...for a black person." As Brown University Africana Studies professor Tricia Rose pointed out, "Al Sharpton is incredibly articulate, but because he speaks with a cadence and style that is firmly rooted in black rhetorical tradition you will rarely hear white people refer to him as articulate."[14] Speaking on MSNBC in early 2007, Al Sharpton's own comments showed even further complexity behind the "compliment" with this concise but loaded one-liner: "I take a bath everyday."[15] (More on this later.)

After Joe Biden and George W. Bush, a third White man entered the "articulate" narrative but in a slightly different way. This time, it was majority leader Harry Reid, the Democratic senator from Nevada. In one of the most talked about political books of the year, *Game Change* by *Time*'s Mark Halperin and *New York Magazine*'s John Heilemann, *articulate* was given new life through a direct linkage between language and race. According to their book, Reid thought that Americans [read: White Americans] might finally be ready to elect a Black president. Then he commented privately that this was especially true because Obama was, relative to other Black candidates like Jesse Jackson and Al Sharpton, "light-skinned" and spoke "with no Negro dialect, unless he wanted to have one."[16] While the media went into another tizzy, Obama once again brushed that dirt off his shoulder, knowing that these comments were not intended as Reid's personal beliefs. Rather, accurately or not, they were made within a context of what Reid believed to be White America's attitude toward Obama and Black candidates in general.

Beyond being out of touch with current nomenclature (you basically gotta be older than dirt to use "Negro" as a racial term of reference), Reid's comments suggest several current realities about race in America. First, many White leaders hold the belief that America's dream of postraciality is far from its racial reality. Second, some Americans might, in fact, be hyperracial if voting is based in part on color of skin and shades of color within that. Third, if a Black man was ever going to be elected, it was gonna have to be an "exceptional" Black man. To spell it out even more clearly, that Black man would have to be damn near White—as light as possible, with White biraciality being a big plus, and speaking in a way modeled on middle-class White linguistic norms and as far away from Black norms of speaking as possible. As one sista joked, pretending to be a White customer in an imaginary political coffee shop, "I'd like to order a 'Black man' please, with *lots* of cream, some chocolate and *plenty* of milk, oh, and with as little detectable 'Negro dialect' as possible!" President Obama himself commented on America's racializing hegemony, the set of ideologies that make Whiteness invisibly "normal" while highlighting all non-Whites as different, meaning less than. The closer one is to a "White ideal," the more palatable they will be to many Americans.[17]

The fourth and fifth White men to enter this tale of "articulate" come later in the game but show how this "articulate" frenzy continues into the 2012 presidential election season. This time, we have Republican representative Joe Walsh from Illinois. (This White view of Black articulateness appears to be one of the few bipartisan issues in Washington these days!) Walsh adds a slightly different twist to the tale, suggesting that Barack Obama's election was linked to both race and language, as well as "white guilt," as if Obama were the presidential politics version of an "affirmative action baby":

> Why was he elected? Again, it comes down to who he was. He was black, he was historic. And there's nothing racist about this. It is

what it is. If he had been a dynamic white state senator elected to Congress he wouldn't have gotten in the game this fast.... [The media] was in love with him because he pushed that magical button: a black man who was articulate, liberal, the whole white guilt thing, all of that.[18]

Aside from the now classic, almost satirical, White rhetorical script of "I'm not racist, but" followed by racist commentary,[19] Walsh's "magical" discourse ties in neatly with the fifth White man to enter the narrative, conservative talk radio host Rush Limbaugh.

Rush Limbaugh, perhaps more directly than any of the other actors in this storyline, makes it painfully obvious that many White Americans vigilantly monitor and police Black Language to the point of obsession. He also makes it clear that there must be no "traces" of Black Language in your speech if you are a Black candidate for President. On his radio show, Limbaugh played a snippet of Barack Obama's speech over and over again, urging his audience to listen really closely because they might miss something. Obama was addressing the National Governors Association when he said, "As a condition of receiving access to Title I funds, we will ask all states to put in place a plan to adopt and certify standards that are college and career ready in reading and math." Limbaugh stops the tape and asks, "D-ahhhh, did you catch, did you catch that there? Did you catch that? No? You missed it.... See, you're listening to the substance here. You *missed* this." After replaying it, he gives Harry Reid's comments new life:

> This is what Harry Reid was talking about. Obama can turn on that black dialect when he wants to and turn it off. The President of the United States just said here, 'As a condition of receiving'— and I wonder if this was on the teleprompter—'As a condition of receiving access to Title I funds we will *aks* [pause] all states' Who is he trying to reach out here to, the Reverend Jackson, the Obama criticizer? Now, if I use the word *aks* for the rest of the day, am I gonna get beat up and creamed for making fun of this clean, crisp, calm, cool, new, articulate [pause] President?...I'll *aks* my advisors. And I might even *aks* Governor *Cumo*, as the Reverend Jackson pronounced his name.[20]

Beyond the obvious race baiting and mockery, Limbaugh displays multiple forms of ignorance here. First, listening to the tape as trained linguists, we noted that Obama's articulation of "ask" was actually "aksk", which threw his timing off, making it more likely that Obama made an error given that the word "access" came shortly before "ask." Anyone who has listened to

Barack Obama speak knows that "ask" is not rendered "aks" in his speech. Second, those like Limbaugh, who berate Blacks for saying "aks" instead of "ask" (including some Black folks like Bill Cosby, Shelby Steele, and others demonstrating linguistic shame) are completely unaware of the linguistic history of the verb. Writing in *English with an Accent: Language, Ideology, and Discrimination in the United States*, Rosina Lippi-Green breaks down the phonological [pronunciation] variation in regard to *ask* in the United States:

> The *Oxford English Dictionary* establishes this variation between [ask] and [aks] as very old, a result of the Old English metathesis *asc-, acs-*. From this followed the Middle English variation with many possible forms: *ox, ax, ex, ask, esk, ash, esh, ass, ess*. Finally, *ax* (aks) survived to almost 1600 as the regular literary form, when *ask* became the literary preference.[21]

Most Americans, including those who mock African Americans for using the historically "preferred literary form" of *ask,* are woefully ignorant of its history. Further, as Lippi-Green notes, this variation is also found in the speech of White Americans in Appalachia, in some urban regions of New York, and in some regional varieties of British English. This last point is important, as many are not aware of that fact that often what makes Black Language unique has less to do with the "ignorance" of its speakers and more to do with the ways that African and British language varieties merged in the process of Creolization.[22]

The Limbaugh story is important because it reveals the general ignorance (not just Rush's) about Black Language and exposes those who manipulate existing White fear of anything or anyone deemed "too Black" (or "not White enough"). It was Rush Limbaugh, not Republican representative Walsh (even though he used the term more recently), who popularized the use of *magic* to describe Barack Obama among Republicans. He broadcast the song "Barack the Magic Negro" (based on "Puff the Magic Dragon") on his radio show, and it was later sent out to members of the Republican National Committee.[23] Barack Obama, depicted as the "Magic Negro" by White Republicans is beyond offensive for a number of reasons, not the least of which is the purposeful use of the word *Negro* to describe Obama. With its usage here, we also see yet another way that Barack Obama has been framed as the "exceptional Negro," standing on call, ready to alleviate White fears and enlighten them on issues of race.

The final point to mention here is something that too often flies under the radar. When White people (whether it's Rush Limbaugh, Joseph Biden, or George W. Bush) give Black people the "compliment" of being "articulate," they often juxtapose it with other adjectives like "good," "clean," "bright," "nice-looking," "handsome," "calm," and "crisp." This aspect of the use of *articulate* is what makes it really feel like a backhanded compliment. When Reverend Al Sharpton responded, "I take a bath everyday," he was pointing out the insidiousness (no matter how inadvertent) of these kinds of juxtapositions. Black folks' assumption is this: If one needs to consistently point out that an individual Black person is "good," "clean," "bright," "nice-looking," "handsome," "calm," and "crisp," it suggests that White private opinions about Blacks, in general, hold that they are usually the opposite— "bad," "dirty," "dumb," "mean-looking," "ugly," "angry," and "rough." So, it's not merely the use of *articulate* that's problematic, nor the expression of surprise or bewilderment that makes it suspect, it is also the fact that its adjectival neighbors describe qualities that help create these exceptionalizing discourses.[24] These common linguistic patterns open *articulate* up to challenges of subtextual racism, one that speakers may not even realize that they hold and perpetuate.

Is This Really about Race, Though? The Media Refer to White Men as Articulate All the Time

In a recent blog post, a Black woman in her late thirties wrote about the White use of the word *articulate*. In her post, she epitomized the Black folk theory about *articulate*'s social meaning:

> To me, whenever someone describes another person as "articulate," even if I just see this in written form, I automatically assume that the person doing the describing is white, and the person being described is black. Articulateness is never pointed out between other groups of people. Therefore, I see "articulate" as some sort of negative euphemism about black people in general. I see it as saying this as a way to actually negate the black person's intelligence. Like they managed to sound articulate by accident or something.

> Recently I was watching the show *Snapped,* which chronicles true crimes committed by women. The show interviews relevant parties, including the law enforcement officials involved in the case. One story was about a black woman who had a Ph.D. in chemistry and was an especially successful chemist. The interviewees couldn't shut up about how highly educated she was. One detective described with obvious admiration—an unusual attitude

when talking about a murderer—about how despite all the evidence against her, "She made an excellent witness—she was so articulate on the stand!"

Why was that something to point out? That a woman with a Ph.D. was articulate? Very troubling word.[25]

This example presents a strong interpretation of the *articulate*-as-White-racism theory and raises some interesting questions. Is the person doing the describing always White? More importantly, is the person being described always Black?

A blogger who refers to himself as the "Undercover Black Man"[26] (most probably because he's White), responds to this interpretation of *articulate* by saying, "I must say, with all due respect: Buuullshit!" The White folk theory on *articulate* usually uses a number of tactics to deny that there is any racism involved. Adherents of this folk social analysis claim White people are angry at the insinuation that you never hear anyone referring to a White person as articulate. It's just not true, they say. They are quick to point out that the media has referred to White politicians as "articulate," and therefore, it cannot possibly be about race, Blackness, or Barack Obama. In its denial of the racially significant meanings of *articulate,* the argument relies on logic that ignores the social and structural patterning of these events altogether. The argument uses the relatively infrequent examples of *articulate* being used to describe White politicians in order to "debunk" and deny any possibility of racism. As Undercover Black Man writes, "We have the handy example of another well-spoken Democratic candidate in this very presidential race...John Edwards."

After a half dozen examples of the media referring to John Edwards as "articulate," Undercover Black Man rests his case: "You know what? I don't think John Edwards or his sympathizers consider it a freakin' *insult* that he keeps being called 'articulate.'" Of course, right there in his list of quotations (his evidence to support a nonracist reading of *articulate*) is this one: "Edwards is a young, smart, articulate, and a good Southerner with moderate tendencies and a heart for traditional Democratic issues (December 28, 2006)." Undercover Black Man fails on two major points. One, he fails to contexualize these readings of John Edwards, a southern candidate for President, within the pervasive U.S. ideologies about "dumb," "slow", or "slovenly" southern speech. He doesn't consider that John Edwards is also being singled out as "articulate" because—as many speakers of southern varieties of English can attest—northern folks often compliment them because they expect them to speak like Gomer Pyle!

Just as with the racializing hegemony evident in Obama's case, "regionalizing hegemony" in the United States marginalizes southern speech varieties in relation to the supposedly nonaccented midwestern varieties of English one hears on the evening news. So both bloggers' perspectives are incomplete, partial readings. Black people are not the only ones to be "complimented" as articulate in this backhanded way, nor does the use of the "compliment" toward White people negate the racial and discriminatory patterning. These kinds of exceptionalizing discourses are not only used against Blacks and southerners, they often appear in conversations about immigrants, especially undocumented immigrants. Just recently, in July 2011, National Public Radio (NPR) host Terry Gross was speaking about undocumented Filipino immigrant and Pulitzer prize winning *Washington Post* writer Jose Antonio Vargas. Many well-intentioned supporters exceptionalize Vargas by making a case for a pathway to citizenship because he is "the kind" of immigrant that "we" should be helping become an American. They often point to the "articulate," "bright," and "hardworking" undocumented immigrants (especially the DREAMers), exceptionalizing them compared to their presumed unintelligent and lazy counterparts who speak a variety of English accented by their primary languages. In short, the use of *articulate* plays well into exceptionalizing discourses of race and other marginalized social and linguistic identities. So, to answer the question, Is this really about race, though? Well, it's about race and about more than race.

Reading *Articulate* as an Exceptionalizing Discourse: White, Black, and Multiracial Perspectives

In order to push on some of these theories of *articulate* a bit more, we asked a group of approximately 50 racially and ethnically diverse American college undergraduates one question: "If someone referred to you as 'articulate,' how would you feel? Explain your answer." They were also asked to submit information about their age, race, ethnicity, gender, and biographical background. Overall, the results reflect four major factors. They: (1) Confirm folk theories of *articulate* as racist discourse, (2) Complicate the conversation by looking across racial and ethnic groups in the United States, (3) Demonstrate the multiple problematic links between "articulateness" and "Whiteness" and "articulateness" and "intelligence" across groups, and (4) Reveal that language, in general, and exceptionalizing discourses, in particular, are anything but neutral. Rather, language is often socially charged, loaded with issues of race, class, citizenship, and other forms of social identification.

One general finding is that while there were Americans across all racial and ethnic groups who viewed the adjective as an unproblematic compliment, this group was predominantly White. Many White respondents expressed "pride" and "happiness" at being considered articulate, as exemplified by this student's response: "In reference to someone describing me as articulate, I believe that I would feel proud. I think I'd feel this way because to me, articulate means being able to express yourself clearly with knowledge of the connotation and meaning of every word you're saying. I like to be able to express myself in a way that is clear to others."

A second general finding is that the overwhelming majority of Black Americans found *articulate* to be problematic, with some downright offended and insulted. In general, Black respondents seemed to go beyond dictionary definitions of the word to think more critically about the social meanings of the word across contexts. The social meanings, the kinds of social messages encoded in the word's use, seemed far more salient for Black Americans. For example, this respondent recalled an early childhood experience:

> I remember the first time that someone did refer to me as articulate, I was about nine and had no idea what it meant. Upon finding out its definition I was flattered. I feel that labeling a child as articulate might be appropriate in many contexts because they might display a level of speaking and conveying their ideas above what you would have expected. However, to label an adult as articulate can be very insulting. It implies that you didn't expect them to be able to express their feelings and ideas with such fluency or clarity. I personally would be especially offended if someone non black called me articulate now because it implies that they expected less of me.

This respondent hailed from Chicago and described himself as an "African American (Descendant of slaves in America)...with a very close extended family," with much of them "from the South as well."

Beyond these expected results, a third general finding of the survey suggested that multiracial Americans seemed not to possess strong interpretations of either side of the *articulate* debate. Further, the data suggests that those Black Americans who identified as Black but were also multiracial— and were socialized in predominantly non-Black communities—also did not view *articulate* as definitively problematic. While we don't want to make too much out of these few responses, they do muddy the clear waters a bit. One example comes from a respondent who self-identifies as "Black" and "African American," yet he also described himself as having a "black father" and a "white mother." He was "usually one or one of a few black students in class in school" where the "majority of the school were Mexican and Asian." His response shows no awareness of *articulate* as part of an exceptionalizing discourse:

> I would feel very uplifted and proud of myself if someone else considered me "articulate." I believe that being described as articulate means that I am good at framing what I want to say into a way that sounds convincing, sometimes, even if my opinion is totally off or wrong. Great use of diction and syntax come with being described as articulate.

This respondent was the only self-identified Black respondent to not consider the complex social meanings of *articulate*.

Another example comes from a respondent who self-identified as "Asian, African American, Native American, Caucasian" and expressed an almost equally uncritical view:

> I take great pride in being called articulate and have been called articulate. Both of my parents are extremely well educated people who have had to give many a speech and were both lawyers who had to speak effectively and persuasively to prove a point in the courtroom. I am certainly guilty of mumbling around my friends.... Yet when I got up to give an oral presentation for my class, I enunciated every word, let my personality shine through my speech, and received glowing reviews. My parents tell me all the time, "We know you can articulate, so why not do it all the time?" In the last couple of years I have become much better at enunciating all the time, and from the day I arrived [on campus] ... others pinned me as an intelligent and articulate person based on the content and delivery of my comments.... If someone looked at me and were shocked that I was articulate, I might be slightly offended, but so far, the situations in which I've been called articulate have only succeeded in making me proud.

While taking great pride in being labeled "articulate," this young woman might be only "slightly" offended by the "compliment" but, more often than not, would accept the praise as well deserved.

The survey further revealed that American ideologies of articulateness are even more complex and nuanced than they appear. First, it seems that some Asian, Latino, Middle Eastern, and other Americans also view *articulate* as problematic but for different reasons. To this group, articulateness is sometimes principally about making them the exception to a (racist) rule, and other times, it's about casting them and their speech behavior as White, an identity category they resist. While this was implicit in some Black responses as well, and much of the educational literature focuses on Black youth resisting "acting White" and "sounding White," these responses allow us to highlight the nuances of the problematic link between "articulateness" and "Whiteness" in other groups. The first example comes from a Mexican-American self-identified "Hispanic/Latina." She writes that being referred to as "articulate" would be a "compliment," especially in academic settings. Feeling marginalized in these contexts, she reports that it would allow her "to claim an identity as a student who 'belongs' and 'fits in' with the world of academia." Then she adds another perspective about her home community in northern California: "Talking as I am writing for this response is asking to be ridiculed where I grew up....Most of my classmates would be quick to say that both the sound of my voice when I speak English and the vocabulary I use make me sound like a white girl. In this case, being articulate is an insult because it gets me the label of sounding white."

The second example is from someone who describes her race as "Asian" and her ethnicity as "Native Hawaiian." Like the Mexican American respondent above, she is able to see both sides of the *articulate* problem; she also resists being racialized as "White" (and classed as "middle"). She writes:

> I think being described as "articulate" is a great thing—to me it means that I can clearly express my feelings and thoughts to others in words....However, I guess there's a flip side where being articulate means speaking clearly and crisply and very prim and proper. This seems very white and middle class. I wouldn't necessarily take *that* as a compliment, especially if "someone" was referring to my everyday way of speaking.

These last two responses show how, in the United States, powerful language ideologies link articulateness with "standard" English with Whiteness. This occurs largely because race and class inequality overlap to the point at which the language variety that folks think of as "standard" English is straightforwardly (if not problematically) constructed as "White English." For many Americans, these ways of speaking become associated with White folks, especially those born with a "silver spoon" in their mouths. As emblems of dominant White cultural privilege, then, sounding "articulate" or sounding "White" is sometimes rejected by those who have been racialized as Others their entire lives.

"Forcing Our Tongues to Fit into a Western System": Insights from Those on the Linguistic Margins (Bi- and Multilinguals)

Asian, Latino, Middle Eastern, and other Americans complicated our survey results in other unexpected ways. In terms of reading the social meanings of *articulate*, some respondents expressed a "split view" that depended on their linguistic background as much if not more than their race. In many cases, respondents do not view *articulate* as problematic in English, but their responses grow more critical when speaking about the language of immigrants, their family members, or those with "accents." Because these Americans are located on the linguistic margins—either they or their parents learned English as a second language—some felt honored to be referred to as articulate, since it meant that they had fully mastered English. At the same time, however, these Americans were also able to point out the challenges of belonging to communities where "accents" from languages other than English are linguistically marginalized.

This example comes from a respondent who describes herself as "Filipino by culture (little blood) and Lebanese by blood (no culture)" but as having grown up "in a predominantly Mexican community" in Texas. She begins, "If someone described me as 'articulate,' I would feel like I had received a great compliment....I believe that the term articulate can apply across languages and the situations they are used in to mean a clear presentation of complex ideas. Therefore, I view articulate as a compliment." Then, in what she describes as "a complete side-note," she provides further information about her mother's language:

> I called my mother at her work today. As she works in an office and several people could have potentially answered the phone, I was not sure if it was her who picked up. To be quite honest, when I heard the woman's voice on the other end of the phone, my immediate thought was, *Nope, that's not mom*. I asked to speak to Soraya, and she said, "Hi!" I said, "Mom! I didn't recognize you..." Her response? "I know. Different when I talk right, huh?"...I had never considered my mother's way of speaking as "not right." Granted, she has a Filipino accent (so I've been told), but her own assertion that her way of speaking is wrong made me realize even more how powerful language really is.

In this next example, from a self-identified "biracial (Hispanic and white)" respondent, we see how the split view of those between linguistic worlds gives *articulate* different meanings. She does not see *articulate* as problematic in English but makes some complex connections in relation to "color" when speaking of Spanish:

> I speak the English that my parents do, so I've never faced the additional challenges of feeling like the only "articulate" person in, for example, an immigrant family that doesn't speak English or a family without parents who are lawyers....Also, I identify as biracial (Hispanic and white) so I've never felt the need to speak the same way as people who look like me. Interestingly, I have felt pressure to speak Spanish because I ended up with the darkest skin of any of my siblings. I have not felt a similar pressure to speak a certain type of English.

For this respondent, the link between language and race is not as salient as the link between language and "color." She does not experience pressure to speak a particular variety of English, but because of her "darker" skin, she has felt social pressure to speak Spanish, as if a higher melanin count leads to higher degrees of Spanish fluency. This respondent's description is similar to existing ideologies of language and race/color expressed by some within Spanish-speaking Latino communities, those that assume that darker-skinned Latinos should or must speak Spanish while giving lighter-skinned Latinos a "pass."[27]

These next two examples provide heavy insights into the complex nature of the *articulate* debate. They also help to show that the underlying cause of Black suspicion and offense when it comes to the word is due to broader, ongoing social processes that relate as much to the deprecation of Blackness as they do to linguistic marginalization in general. The following insight comes from someone who self-identifies as "½ Korean, ½ mixed white" and represents a great case of the split view. Due to her position on the racial and linguistic margins, she claims that she is not "articulate" and often feels like "she can't gather her thoughts to be expressed in an articulate manner." So, her first response to being referred to as articulate "would be surprise, but also pleased that I'd come across that way." She later complicates her own view by providing an Asian American vantage point to the discussion: "I think, though, that the word contains a bit of surprise in it, as if one is exceeding expectations...if someone told me I was 'articulate' after asking where I was from, or if I spoke English, or anything else pointing to my race/ethnicity, then I'd be annoyed." She then explains why this might be particularly frustrating for Asian Americans, who are often having to battle the "forever foreigner" stereotype.[28]

Asian-American speech doesn't get stereotyped as inarticulate like black and Latino speech does, but it does sometimes get stereotyped as accented. Maybe the person was trying to give me a compliment, but Asian immigration to the U.S. is not new, the U.S. as a multiracial society is not new, and multiracial people aren't new. I would feel Othered and out of place, even though this is my place.

The final response in this section is worth quoting in full as it reveals further complexity and the often unacknowledged emotional pain of growing up on the linguistic margins of America. This respondent is an indigenous speaker of Hawai'i Creole English, a stigmatized variety of American English:

Answering this question is difficult. I spent the majority of my childhood trying to prove my intelligence. Growing up in an alternative school was difficult. I didn't learn to read or write in English until the 6th grade and even though I was different from my classmates in that most of the community didn't expect us to succeed in a mainstream school I knew from a young age that I had the work ethic and even more important the support to be successful outside of our community. At the same time I struggled with...being judged for speaking primarily Pidgin. We were taught that Pidgin would prevent us from being successful, and prevent people from respecting us. So those of us who could, or cared enough, tried to force our tongues to fit into a western system that would only patronize us for our efforts. Because of this, a part of me, the part that so wanted to be successful as a child would feel honored almost at the thought of someone calling me articulate. But the version of me that has learned about the motivations for consolidating communities into a singular language variety makes me feel offended to be placed under that hammer. I know that code switching is a sign of intelligence, even if it's not recognized as one. I know that I have the ability, because of my background to effectively communicate with people from a broad range of backgrounds in a way that is meaningful to them. I would call this skill articulate if it weren't already tainted with expectations of covering up any language variety that doesn't agree with what some people call 'Educated English.' So for now, I can do without such compliments—I don't need them.

While speaking from a particular vantage point of the linguistically colonized in Hawai'i, this young woman expresses several shared sentiments of those on the linguistic margins. First, we can see clearly that Americans on the linguistic margins—whether they speak Arabic, Black Language, Span(gl)ish, Tagalog, or Hawai'i Creole English—learn the dominant ideology that links articulateness with intelligence and Whiteness. Second, rather than continue to feel shame, she expresses an alternative ideology that privileges bilingual and multilingual speakers' abilities to switch in and out of multiple languages. Lastly, she frames *articulate* as a political term. Far from neutral, it is loaded with a cultural-linguistic hegemony that imposes itself on people, and praises them for "covering up" their own language varieties rather than rewarding them for speaking multiple language varieties.

White Paternalism, Black Empathy: Nuancing the Black Folk Theory

The Black folk theory of the social meanings of *articulate* is more layered than previously described. In several responses, Black Americans noted that age was a critical factor in their analysis. Most Black folks can get with adult references to children as "articulate." What they can't get with is when Whites refer to Black adults in the same way; it smacks of that same paternalistic attitude that infantilizes Black intelligence, bringing up images of *articulate* being uttered with an accompanying "pat on the head." As one young woman put it, "I would understand a tone of surprise if I was five years old, but at my age (22) it should be an expectation. As an African-American, I am even more sensitive and defensive about how people perceive my linguistic abilities." In other words, to make it plain, there is no normal developmental issue here, where a child is being socialized through praise into adult ways of speaking. Rather, there is a peculiar social issue, where Black people feel similarly rewarded for being socialized into White ways of speaking. Like the previously cited narrative from the Hawai'i Creole English speaker, the assumption is that Black folks should want to leave their language behind and "move on up" to the White highrises like the Jeffersons. Not only can Black people call the lie on that (as if upward mobility was just about language, not race and class), but there is also the almost inexplicable realization that one is being praised for abiding by White norms, or as one respondent put it, "as someone who talks like an upper-class white boy."

These issues of language and racial politics are heightened for African Americans in comparison to many immigrant populations because African Americans do not consider themselves learners of English as a second language. These heightened racial politics also have a long history in the United States and are incredibly enduring. It should not come as a surprise to anyone that Blacks might react so negatively to White paternalistic views of their language. These views formed the core of the early scholarship on the language of Black Americans that theorized Black Language as "baby-talk."[29] Blinded by a firm belief, a science even, of the biological inferiority of Blacks, other linguists took the baby talk theory to new lows. Writing about Black speech communities in the American southeast, one linguist "explains" the differences in Black speech not as caused by the learning of English and influences from African languages but as caused by "[i]ntellectual indolence, or laziness, mental and physical, which shows itself in the shortening of words, the elision of syllables, and modification of every difficult enunciation. It is the indolence, mental and physical...that is its most characteristic feature."[30] Is there any wonder why Black people look suspiciously and contemptuously on White "compliments" of their "articulateness"?

Many in the Black community are aware of how their speech is perceived by White and other Americans. As linguists have noted, there are websites dedicated to the mockery of Black speech and every news report on Ebonics is followed by a litany of disgustingly racist diatribes online.[31] In terms of our *articulate* analysis, we can historicize this linguistic monitoring within the American institution of slavery where we find ample evidence that the policing of Black Language goes hand in hand with the policing of Black bodies. In their postings to capture runaway enslaved Africans, Whites often distinguished between them by their abilities to speak English. An ad in the *New York Evening Post* in 1774 read: "Ran away...a new Negro Fellow named Prince, he can't Scarce speak a Word of English." And take this ad from the *North Carolina Gazette* in 1760: "Ran away from the Subscriber, living near Salisbury, North Carolina...a negro fellow named JACK....He is about 30 years of age, and about 5 feet high, speaks bad English." Contrast these two announcements with this one from Philadelphia's *American Weekly Mercury* in 1734: "Run away...A Negro Man named *Jo Cuffy*, about 20 Years of age...he's Pennsylvania born and speaks good English." Thus, we can see that the White practice of separating "good" and "bad" Black speakers of English is an enduring legacy of the African slave trade. Whites made use of exceptionalizing discourses to refer to their "runway slaves" as speaking "good" or "exceptional" English.[32]

Despite this long and horrid history, survey results showed that at least one or two Black folks stand on principle and express a sense of empathy toward Whites. Rather than automatically reading *articulate* as part of a system of racist, White paternalism toward Blacks, this respondent acknowledges the distinct possibility of a racist subtext and then expresses his internal conflict at length:

> The hard part about reacting to being called articulate is that I don't want my judgment of the speaker's views to be based on a double standard. I am in danger of making an assumption about the speaker's awareness, or lack thereof, of the issues that affect many urban minority areas so that many kids that live there don't get complimented as articulate....I try hard to approach people, especially people I am just meeting, without bias. This situation is even more difficult because being called articulate is often something that happens to me when speaking to someone I'm just meeting for the first time. Although I am using things like context clues and body language, my reaction in these circumstances is almost impossible to do without assumptions about the person I am talking to that have not had time to be confirmed or denied. Therefore, this situation shows its complexity because of its potential for unfair assumptions to be made on both parts.

This respondent recognizes that White "compliments" about his "articulateness" are probably "linked to [his] being black" yet does not want to fall prey to making similar kinds of race-based assumptions about the White person giving the "compliment." He does not want to prejudge people that he meets for the first time, even as "being called articulate is often something that happens to [him] when speaking to someone [he's] just meeting for the first time."

Some readers might expect us to view this example of Black empathy as admirable, as something to be emulated by other victims of racism in order "to break the cycle of hate," as popular White antiracist discourses go. But there's a different point to be made here. While this respondent's heartfelt narrative displays an empathetic, honest struggle with the *articulate* question, it lacks a critical perspective on racism in at least four dimensions. To begin with, the respondent is right in resisting making assumptions about individual utterances. However, what many people are responding to is how utterances are structured socially so that particular patterns appear far more frequently than others. From our previous examples, for instance, it's important to remember that *articulate* is used by members of the dominant culture to describe the speech of those on the social and linguistic margins, such as children, southerners, immigrants, second language learners, and so on. So, there is a salient link between those characterized as articulate and social marginality.

Second, as we previously stated, it ain't really helpful to look at any one particular utterance of *articulate* and attempt to guess the speaker's intention. What is useful, though, is looking across utterances and noticing, for example, patterns in other juxtaposed adjectives. These other neighboring adjectives simultaneously frame the speaker and the group to which the speaker belongs in opposition to each other. The exceptional "peaceful, patriotic, moderate Muslim," for example, versus her "violent, anti-American extremist Muslim community" is one such opposition heard frequently in post-9/11 American public discourses. So, in addition to the broader, interactional patterns of who utters what to whom, we must also consider the more microlinguistic patterns that we use to construct "articulate" exceptions to the racist rule.

Thirdly, within the empathetic frame, racism becomes the property of individuals, something that lives inside one person's head or heart. Racism is constructed as something that can be denied or refuted depending on a person's real intentions. The problem with this, of course, is that racism is perpetually deniable because no one can ever really know if someone else harbors racist thoughts or feelings and, especially, if those thoughts and feelings will lead to racist actions. As noted by Imani Perry in *More Beautiful and More Terrible: The Embrace and Transcendence of Racial Inequality in the United States*, intentionality is no longer a good measure of racism. People can—and often do—"promulgate racist imagery and ideas without having any interest in identifying oneself as racist."[33] Further, as critical race theorists have long argued, racism is more productively viewed not as an individual, emotional problem but as an institutional, systemic one. The question worth asking is not "Does that particular person harbor racist beliefs when they call me *articulate*?" but "How does the repeated, patterned use of *articulate* draw on racist ideologies and (re)produce racial inequalities?" Rather than trying to prove if one person's utterance is evidence of racism, we can more fruitfully examine the ways our everyday discourse is racially structured. So, in a "postintent" era, whether racist "compliments" are intentional or even conscious becomes far less interesting than how these "compliments" are patterned over time and space and how they perpetuate racist ideas.

The empathetic frame—or not wanting to make assumptions of racism based on a single utterance—assumes that words can be lifted up outta their context and still carry meaning, but context is crucial to how we make meaning. The repeated use of particular words by particular people in particular contexts and situations over time is how words come to take on socially charged meanings in the first place. Black speakers, for example, interpret Whites' use of *articulate* within a body of sociohistorical discourses about White ideologies of race and language as well as contemporary experiences with White racism and linguistic discrimination. So, when it comes to *articulate*, we have to attend to microlinguistic and broader interactional patterns of use, yes, but we also have to consider how *articulate* articulates (to use our beloved adjective as a verb) with other sociohistorical discourses and ideologies. Further, we need to develop a more critical perspective on racism as not individual or even necessarily intentional but as institutional and most definitely consequential.

Articulate as a Gatekeeping Mechanism: Racial Segregation, Cultural Assimilation and Linguistic Policing

The *articulate* question is a complex, multilayered one. An in-depth analysis brings with it a whole complicated set of issues that raises questions about American society and the American experiment. As an example of the policing of language—specifically, the White policing of Black Language—our analysis raises questions about the workings of multiple forms of linguistic racism in the United States. The *articulate* question is linked to deeper concerns with stubborn, enduring sociostructural and sociocultural aspects of American society. Specifically, we wanna talk about how *articulate* brings to the fore a set of related issues from racial segregation to cultural assimilation and linguistic policing (from everyday social monitoring to patterned language-based racial discrimination).

Earlier we quoted a survey respondent who noted that she would take *articulate* as a compliment if she was 5 years old. But now that she's 22, it should be an expectation and is, therefore, read as an insult. She then went on to add, "As an African-American, I am even more sensitive and defensive about how people perceive my linguistic abilities." The loaded phrase here is "As an African-American," which suggests that being "complimented" as articulate evokes longstanding White discourses of Black Language (and people) as "deficient." Another respondent felt that he was being "praised" for abiding by White linguistic norms, or as he put it more directly, for talkin "like an upper-class white boy." For this respondent, *articulate* links up not only with discourses of Black deficiency but also with hypocritical discourses of racial assimilation and integration. The combination of these two discourses—Black deficiency and racial assimilation and integration—suggests that in order for a Black person to make it in America, he or she must be an exception to the racist rule of Black deficiency and must prove it by not speaking like "those other Black people." Further, the implication is that, unless you talk like an "upper-class white boy," you will not succeed in America. And this brings us to the real problem with *articulate*, which is the real problem with Black Language.

White America has long insisted on White English (not Chicano English, not Black English, not no other kind of English) as the price of admission into its economic and social mainstream. Even many otherwise liberal and progressive Whites remain rigid and inflexible when it comes to linguistic diversity. While some may deny their complicity in this kind of linguistic hegemony, others earnestly work toward convincing linguistic minorities that the journey to upward mobility will be easier for them once they drop their cultural-linguistic baggage and acquire what they uncritically refer to as "standard" English. (Hey, it sound nicer than saying, "once you talk like me," right?). So, despite America's expressed egalitarian values, linguistic hegemony is framed as beneficial to linguistic minorities rather than harmful, and linguistic homogenization is presented as preferable to linguistic diversity. Black Americans, then, who have developed a language, a way of speaking, that serves as a source of solidarity, cultural pride, creative literary production, artistic expression, and just everyday kickin it are hypocritically asked to abandon that language in order to "make it" in a "White world." So, when White people praise and reward "articulate" Black speakers, they are also celebrating Black movement toward the White mainstream and away from a threatening cultural separatism. As Lippi-Green once put it:

> The real trouble with Black English is not the verbal aspect system which distinguishes it from other varieties of US English, or the rhetorical strategies which draw such a vivid contrast, it is simply this: [Black English] is tangible and irrefutable evidence that there is a distinct, healthy, functioning African American culture which is not white, and which does not want to be white. This is a state of affairs that is unacceptable to many.[34]

She goes on to pose this difficult, complex question: Given America's national discourses of *"one nation, indivisible,"* and the official "end" of racial segregation in "schooling, housing, public places, and the workplace...what does it mean then to say that there is an African American culture distinct enough from other American cultures to have its own variety of English, a variety that persists in the face of overt stigmatization?"[35]

On the other side of this coin are some really troubling facts about racial integration. While most White people claim to want racial integration, it's like they be talkin outta both sides of they mouth. Racial integration in American society is still far from reality, in part, because as Barack Obama observed in *The Audacity of Hope*, "Few minorities can isolate themselves entirely from white society—certainly not in the way that whites can successfully avoid contact with members of other races."[36] In contemporary American society, even in the Obama Era, there is a critical disjuncture between White attitudes and behaviors in regard to racial integration and equity. As Stanford University sociologist Prudence Carter points out in *Stubborn Roots: The Threat of Cultural Inflexibility to Equity in U.S. & South African Schools*, while many middle-class Whites, in particular, have absorbed the discourse of racial integration, their actions militate against it.[37] Racial integration is apparently a nice theory, but in practice, folks find all kinds of ways to resist racial integration in schooling, housing, and so on. So, clearly, the irony—better put, hypocrisy—is that even as Whites promise milk and honey to Blacks willing to accept a particular form of linguistic colonization, they be steady *workin* to deny access to the Promised Land like it was some kinda gentrified gated community!

Since outright racial discrimination is legally banned (though still widely practiced), language has become an even more important vehicle in the denial of access to resources to Blacks, particularly housing. When *articulate* functions as an exceptionalizing discourse, it separates the speaker from other Black people, who are largely working class, the kind of Black people that White gatekeepers want to keep far away from their children and their property values. They are also typically people who "sound Black"—and due, in part, to racial segregation and in part to Black cultural priorities—have not mastered "Ole Massa's" linguistic norms. Over the last several decades, since the outlawing of racist, discriminatory real estate practices, housing discrimination has become more stealth. We have seen the growth of a new form of racism in housing that relies on linguistic cues as indices of someone's race, ethnicity, class, nationality, sexuality, region, and so on. For example, if a landlord receives a call from a prospective tenant and denies that application solely because of the tenant's race, that's straight-up illegal, Racism 1.0. This does not prevent a landlord, however, from making sociological inferences based on the prospective tenant's speech (thinking to oneself, "That tenant sounds Black") and then conjuring up a false reason ("it's been rented," for example) to deny the tenant's application: Racism 2.0.

As scholars, our first experience with this kind of linguistic racism occurred a little more than two decades ago. In 1989, Geneva Smitherman was asked to be an expert witness in a housing discrimination case in the Detroit area suburbs. The chief plaintiff in the case, *Young v. Riverland Woods Apartments et al.*, was a Black woman who had appeared at the apartment manager's office in person and was told that there were "no vacancies." This was a sista whose speech was, according to many, "White-sounding." Smitherman's role was to establish that people could and did make accurate racial assessments based on the sound of someone's voice over the phone. To accomplish this, she played tapes of White and Black speakers, most of them colleagues of the plaintiff, to both White and Black listeners from the Detroit metropolitan area. Each speaker was heard on tape saying the same script, a set of statements and questions about renting an apartment. Consistently, listeners were able to identify the "Black-sounding" voices as Black and the "White-sounding" voices as White. Further, both the plaintiff and another Black woman who "sounded White" were also consistently identified as White. However, when the plaintiff had shown up at the apartment building, she was told that there were no vacancies. Between that kind of linguistic evidence and the Black and White testers who visited the apartment complex— in pairs, an hour apart—the jury was soundly convinced that Riverland Woods was guilty of racial discrimination in housing. Cost them a nice piece of change too.

The case of *articulate* is directly relevant to this form of linguistic racism. While Smitherman showed that most speakers, most of the time, are able to correctly identify a speaker's race by the sound of her voice (and volumes of linguistic research have supported this finding), her results also showed the potential for racial misidentification. If Black women, including the plaintiff, were identified as White, then it became possible for landlords to deny their ability to detect race based on voice alone. What is relevant here is that only the Black women who were preidentified as "sounding White" would be likely to receive return calls and/ or to be told on the phone that there were available apartments. Whites rewarded individual "White-sounding" speakers in much the same way that "articulate" speakers are praised, while "Black-sounding" speakers were punished.

Further, this case highlights the complexity of this form of linguistic racism because it demonstrates how race intersects with class in the minds of the listeners on the other end of the phone. More often than not, Black speakers who receive White "compliments" for being "articulate" are highly educated and middle class. Of course, the glaring irony here is that as Whites reward Blacks for being "articulate"—tying promises of upward mobility and desires of racial integration to one's ability to master White linguistic norms—White racist practices often reveal the ambivalence (at best) and hypocrisy (at worst) of this "damned if you do damned if you don't" language politics. The somber reality for many African Americans is that, still, no matter how "articulate" yo ass is, upon visiting in person, can't nuthin fool the landlord now, baby—you Black, Jack!

Ten years after Smitherman testified in Detroit, sociologists Douglas Massey and Garvey Lundy at the University of Pennsylvania documented this type of linguistic racism in the housing market in the Philly area. Similar to Smitherman's experiments, the research team designed a study with male and female speakers of "White Middle-Class English, Black Accented English, and Black English Vernacular."[38] In an article published in the *Urban Affairs Review*, the authors found that "rental agents now use linguistic cues over the phone to assign prospective renters to racial categories and then vary their behavior systematically to discriminate on the basis of inferred race." Compared with Whites, Blacks were "less likely to get through and speak to a rental agent, less likely to be told of a unit's availability, more likely to pay application fees, and more likely to have credit worthiness mentioned as a potential problem for qualifying for a lease." These effects were "generally exacerbated by gender and class" with "the most disadvantaged group" being "lower-class black females."[39]

This real and tangible example of language policing has recently been given the name *linguistic profiling*[40] by Washington University professor John Baugh. H. Samy Alim, as a graduate student at Stanford University, was privileged to be a part of the Linguistic Profiling Research Team from 2001 to 2003, where he was first exposed to perceptual and phonetic studies of linguistic racism. In these studies, linguists concluded that "(a) dialect-based discrimination takes place, (b) ethnic group affiliation is recoverable from speech, and (c) very little speech is needed to discriminate between dialects."[41] Other Linguistic Profiling Research Team members documented the widespread nature of this discriminatory linguistic practice. Ashlyn Aiko Nelson, then graduate student in economics and education, who is currently professor at Indiana University, studied "the sound of equal opportunity" by examining how linguistic profiling worked in terms of credit and housing access for linguistic minorities.[42] In this work, she presents strong evidence "of unequal access to credit for language minorities" and makes a clear link between race/ethnicity, language, and one's ability to build wealth in the United States. Dawn L. Smalls, then a Stanford Law School student, who is currently Executive Secretary to the US Department of Health and Human Services, investigated linguistic profiling in the law by examining "its use in employment discrimination, housing discrimination, and...the criminal law."[43] Since the early 2000s, studies of linguistic profiling have grown in scope, demonstrating the pervasiveness of this practice and its applicability across linguistically marginalized populations, from bilingual speakers to deaf signers. Baugh has edited two volumes of studies that explore this phenomenon in interdisciplinary and global perspective.[44]

Learning to Let Go

In *The Audacity of Hope*, Barack Obama writes that "[i]n general, members of every minority group continue to be measured largely by the degree of our assimilation—how closely speech patterns, dress, or demeanor conform to the dominant white culture—and the more that a minority strays from these external markers, the more he or she is subject to negative assumptions."[45] Perhaps more important is Obama's consideration of the overall impact of dominant, racist ideologies on ethnoracial minorities in the United States. "It's unrealistic to believe that these stereotypes don't have some cumulative impact on the often snap decisions of who's hired and who's promoted, on who's arrested and who's prosecuted, on how you feel about the customer who just walked into your store or about the demographics of your children's school."[46] And we would add, too, how one feels about the voice on the other end of the telephone, the family who just moved into the neighborhood, or the prospective tenant who just walked into the apartment office. More than about simply being acceptable or palatable to White America, President Obama's framing of race and language issues as having tangible consequences for people of Color is of critical importance.

The fact that Racism 2.0 is subtle, rather than blatant, and institutional, rather than individual, makes it all the more insidiously oppressive and effective as a system that maintains unequal access to social and economic resources. As we have shown, the policing of language is a fake-out, an excuse for preventing marginalized groups from accessing power, property, and influence. It ain't ever really about "your verbs agreeing" or "enunciating the ends of your words." Because of the strong links between language and identity, linguistic discrimination is often nothing more than racial and ethnic discrimination by proxy. In light of the reality of language-based racism, we are sure that some of y'all are thinking, "In the face of all of this evidence, why don't Black people just let go of their cultural way of speaking so that at least they can escape Racism 2.0 (linguistic profiling), even if they can't escape Racism 1.0 (being visually identified and denied based on race)?"

First, if we truly believe in the American "experiment," the ideal of American equality and democracy does not require cultural-linguistic homogenization. Quite the opposite: The American value of diversity within democracy is touted as one of our greatest strengths. While Barack Obama's common refrain that "[o]nly in America is my story possible" might be an example of American exceptionalism—setting America apart from and above other nations—it also expresses the value placed on diversity in American society.

Second, as most linguistically marginalized Americans are painfully aware, while some individuals can styleshift and codeswitch to an extent that they are racially unidentifiable, many others simply cannot. Even when some folks speak "flawless standard English," they can still be identified as Black by their voice quality, frequency and pitch, patterns of intonation, and so on. Barack Obama, for example, is sometimes identified as "sounding Black" just by the "baritone of his voice." (We in some deep ishhh if our very own pres-o-dent can't escape linguistic profiling!). In the Massey and Lundy study previously mentioned, their inclusion of "Black Accented English" speakers allowed them to test results for middle-class Blacks who could codeswitch into more "standard" varieties of English (in other words, those most often on the receiving end of *articulate*). Those speakers, though, were also identified as Black due to the pronunciation of certain words (pronouncing *advertised* as *advertahsed*, for example).

Third, language and culture are not things that people can just "let go" of. Speakers of marginalized language varieties—shoot, of any language variety—learn language from the community of speakers within which they are socialized. Linguistic styles and accents are not genetic; they're social. Not to state the obvious, but a Black child does not "sound Black" because he or she is Black. Take that same child and raise him or her in upper middle-class White suburbia or in an isolated rural village in the Japanese countryside, and lo and behold, the child will come up speaking the language varieties of the local speech community. The unfairness of the demand to "just let go" of one's language should be obvious then. Asking people to unlearn or abandon their language is like asking them to go back magically in time and select a different speech community to be raised in. How does one accomplish that? And since this point is often difficult to grasp, consider this: How many White speakers, for example, would be able to pass the test of sounding "authentically" Black? Chances are that most would sound like straight-up posers unless they grew up in Black communities and/or have intimate Black friendship networks. There is little, if any, chance that a White person can "let go" of the markers of his or her Whiteness and even less chance of successfully getting a job or housing or a small business loan, for example, if achieving any of these depended on one's mastery of Black linguistic norms.

Being socialized into a language, into a community of speakers, is also being socialized into a culture. Many Black Americans grow up in a culture that privileges alternative meanings of being "articulate," including those that focus on "speaking clearly" as well as those that emphasize the *art* in articulate. The artful use of language, as we saw in the Chris Rock skit, for example, is a source of pleasure, entertainment, reflection, and of course, socialization. It's not only where you learn to speak the language of those you love; it's where you learn to love and be loved. It's where you have your first formative experiences of being a member of a family, a community, a culture. It's where you develop your first notions of who you are and who you might become. And if you're an ethnoracial minority in the United States, it may also be one of the few spaces where you feel both connected and respected. All of that and more are communicated through language. Why, then, should any American be forced to abandon his or her language variety because of dominant culture's discriminatory practices? If you ask us, it ain't the language and culture that we should be lettin go of; it's these messed-up racist practices.

NOTES

1. Joseph Biden made these remarks in the *New York Observer* in 2007 back when he was running against Barack Obama and Hillary Clinton for the Democratic nomination. For the full story and video, check out: http://www.cnn.com/2007/POLITICS/01/31/biden.obama. Last accessed: 09-01-11.
2. Barack Obama's written statement is quoted in the same CNN article above.
3. This skit is part of Chris Rock's HBO special "Bring the Pain," which appeared in 1996. Rock took home two Emmys for his performance, one in Outstanding Variety, Music, or Comedy Special, and the other in Outstanding Writing for a Variety of Music Program. Throughout his career, Chris Rock has been known for his insightful, sharp, witty commentary on race relations in the United States. On November 29, 2007, Chris Rock, along with leading Black race theorist and then-Princeton University professor Cornel West, introduced then presidential candidate Barack Obama at the Apollo Theatre.
4. From Barack Obama's *The Audacity of Hope: Thoughts on Reclaiming the American Dream* (New York: Crown Publishers, 2006, 235).
5. Wise is one of the most prominent White antiracist voices in the United States. His ability to explain White privilege to White people has been noted since the publication of his first book, *White Like Me: Reflections on Race from a Privileged Son* (Berkeley, CA: Soft Skull Press, 2004). His discussion of "racism 2.0" can be found in the preface of *Between Barack and a Hard Place: Racism and White Denial in the Age of Obama* (San Francisco: City Lights Books, 2009, 8–11).
6. Wise (2009), 9.
7. For Harris-Perry's full comments, see: http://articles.cnn.com/2010–01–11/opinion/harris.lacewell=PM:OPINION. Last accessed: 09-01-11. Also, Stanford University professor of psychology Jennifer Eberhardt and her associates have shown how racist stereotypes continue to haunt Americans. And for Black Americans, racism continues to be a life-and-death matter. Check out these two articles by Eberhardt et al. as a starting point: "Looking Deathworthy: Perceived Stereotypicality of Black Defendants Predicts Capital Sentencing Outcomes" in *Psychological Science*, 17, 383–386, 2006, and "Seeing Black: Race, Crime, and Visual Processing" in *Journal of Personality and Social Psychology*, 87, 876–893, 2004. And if that don't blow your mind, see also, Goff et al. "Not Yet Human: Implicit Knowledge, Historical Dehumanization, and Contemporary Consequences" in *Journal of Personality and Social Psychology*, 94, 292–306, 2008.
8. Check: http://www.cnn.com/2007/POLITICS/01/31/biden.obama. Last accessed: 09-01-11. In the article, Biden is also quoted as making other questionable comments: "In a June 2006 appearance in New Hampshire, the senator commented on

the growth of the Indian-American population in Delaware by saying, 'You cannot go into a 7–11 or a Dunkin' Donuts unless you have a slight Indian accent. Oh, I'm not joking.'"

9. For Bush's comments, see: http://www.washingtonpost.com/wp-dyn/content/article/2007/01/31/AR2007013101304.html. Last accessed: 09-01-11.

10. See: http://www.nytimes.com/2007/02/04/weekinreview/04clemetson.html. Last accessed: 09-01-11.

11. See Philip Arthur Moore in *Racialicious*, http://www.racialicious.com/2007/01/25/barack-obama-is-awb-articulate-while-black/. Last accessed: 09-01-11.

12. In: http://www.nytimes.com/2007/02/04/weekinreview/04clemetson.html. Last accessed: 09-01-11.

13. Check: http://www.cnn.com/2007/POLITICS/01/31/biden.obama. Last accessed: 09-01-11.

14. In: http://www.nytimes.com/2007/02/04/weekinreview/04clemetson.html. Last accessed: 09-01-11.

15. Check out: http://www.time.com/time/quotes/0,26174,1584608,00.html. Last accessed: 09-01-11.

16. See: http://politicalticker.blogs.cnn.com/2010/01/09/reid-apology-for-negro-dialect-comment/. Last accessed: 09-01-11.

17. Barack Obama's *Audacity of Hope*, 235.

18. In: http://www.washingtonpost.com/blogs/plum-line/post/gop-rep-walsh. Last accessed: 09-01-11.

19. This and other White discursive strategies to deny racism have been noted again and again by social science research on language and race, from discourse analyst Teun van Dijk's *Communicating Racism: Ethnic Prejudice in Cognition and Conversation* (Amsterdam: John Benjamins, 1987) to linguistic anthropologist Jane Hill's *The Everyday Language of White Racism* (Malden, MA: Wiley-Blackwell, 2008) to sociologist Eduardo Bonilla-Silva's *Racism without Racists: Color-Blind Racism and Racial Inequality in Contemporary America* (Lanham, MD: Rowman & Littelfield, 3rd edition, 2010).

20. Check the video yourself at: http://mediamatters.org/mmtv/201002220031. Last accessed: 09-01-11.

21. From Rosina Lippi-Green's *English with an Accent: Language, Ideology, and Discrimination in the United States* (London/New York: Routledge, 1997, 179). This work continues to be one of the most influential books within and beyond the academy in the area of language and discrimination. Lippi-Green's model of language subordination shows how linguistic discrimination functions in diverse contexts from the classrooms to the courts to corporate culture and cable television. The new edition, released in late 2011, includes a brief section on the media's monitoring of Obama's language.

22. *Creolization* is a technical linguistic term that refers to the linguistic restructuring that occurs when two language varieties come into contact. The uniqueness of Black Language in the United States is due, in part, to its roots as a contact language that developed in the sociopolitical context of the African slave trade. For a brilliant introduction to concepts such as Creole formation, language mixing, second language learning, and so on, see Donald Winford's *An Introduction to Contact Linguistics* (Malden, MA: Blackwell, 2003).

23. The term *magical Negro* was popularized by Black filmmaker Spike Lee, "super-duper magical Negro" in 2001 (http://www.yale.edu/opa/arc-ybc/v29.n21/story3.html). Last accessed: 09-01-11. It usually refers to a stock character who uses special insights or powers to help, not himself, but the White protagonist and is more generally about the misrepresentation of Black characters in film. For a more complete discussion, see Krin Gabbard's *Black Magic: White Hollywood and African American Culture* (New Brunswick, NJ: Rutgers University Press, 2004) and Matthew Hughes's "Cinethetic Racism: White Redemption and Black Stereotypes in 'Magical Negro' Films" in *Social Problems*, *56(3)*, 543–577, August 2009.

24. In her chapter, "Exceptionally Yours: Racial Escape Hatches in the Contemporary United States" (from her book, *More Beautiful and More Terrible: The Embrace and Transcendence of Racial Inequality in the United States*, NYU Press, 2011), Imani Perry explains that "racial exceptionalism is the practice of creating meaning out of the existence of people of color who don't fit our stereotypic or racial-narrative-based conceptions....The phenomenon of exceptionalism ultimately serves to support a general stereotyping of the larger populace...and justifies that stereotyping within a social context in which racial egalitarianism is proclaimed....When the normal state of people of color is assumed deficient, then the departure from that state puts one into a 'state of exception'" (130–131). In relation to Barack Obama, Perry reads Joseph Biden's "inartful" comments as evidence of "a thematic in American culture in which the idea of Blackness is dissonant to excellence and achievement and in which, in those instances in which excellence and achievement are found in Black bodies, those individuals are cast as necessarily extraordinary and distinguished" (127).

25. From www.dap.com. [No longer accessible].

26. See: http://undercoverblackman.blogspot.com. Last accessed: 09-01-11.

27. These language ideologies insist that darker-skinned Latinos (especially those who look "mas indio," or more indigenous) who do not speak Spanish are only "pretending" not to do so, or that they must be speakers of a stigmatized indigenous "dialecto." Alim has heard this ideology expressed numerous times among Mexicans in California, usually accompanied by a hand gesture touching the forehead, "¿¡Cómo que no puede hablar español cuando trae el nopal en la frente?!" [Loosely, "How come he/she can't speak Spanish when he/she looks unmistakably/stereotypically Mexican?!"]. Another example of this is found in linguistic anthropologist Jonathan Rosa's University of Chicago dissertation, *Looking Like a Language, Sounding Like a Race: Making Latino Panethnicity and Managing National Anxieties* (2010), in which he discusses a relatively light-skinned student who joked that the number of people who spoke to him in Spanish increased during the summer time when his skin was darker. An already classic volume on how these language ideologies work across contexts is Bambi B. Schieffelin, Kathryn A. Woolard, and Paul Kroskrity's (eds.) *Language Ideologies: Practice and Theory* (New York/Oxford, UK: Oxford University Press, 1998).

    Alice Ashton Filmer describes this race/color/nationality/language association as *acoustic identity* in her 2007 article, "Bilingual Belonging and the Whiteness of (Standard) English(es)," *Qualitative Inquiry*, 13, 747–765. Looking across racial and ethnic groups and across various national contexts, she concludes by noting that "[i]n every case, the speaker's acoustic identity and sense of bilingual belonging are negotiated and defined within a complex set of historical/sociopolitical/cultural relations and expectations that ultimately conflate the use of (Standard) English(es) with Whiteness and Western imperialism. In light of this evidence, to insist that Standard Englishes are neutral forms of communication capable of unifying multiracial/ethnic/cultural societies is to fail to recognize these prevalent, and generally unconscious assumptions and expectations. This brand of linguistic ethnocentrism—a major legacy of Euro-American colonialism—is unethical and must be challenged on the grounds of human and civil rights." (761–762).

28. The various stereotypes that circulate in the United States about Asian Americans are discussed in linguistic anthropologist Angela Reyes's book, *The Other Asian: Language, Identity, and Stereotype among Southeast Asian American Youth* (Mahwah, NJ/London: Lawrence Erlbaum Associates, 2007). Drawing on the classic work of Edward Said, Reyes explains that the "forever-foreigner" stereotype "draws on discourses of Orientalism, ideologies which shape the image of Asian and Middle Eastern peoples as Other and thus unassimilable due to innate East-West differences that cannot be resolved." (7–8).

29. See J. A. Harrison (1884). "Negro English." *Anglia*, 7, 232–279.

30. See J. Bennett (1908), "Gullah: A Negro Patois." *South Atlantic Quarterly*, 7, 332–347 and Bennett, J. (1909), "Gullah: A Negro Patois." *South Atlantic Quarterly*, 8, 39–52.

For a full breakdown, see Geneva Smitherman's "Discriminatory Discourse on African American speech" in Smitherman's *Talkin That Talk: Language, Culture, and Education in African America* (New York/London: Routledge, 2000, 67–92).

31. See John R. Rickford and Russell Rickford's *Spoken Soul: The Story of Black English* (New York: Wiley & Sons, 2000) and Rosina Lippi-Green's *English with an Accent*, 2nd edition (New York/London: Routledge, 2011), among several others. Rickford and Rickford's *Spoken Soul* is particularly informative for folks who wanna read up on Black Language in the United States and remains a central text in the field.

32. For more on the development of Black Language in the United States and the racial politics of speaking it, see Geneva Smitherman's now classic text, *Talkin and Testifyin: The Language of Black America* (Boston: Houghton Mifflin, 1977; [republished in 1986, Detroit: Wayne State University Press]). See pages 10–15 for more on these newspaper announcements describing the language of enslaved Africans.

33. Check Imani Perry's *More Beautiful and More Terrible* (New York: NYU Press, 2011), 22.

34. See Lippi-Green's *English with an Accent*, 1997, 178.

35. Ibid.

36. Barack Obama's *The Audacity of Hope*, 2006, 236.

37. See sociologist Prudence Carter's *Stubborn Roots: The Threat of Cultural Inflexibility to Equity in U.S. & South African Schools* (New York/London: Oxford University Press, 2012).

38. D. S. Massey and G. Lundy (2001). "Use of Black English and Racial Discrimination in Urban Housing Markets: New Methods and Findings," *Urban Affairs Review*, *36(4)*, 452–469. The authors described "Black Accented English" and "Black English Vernacular" as differing in their grammar. So, "Black Accented English" was their label for (usually middle-class) Black folks who may have "sounded Black" on occasion but spoke without any Black grammatical features. Those who may have "sounded Black" and spoke with Black grammatical features were labeled as "Black English Vernacular" speakers. Similarly, "White Middle-Class English" speakers were those who spoke with no features of "Philadelphia's distinctive working-class accent." (456). The authors did not have access to any working-class speakers so they were not able to see the effect of class within White speakers.

39. D. S. Massey and G. Lundy (2001), 466–467.

40. See sociolinguist John Baugh's "Linguistic Profiling" in Makoni, Smitherman, Ball, & Spears, (eds.), *Black Linguistics: Language, Society, and Politics in Africa and the Americas* (New York/London: Routledge, 2003, 155–168). Baugh's work and media appearances have raised the nation's consciousness about this issue. His research has influenced public service announcements by the National Fair Housing Association and garnered him the second annual Pioneer of Fair Housing Award from the US Department of Housing and Urban Development in 2004.

41. See T. Purnell, W. Isardi, and J. Baugh (1999). "Perceptual and Phonetic Experiments on American English Dialect Identification." *Journal of Language and Social Psychology*, *18*, 10–30.

42. See her chapter, "The Sound of Equal Opportunity: Credit and Housing Access for Language Minorities," in John Baugh's *Linguistic Profiling in Interdisciplinary Perspective, Volume 2: Social Science and Legal Dimensions* (Final Report: Prepared for the Ford Foundation. African and African American Studies: Washington University in St. Louis, 2009). See also A. A. Nelson (2009). "Credit Scores, Race, and Residential Sorting." *Journal of Policy Analysis and Management*, *29(1)*, 39–68.

43. See D. L. Smalls (2004). "Linguistic Profiling and the Law." *Stanford Law and Policy Review 15(2)*, 579–604. One of the most troubling findings in Smalls's legal note is that there is a "blatant lack of consistency" in the way courts treat linguistic profiling testimony. As she writes, "Particularly problematic is the fact that linguistic profiling testimony appears to be subject to a higher standard in the civil context than in the criminal context; whereas courts express doubt about a person's ability to distinguish

a speaker's race in the realm of housing discrimination, courts often categorically accept this premise in the criminal law." (603). In other words, our judicial system avoids placing blame on landlords and rental agents (because they can't infer someone's race by voice 100 percent of the time) but will readily convict a person of color because ear-witness testimony describes them as "sounding" like a particular race. The denial of individual racism upholds institutional racism yet again.

44. See John Baugh's *Linguistic Profiling in Interdisciplinary Perspective, Volume 1: Linguistic Foundations* and *Volume 2: Social Science and Legal Dimensions* (Final Report: Prepared for the Ford Foundation. African and African American Studies: Washington University in St. Louis, 2009).

45. Barack Obama's *The Audacity of Hope*, 2006, 235.

46. Ibid., 235–236.

3

Makin a Way Outta No Way

The "Race Speech" and Obama's Rhetorical Remix

When our days become dreary with low hovering clouds
of despair, and when our nights become darker than a
thousand midnights, let us remember that there is a
creative force in this universe, working to pull down
the gigantic mountains of evil, a power that is able *to
make a way outta no way* and transform dark days into
bright tomorrows. Let us realize that the arc of the moral
universe is long but bends toward justice.[1]
—Dr. Martin Luther King Jr., 1967 [Italics ours]

Reverend Wright and other African Americans of
his generation...came of age in the late fifties and
early sixties, a time when segregation was still the
law of the land and opportunity was systematically
constricted. What's remarkable is not how many
failed in the face of discrimination, but rather how
many men and women overcame the odds, how
many were able *to make a way out of no way* for
those like me who would come after them.[2]
—Barack Obama, 2008 [Italics ours]

At a crucial historical moment in the 2008 presidential campaign, then-senator
Barack Obama was forced to directly confront America's most treacherous
social, cultural, and political minefield—race. While Obama had been relatively silent on the issue of race, there came a point in the campaign when
he had no other choice but to address the nation. During the months of
heated primary debates with his then-opponent Hillary Clinton, a series
of controversial sermon sound bites from Reverend Dr. Jeremiah Wright
emerged and were looped 24-7 across all media outlets. Reverend Wright
had been Obama's pastor for some 20 years, performed Obama's marriage
ceremony to Michelle, baptized Obama's two children, and was currently

serving as a member of the Obama campaign's African American Religious Leadership Committee. His pastor's controversial sermonizing had taken Obama's silence around the racial dynamics of his campaign and shouted these dynamics from the rooftops. To paraphrase T. Denean Sharpley-Whiting in her introduction to *The Speech: Race and Barack Obama's "A More Perfect Union,"* many White Americans were lookin at Barack like, "Well, before you start movin your furniture into the White House, homie, you got some splainin to do."

As White calls for an "explanation" grew and the daily media coverage began turning into a public relations nightmare, many Hillary Clinton supporters, joined by nearly all conservative pundits and talking heads, declared this the end of the Obama campaign. Heading into March 2008, some Black supporters of Obama lamented, "Might as well stick a fork in dude, he's done." The numbers told a similar story. Obama watched his six-point lead in the Gallup tracking polls turn into a seven-point deficit. Journalist and cultural critic Joan Morgan summed up the situation like this:

> By all accounts, the Wright debacle was a live grenade that threatened to damage an essential tenet of the Obama campaign: the sexy new multiracial, youth-driven, socioeconomically diverse, bipartisan 'CHANGE' he was promising America....The question was never *if* race would morph from the pink elephant in the room into the raging tiger that needed to be sedated and tamed. It was always when and who, if anyone, would emerge intact once the beast was unleashed.[3]

The Black Elephant in the Room: Navigating America's Most Treacherous Minefield

Paradoxically, the Obama candidacy was a "postracial" moment. While it represented a symbolic break from the "whiteout" on the US presidency, it was also, obviously, the most racialized campaign in American history. There were, of course, all the folks at the rallies for Obama's opponents who showed up with stuffed monkeys, or Curious George T-shirts, or with racist images of watermelons and fried chicken, and folks who sang "Barack the Magic Negro" along with Rush Limbaugh. But race had become an issue even in the primary battle with Hillary Clinton. Barack Obama noted:

> This is not to say that race has not been an issue in this campaign. At various stages in the campaign, some commentators have deemed me either 'too black' or 'not black enough.' We saw

racial tensions bubble to the surface during the week before the South Carolina primary. The press has scoured every exit poll for the latest evidence of racial polarization, not just in terms of white and black, but black and brown as well.[4]

Obama's South Carolina primary comment reminds us of former president Bill Clinton's racial-referencing of Obama's candidacy. By Bill's logic, the fact that Barack defeated Hillary by receiving an overwhelming majority of the Black vote in South Carolina made Barack "a Black candidate." Astute observers knew that Clinton was employing race to try to box Barack in verbally so that he could not appeal to the broader American public. As author and political commentator Keli Goff noted and certainly as the Clintons knew, "Obama had spent his campaign trying to avoid being pigeon-holed as 'the black candidate,' or worse, being viewed as the typical black candidate—one whose candidacy is predicated primarily on running as a black person there to advance black issues or to air black grievances."[5] Most Black Americans, while understanding Bill's support for his wife, read Bill's move as a racially loaded betrayal, deserving of a revoking of his honorary Black status. Further, Hillary Clinton used Obama's Blackness to demand that he "denounce"—and then further "reject" (big difference there, right?)—everything "militantly Black" from Minister Louis Farrakhan to Reverend Dr. Jeremiah Wright. Geraldine Ferraro cited Obama's Blackness as the reason that he had even made it this far.[6] Clearly, for Obama to navigate America's treacherous minefield of race was more than complex, it seemed downright impossible.

The enormity of the challenge lay in not just navigating the treacherous terrain of race in the United States, in general, but also Reverend Wright's Black Liberation Theology and Black community politics, in particular. Yet, after doing a string of talk shows and media appearances attempting to extinguish Reverend Wright's racial firestorm, Obama told his senior advisor, David Axelrod, "I want to do this speech on race. I want to put this thing in its proper perspective....I think this is an important moment, and people may accept what I have to say or not, but it's an important moment in terms of dealing with the elephant in the room."[7]

President Obama's "A More Perfect Union" speech, which has come to be known as the "Race Speech," was delivered at the National Constitution Center in Philadelphia, Pennsylvania, on March 18, 2008, nearly eight months before the November election. When the motion of history presented Obama, and America, with this gut-wrenching political moment, Obama did not retreat from the difficult, problematic, ultrasensitive topic of race. Rather, he faced the matter of race and US racism head on, making a strategic decision to talk openly, boldly, honestly—and personally—about

race. In doing so, he offered us a new twenty-first-century model for political discussions about race in the United States.

"Unashamedly Black": Black Preaching and the Reverend Dr. Jeremiah Wright Controversy

Soundbites from Reverend Wright's sermons began wide circulation in the
media in March of 2008, broadcast 24–7 in, as Obama called it, "an endless
loop," accompanied by negative commentary. Not only were these excerpts
decontextualized, they were offered to the American public without explan-
atory cultural background about Traditional Black Church preaching, in
general, and the social gospel, in particular. Further, rarely was there ever
any discussion of Reverend Wright's family background, educational and
theological training, life experiences (including military service), or con-
tributions to the Chicago and national Black community. If media depic-
tions served as one's only source of information about Wright, "one would
expect him to be a militantly black supremacist hater of America and all
she stands for," as professor of Biblical interpretation Obery M. Hendricks
Jr. put it in "A More Perfect (High-Tech) Lynching: Obama, the Press, and
Jeremiah Wright."[8]

Hendricks notes that Reverend Wright's parents were highly respected
members of the Philadelphia community where he was born, his father, a
long-serving Baptist minister and his mother, an educator who broke racial
barriers as the first Black teacher at Germantown High School and later
first Black vice principal at Girls High School. The Philadelphia high school
from which Wright graduated, Central High, at that time overwhelmingly
White, accorded him great respect. Unlike others of his generation, he did
not exercise his college deferment but volunteered for the military, serving six years, both in the Marines and the Navy, where he was trained
as a cardiopulmonary technician. He was part of the medical team during
Lyndon Johnson's surgery while Johnson was president and received a letter
of thanks on behalf of President Johnson. A highly educated man, Wright
has been awarded eight honorary degrees and is the holder of four earned
degrees. He attended Virginia Union University, Howard University, and
the University of Chicago Divinity School, from which he earned a master's
degree, and United Theological Seminary, where he studied under the illus-
trious theological scholar Samuel DeWitt Proctor (mentor to Martin Luther
King Jr.) and from which he earned a Doctor of Ministry.

Additionally, Wright is A.B.D. (all but dissertation) in the Ph.D. program in History of Religions at the University of Chicago. He stopped work
on his dissertation to devote all his energies and time to building a new

church for Trinity United Church of Christ on Chi-Town's South Side where he was called to pastor in 1972 and where he built the congregation from 87 members to more than 8,000 by the time of his retirement in 2008.[9] Over the years, Wright had spoken not only at Black churches around the country but also at numerous universities and academic conferences.

Media pundits attacked Wright as a racist, hatemonger, and leader of a church that denounces White people. Yet, as Hendricks notes, the United Church of Christ, of which Wright's Trinity is a part, is a predominantly White denomination, and Trinity does have White members. Trinity's motto is "unashamedly Black," and its symbols and much of its literature are African-Centered. Similar to the history of African American Studies in the academy and African-Centered Education in K–12 schools, it is difficult for non-Blacks to wrap their minds around the fact that pro-Black is not anti-White. As University of Chicago (White) Professor Emeritus Martin Marty explained: "For Trinity, being 'unashamedly black' does not mean being 'anti-white,' but rather is a discursive tactic to address the abiding sense of shame in many African Americans that is a legacy of slavery and Jim Crow segregation."[10] Further, the United Church of Christ ministers and leadership (many of them White) rose to Wright's defense. Reverend John Thomas, the General Minister and President of the United Church of Christ, declared at a press conference held at Trinity in early March 2008:

> It has saddened me to see news stories reporting such a caricature of a congregation that has been such a blessing.... Those who sifted through hours of sermons searching for a few lurid phrases and those who have aired them repeatedly have only one intention. It is to wound a presidential candidate. In the process a congregation that does exceptional ministry and a pastor who has given his life to shape those ministries is caricatured and demonized. You don't have to be an Obama supporter to be alarmed at this.[11]

So what was the message in those sermons and sound bites that so inflamed and infuriated White folk? More so than the message, it was the rhetorical style and linguistic discourse in which the message was conveyed. Points in Wright's sermons that had to do with US culpability and wrongdoing at home and abroad had been made by others, and—check it out—can even be found in Obama's "Race Speech." However, whereas Obama tempered and significantly departed from the Black jeremiadic style in his sermons, Wright was rhetorically relentless in maintaining both the caustic Black and the damning Biblical jeremiadic style.

The Wright sermons that were the source of the soundbites were his "The Day of Jerusalem's Fall," preached September 16, 2001, and "Confusing God and Government," preached on April 13, 2003. In the September 16, 2001 sermon, among the words Wright preached were:

> I heard Ambassador Peck on an interview yesterday....He was on Fox News. This is a White man, and he was upsetting the Fox News commentators to no end. He pointed out...a White man, he pointed out...that what Malcolm X said when he got silenced by Elijah Muhammad was in fact true—America's chickens are coming home to roost....We bombed Hiroshima, we bombed Nagasaki, and we nuked far more than the thousands in New York and the Pentagon, and we never batted an eye...and now we are indignant, because the stuff we have done overseas is now brought back into our own front yards. America's chickens are coming home to roost....Violence begets violence. Hatred begets hatred. And terrorism begets terrorism. A White ambassador said that y'all, not a Black militant. Not a Reverend who preaches about racism. An ambassador whose eyes are wide open and who is trying to get us to wake up and move away from this dangerous precipice upon which we are now poised. The ambassador said the people that we have wounded don't have the military capability we have. But they do have individuals who are willing to die and take thousands with them. And we need to come to grips with that.[12]

In the April 13, 2003 sermon, among the words Wright preached were:

> Where governments lie, God does not lie. Where governments change, God does not change...The government lied about their belief that all men are created equal. The truth is they believed that all White men are created equal. The truth is they did not even believe that White women were created equal, in creation or civilization. The government had to pass an amendment to the Constitution to get White women the vote. Then the government had to pass an equal rights amendment to get equal protection under the law for women...[The] government, when it came to treating the citizens of Indian descent fairly, she failed. She put them on reservations. When it came to treating her citizens of Japanese descent fairly, she failed. She put them in internment prison camps. When it came to treating her citizens of African descent fairly, America failed. She put them in chains...in

slave quarters...on auction blocks, in cotton fields...in inferior schools...substandard housing...in scientific experiments...in the lowest paying jobs...outside the equal protection of the law, kept them out of their racist bastions of higher education and locked them into positions of hopelessness and helplessness...gives them the drugs, builds bigger prisons, passes a three-strike law and then wants us to sing "God Bless America." No, no, no! Not God Bless America. God damn America—that's in the Bible—for killing innocent people. God damn America for treating our citizens as less than human. God damn America as long as she tries to act like she is God, and she is supreme.[13]

As several theologians pointed out, Reverend Wright is preaching out of the Biblical jeremiadic tradition. In that tradition, it is the preacher's obligation to warn his flock when they are going astray and in danger of incurring the wrath of God. According to Rabbi Sharon Kleinbaum of Congregation Beth Simchat Torah in New York City, Reverend Wright's sermons were "deeply traditional, carefully composed and structured talks in the Biblical tradition of such venerated sources as Isaiah, Jeremiah, and Deuteronomy...solidly in the tradition of the ancient prophets, who would catalogue the sins of the people and invoke the Divine litany of curses upon people who [had] wandered from the righteous path prescribed in Scripture."[14] White Minister Paul Davis put it this way:

As a minister, I do not find the Pastor's sermons disturbing in the least. After all a good sermon should afflict the comfortable and comfort the afflicted...I agree wholeheartedly with everything Pastor Wright said here. If American history turns Rush Limbaugh's stomach, perhaps he should get a little more intestinal fortitude... Don't side with pro-war conservatives, an oxymoron in itself considering the trillion dollar expenditure of killing in foreign theaters of war, and then hide from the consequences of your foreign policy.[15]

As Hendricks points out, the function of Wright's Biblical jeremiad "is to remind Americans, lest we become self-righteous in our righteous indignation, that we too have engaged in mass destruction of innocents."[16]

In the sacred world of the temple, the Judeo-Christian leader/pastor/priest/rabbi is supported by thousands of years of Biblical tradition, prophesy, prophetic teaching, and beliefs subscribed to by all. By contrast, Obama's "Race Speech" was delivered in the secular world where the swirling, changing state of sociopolitical realities, varying beliefs, and multiple demographics make the rhetorical pathway not so clear. How does one speak the truth to a people who are diverse and speak many tongues? How does one speak the truth about race in America—and in a single speech—when having an honest discussion is like navigating a minefield? And how does a man who is racialized as Black—the bottom rung on America's (and the world's) racial hierarchy—address these real and difficult tensions when both Black and White racial resentment is heightened by the divisive discourse incited by the very act of his presidential bid? This was the challenging, formidable charge to Barack Obama, with commentators on both sides looking for any signs of either too much sympathizing with Black people (a "Black Messiah") or too much shuckin and jivin to the White power structure (an "Uncle Tom"). The rhetorical situation called for someone who could be, as commentator Keli Goff put it, "somber yet transcendent, painfully honest yet awesomely inspiring...but most of all he would have to find some way to unify and uplift and connect, not alienate."[17] This is what Goff was hoping for, yet she considered it "virtually impossible," that is, until she heard the "Race Speech." Barack Obama not only met the rhetorical demands of the "Race Speech," he did the impossible—he made a way outta no way.

"Black and More Than Black": The Rhetorical Demands of the "Race Speech"

Obama was confronted with a rhetorical situation in which Black and White perceptions and past and present experiences of race are often at odds. In great measure this is attributable to a long, brutal history of enslavement, followed by an additional century of neoenslavement and today's continuing racial separation—for example, in housing, schooling, and other institutions.[18] In and of itself, the fact that Obama would seek to deliver a speech about race was nothing new. African descendants in the United States have been engaging in public discourse about racial oppression at least since David Walker, born to a slave father and a free mother in Wilmington, North Carolina, in 1785, issued *David Walker's Appeal, in Four Articles; Together with a Preamble, to the Coloured Citizens of the World, but in Particular, and Very Expressly, to Those of the United States of America* (1829).[19] What was new was a race speech delivered in our time, in what many Americans believe is a "postracial" (or "colorblind") society, one in which problems of race and racism are widely believed to no longer exist. (People can see color in everything from roses to rainbows but somehow can't see it in race.)

The argument is that these issues were addressed and dealt with in the last century and owing in great measure to the "success" of the Civil

Rights Movement, African Americans have made major advancements on all fronts—educational, economic, social, political. Those who hold this position contend that there is no longer a need for a "Black Movement" and speeches of protest against White oppression. Whether or not one agrees with this interpretation of current Black social reality, it is a fact that, except for an occasional public talk by Reverend Jesse Jackson on corporate responsibility to Blacks or the Reverend Al Sharpton on the shooting of yet another hapless young brotha by police, the longstanding genre of Black protest oratory is all but dead in the twenty-first century. So many Americans were sitting at the edge of their seats precisely because, as noted by Derrick Z. Jackson, this speech presented to us the very rare occasion to hear a Black man talk about race on the national stage.[20]

To be sure, today's sociopolitical context is decidedly different from that of nineteenth-century Black leaders such as former slave turned abolitionist, Frederick Douglass, or twentieth-century Civil Rights and Black Power activists, such as Martin Luther King Jr., Malcolm X, and Kwame Ture.[21] The blatant symbols of racial oppression—for instance, White-only access to hotels, theaters, and public facilities, police dogs and water hoses spraying nonviolent protestors—are no longer with us. There is now a sizable, highly educated Black middle and upper class. The NBA, the NFL, Hip Hop, and other forms of Black popular culture have contributed to the development of the image of a bling-bling, livin large Black elite, with Benjamins to burn. Moreover, late twentieth-century periods of "benign neglect" and the end of the "Second Reconstruction" virtually succeeded in the erasure, from America's social agenda, of Black concerns about social justice, poverty, and educational inequities.[22] In short, this was a 2008 White audience for a speech about race, not a 1968 one, a situation that called for a new kind of Black oratory, a reinvention of the Tradition.

While the Black audience for such a speech was also a twenty-first-century one, these people who are "darker than blue" (as the late Curtis Mayfield often sang) have long, painful memories of betrayal by both Black and White politicians and leaders. Moreover, even those who seek to invoke historical amnesia in order to keep on keepin on in their overworked, paperchasin struggle to survive are forced to bear witness to the historical impact and presentness of the past—the resegregation of schools, the seemingly intractable poverty in urban wastelands, and the skyrocketing incarceration rates of Black men.[23] For many Blacks, the reality of their condition could not be swept under the rug, it cried out for acknowledgment and recognition. Blacks—and Obama himself—had painfully understood the good Reverend's fiery, Biblically grounded sermonic exhortations about America's misdeeds and failings. But still, for some Blacks there was that nagging question about Obama's Blackness. Is he Black enough? Is he culturally Black? Is he attuned to The Tradition?

Given the demands of these two different—and on some levels, diametrically opposed audiences—the historical moment called for a race speech that could be explicatory, but it could not be condemnatory as was the case with much of the racial rhetoric of the previous century. While the rhetorical task required a speech crafted by an African American, it had to be an "American", not just an "African American" speech.[24] Or in the words of Obama, it had to be "black and more than black."[25] Given his background and upbringing, his "improbable" journey in America, Obama seemed especially suited—dare we say called?—for this task. He was, after all, an American who is neither "White" nor "Black" (in the narrow stereotypical American sense). At the same time, paradoxically, he was an American who is and has lived both "Black" and "White," who thus is uniquely positioned to see and feel both dimensions of the Black-White binary.

One of the authors of this book, Smitherman, is the daughter of a baptized-in-the-fire Baptist preachaman, who has, on many occasions, shouted and clapped to the stirring power and visionary message in a Reverend Dr. Jeremiah Wright sermon. Smitherman is also a sociolinguist who teaches courses in African American Language and Culture and has used Wright's oratorical brilliance—as in his "Demons and Detractors" sermon, which is also excerpted in her *Word from the Mother: Language and African Americans* (2006)—to teach the rhetoric of what late linguist Grace Sims Holt referred to as "stylin' outta the Black pulpit."[26] Stanford University sociolinguist John R. Rickford uses Wright's "When You Fail in Your Trying" sermon for a similar pedagogical purpose (see Rickford and Rickford's award-winning book, *Spoken Soul: The Story of Black English*, 2000). As a member of the generation that came of age in the twentieth-century Black Freedom Struggle,[27] Smitherman has also shouted and clapped to the flamboyant speechifying and insightful calls to action in a M. L. King, Kwame Ture, or H. Rap Brown speech.[28] Curiously, she found herself awed by Obama's speech, despite the fact that it didn't appear to reflect the Black protest oratory she intellectually and emotionally knew so well. This wasn't your traditional Black speech. Millions of others were also awed—audiences all over the country, Black, White, Asian, and Latino, male and female, of different generations and classes—because it was not your typical political speech either. How could it be that his speech satisfied the complex psychosocial demands of Whites, Blacks, and other folks while at the same time it candidly spoke the truth to the people?

We believe the answer lies in the strategic rhetorical choices made by Barack Obama. Verbal persuasion is both an art and a science. The rhetor must have the ability to discern the most effective means of persuasion at his or her disposal. Accurate audience assessment and analysis are critical, as is skill in appropriating available persuasive strategies. For example, the historical annals of Black oratory record that in the Nation of Islam (NOI), Malcolm X reached heights of dazzling speechmaking while Elijah Muhammad was considered ho-hum. In the Civil Rights Movement, Martin Luther King Jr. scaled the rhetorical mountain while Ralph Abernathy never got off the ground. In all of these cases, the success of the orator was never based solely on the content of the speech (for the message was fairly consistent); rather, it was always also judged by the linguistic and rhetorical style of the speaker.

Makin a Way Outta No Way: Obama's Symbolic Use of Black Language

While most commentators before and after the "Race Speech" focused on what Obama needed to say, actually said, or should have said, few, if any, paid attention to how he said what he said. Given that commentators had deemed the speech's success an impossibility or suggested that nothing short of a miracle was needed, Obama's "Race Speech" symbolized his own ability "to make a way outta no way." A longstanding idiom in African American Language, makin a way outta no way is grounded in The Tradition. It reflects the Black struggle to survive, as the late, great Tupac Shakur once said, "against all odds." It is the paradox of the indomitable drive to find a solution when there is no way out. As a Black folk expression, makin a way outta no way is summoned up to characterize even such everyday experiences as Blacks creating culinary delicacies from Ol Massa's scraps and leftovers (e.g., chitlins). Against the panoramic span of Black people's continuously evolving history, makin a way outta no way announces that, even when given very little to work with or when all the cards seem stacked against us, we will find a way to survive—and thrive. Makin a way outta no way refers to a hope, a deep, abiding faith, that, as Reverend Dr. Martin Luther King Jr. put it, even when our "days become dreary with low hovering clouds of despair, and when our nights become darker than a thousand midnights," the bright day of justice will soon come.

In "Makin a Way Outta No Way: The Proverb Tradition in the Black Experience," Smitherman, Daniel, and Jeremiah (1987) interviewed Blacks in the United States and in the Caribbean to demonstrate that proverb use is a crucial source of strategies for makin a way outta no way.[29] As in other communities worldwide, Black American proverbs serve an important socializing function, quoted by parents to their children, or to friends and siblings, as a way to teach rapidly and in no uncertain terms about life and living. Often used proverbs—not necessarily African derived—and the proverbial wisdom and life experiences they embody contain guides and Black belief sets for survival and development. As described by Smitherman et al., "[Proverbs] represent the wisdom [of the people]...these sayings are like honeycomb; sweet to the soul, and health to the bones...Black beliefs that reflect fundamental perceptions of reality...essential value orientations and most basic rules for living....Proverbs are significant...as a legacy that has enabled African people to 'make a way outta no way.'"[30]

For Reverend Dr. Martin Luther King Jr.—as well as Reverend Dr. Jeremiah Wright and millions of African Americans—makin a way outta no way is embodied in the "faith of the Fathers," a belief in a God-centered universe and the social justice of Christianity. Through the centuries, the Black Church has been influential in sustaining this cultural ethos and value system among Blacks—notwithstanding the fact that not all Blacks are ardent or, for that matter, even regular, churchgoers. However, this accounts for the historical legacy and continuing significance of the Black Church, a past and present refuge for Blacks. Explaining how he came to understand and embrace faith, in *The Audacity of Hope,* Obama draws on the Black proverb tradition and writes:

> Out of necessity, the black church had to minister to the whole person. Out of necessity, the black church rarely had the luxury of separating individual salvation from collective salvation. It had to serve as the center of the community's political, economic, and social as well as spiritual life; it understood in an intimate way the biblical call to feed the hungry and clothe the naked and challenge powers and principalities. In the history of these struggles, I was able to see faith as more than just a comfort to the weary or a hedge against death; rather, it was an active, palpable agent in the world. In the day-to-day work of the men and women I met in church each day, in their ability to "make a way out of no way" and maintain hope and dignity in the direst of circumstances, I could see the Word made manifest.[31]

We consider makin a way outta no way a metaphor for Obama's overall strategic success in the "Race Speech." Employing this familiar, culturally rooted Black Vernacular trope, he thus symbolically indexes his Black identity, represents his Black cultural affinity, and advances a political stance that frames the Black condition in terms of success, not failure ("What's remarkable is not how many failed in the face of discrimination, but rather how many men and women overcame the odds, how many were able to make a way out of no way for those like me who would come after them").

While this rhetorical strategy probably flew right over the heads of most White and other non-Black listeners, to Black folks, it signaled a cultural-linguistic connection and a political worldview that validates the perspective of Black survival under extraordinarily adverse circumstances.

Simultaneously, however, Obama articulated this vernacular idiom in the formal voice of the LWC (Language of Wider Communication, or as some would have it, the Language of Whiter Communication).[32] Linguistically speaking, while most Black speakers using this idiom pronounce it with a particular Black prosody and rhythm and render "out of" as "outta," for example, Obama utters this phrase in a highly formal register, enunciating every syllable. Drawing on a culturally salient and politically important proverbial Black Idiom in The Tradition but formally pronouncing it, Obama articulates Blackness anew. He found a way to articulate Blackness on a national stage—quietly communicating an important ideological message to the Black electorate—but doing so in a form that was digestible to non-Black America.[33]

The Old: The (White) American and African American Jeremiad

> But if ye will not hear these words, I swear by myself, saith the Lord, that this house shall become a desolation....And many nations shall pass by this city, and they shall say...[w]herefore hath the Lord done thus unto this great city? Then they shall answer, Because they have forsaken the covenant of the Lord their God. (Jeremiah 22: 5-9)

The term *jeremiad* is derived from Jeremiah, an Old Testament prophet who accounted for Israel's trials and tribulations as punishment for departing from their covenant with God. However, even as he critiques Israel for its wayward, ungodly behavior, he reminds the people of their status as God's chosen people and foreshadows their return to greatness following repentance. The American jeremiad is a speech, sermon, or other form of public discourse in which the speaker critiques the society for its misdeeds and wrongdoings while holding out hope that this fall from Grace can be reversed if the country corrects its behavior and lives up to its divine mandate. It has its roots in the European jeremiad, which, in turn, has its roots in the Biblical jeremiad and began as a political sermon in the Puritan era. Like the Old Testament Israelites, seventeenth-century Puritans believed that they, too, were God's chosen people. They had been delivered out of Europe and called by God to establish a new order, to create in this new world a nation that would be a symbol of liberty, freedom, and hope for peoples around the globe. (Notwithstanding this grand vision for the new order, no thought was given to the fate of the Indigenous peoples of the land—American Indians.[34])

Puritan leaders used the rhetorical framework of the American jeremiad to remind the colonists of God's divine plan for America and their role in the fulfillment of the new nation's destiny. Cultural historians, such as Sacvan Bercovitch in *The American Jeremiad* (1978), track the continuing belief in and discourse of American exceptionalism to its beginnings in the American jeremiad of the Puritan era. Bercovitch contends that the jeremiad has persisted for centuries and has "played a significant role in the development of...modern middle-class American culture." He notes that the "prophetic history" and "mission" of America as a special, unique country is writ large, not only in sermons and speeches but also in literature, culture, and core values, such as the "devaluation of aristocracy, opening up of political, educational, and commercial opportunities to a relatively broad spectrum of the population."[35] (Notwithstanding Bercovitch's astute, scholarly account of the "process of Americanization," at points he is surprisingly honest in his assessment of what he calls the "patent fiction" that is the "American mission."[36])

Jeremiadic speeches and sermons had a set tripartite formula: (1) The speaker intones America's promise as a beacon of liberty, equality, and social justice; (2) He (or she, but it was almost always a he) details and castigates America's misdeeds, its grave departure or "retrogression" from the promise; (3) The speaker reaffirms the prophesy that America will complete its mission and redeem the promise.[37] This rhetorical structure helped the speaker to simultaneously chastise and uplift his audience. "The jeremiad...was filled with underlying optimism about America's fate and mission....[Its] dark portrayal of current society never questioned America's promise and destiny....The unfaltering view is that God will mysteriously use the unhappy present to spur the people to reformation and speedily onward to fulfill their divine destiny."[38]

As an archetype of the American jeremiad, Bercovitch analyzes "Brief Recognition of New England's Errand into the Wilderness," a speech by Samuel Danforth delivered in 1670. He notes that Danforth's speech "condemns the colonists' shortcomings and justifies their afflictions." The charge is that "[w]e have...in a great measure forgotten our errand." Danforth "underscores this meaning by comparing New England's 'howling wilderness' with that of Moses and John the Baptist." He goes on to "assure the colonists of success not because of their efforts, but God's: 'the great Physician of Israel hath undertaken the cure...he will provide...we have the promise.'"[39]

Just as there was a Black nation within the White nation, there was a concomitant Black jeremiad within the White jeremiad. Beginning in the Antislavery Movement, Black leaders adapted the White jeremiad for the purpose of protest against enslavement and later discrimination and racism. In the Black version, the rhetoric envisioned US descendants of enslaved Africans as also being God's chosen people. God's mandate became a charge to the White nation to live up to its divinely inspired calling and provide equality and social justice for the Black nation. Historian Wilson Jeremiah Moses, who is believed to have coined the term *Black jeremiad,* argues in his *Black Messiahs and Uncle Toms: Social and Literary Manipulations of a Religious Myth*: "If the bondage of the Colonies to England was similar to the enslavement of Israel in Egypt, was not the bondage of blacks in America an even more perfect analogy? If Americans, by virtue of the ideals of their revolution, were in fact a covenanted people and entrusted with the mission to safeguard the divine and natural laws of human rights, was there not a danger to the covenant in perpetuating slavery?"[40]

Following the tripartite structure of the American jeremiad, the Black speaker lauds America for its founding principles and promise ("life, liberty, pursuit of happiness," "all men are created equal"), details and denounces the society for its failure to live up to that promise (e.g., enslavement, denial of equal opportunity, Jim Crow), and calls on the country to recommit to its historical mandate and divine promise by alleviating Black oppression. A classic example of the Black jeremiad is Frederick Douglass's oration delivered in Rochester, New York, on July 5, 1852, which has come to be known as his "Fourth of July" speech. This former slave, who became a powerful force in the Abolitionist Movement and a revered leader of African slave descendants in his time, acknowledges and celebrates the significance of July 4, but he is ultimately dismissive of the holiday since it is meaningless to those still in bondage.

Douglass employs Biblical metaphors, as in the White jeremiad, to recall America's prophetic mission and promise. "This, to you, is what the Passover was to the emancipated people of God." As he continues, he contrasts the lofty ideals and liberatory promise of America with the capture of Africans, the horrors and brutalities of bondage, and his own personal tribulations during enslavement. Although he frames his argument with overtones of the Biblical narrative, his language is caustic and accusatory, his metaphors bitter and brutal.

> Are the great principles of political freedom and of natural justice, embodied in that Declaration of Independence, extended to us?..."By the rivers of Babylon, there we sat down....We wept when we remembered Zion....They that carried us away captive,

required of us a song; and they who wasted us required of us mirth, saying, Sing us one of the songs of Zion. How can we sing the Lord's song in a strange land?"...What, to the American slave, is your 4th of July?...Your celebration is a sham; your boasted liberty, an unholy license; your national greatness, swelling vanity...your denunciation of tyrants, brass fronted impudence; your shouts of liberty and equality, hollow mockery; your prayers and hymns, your sermons and thanksgivings, with all your religious parade and solemnity, are to him...a thin veil to cover up crimes which would disgrace a nation of savages. There is not a nation on the earth guilty of practices more shocking and bloody than are the people of the United States....This Fourth of July is *yours*, not *mine*. *You* may rejoice, *I* must mourn.[41]

Calling the question of America's promise, as embodied in its founding documents, Douglass foreshadows the end of enslavement and expresses his belief that Whites will rise to the greatness in that promise. His tone reflects what Obama, borrowing from Reverend Dr. Wright, who, in turn, borrowed from late Reverend Frederick Sampson of Detroit, might have called the "audacity of hope."[42]

Now, take the Constitution according to its plain reading, and I defy the presentation of a single pro-slavery clause in it. On the other hand, it will be found to contain principles and purposes, entirely hostile to the existence of slavery...Notwithstanding the dark picture I have this day presented...[I] draw...encouragement from "the Declaration of Independence," the great principles it contains, and the genius of American Institutions.

Perhaps the quintessential Black Jeremiad is Dr. Martin Luther King Jr.'s oft-quoted "I Have a Dream" speech, delivered August 28, 1963, in the Nation's capitol. Following the well-worn Jeremiadic script, King invokes the prophetic vision of America: "When the architects of our Republic wrote the magnificent words of the Constitution and the Declaration of Independence, they were signing a promissory note to which every American was to fall heir...a promise that all men—yes, black men as well as white men—would be guaranteed the unalienable rights of life, liberty and the pursuit of happiness." However, the society has failed to fulfill its "sacred obligation...The Negro is still badly crippled by the manacles of segregation and the chains of discrimination...The Negro lives on a lonely island of poverty in the midst of a vast ocean of material prosperity." Like Jeremiahs before him, King foreshadows doom so long as America fails to address the racism and oppression of Blacks and thus remains unrepentant:

> We can never be satisfied as long as our bodies, heavy with the fatigue of travel, cannot gain lodging in the motels of the highways and the hotels of the cities...We can never be satisfied as long as our children are stripped of their adulthood and robbed of their dignity by signs stating "For Whites Only"...We cannot be satisfied as long as the Negro in Mississippi cannot vote and the Negro in New York believes he has nothing for which to vote...There will be neither rest nor tranquility in America until the Negro is granted his citizenship rights. The whirlwinds of revolt will continue to shake the foundation of our nation until the bright day of justice emerges.

Later, and with the "fierce urgency of now" (another Martin Luther King phrase often cited by Obama), King calls for re-commitment to the promise, exhorting America to "rise up, live out the true meaning of its creed: 'We hold these truths to be self-evident, that all men are created equal...' This will be the day when all of God's children will be able to sing with new meaning: 'My country, 'tis of thee, sweet land of liberty, of thee I sing. Land where my fathers died, land of the pilgrim's pride, from every mountain side, let freedom ring.'"[43]

While Obama's "Race Speech" relied on fundamental rhetorical principles that Aristotle taught centuries ago, principally *ethos* (persuasion based on a speaker's personal character) and *logos* (persuasive appeal based on reason), more importantly he selected a familiar rhetorical paradigm, the jeremiad, and skillfully adapted this centuries-old framework to accommodate a postmodern, post–Civil Rights, twenty-first-century Black and White audience.

This. Is. The Remix: Barack Hussein Obama's Jeremiad

As a powerful and eloquent public discourse on race, Obama's speech is clearly situated in the jeremiadic tradition, but he puts his own innovative imprint on the game, remixing the classic traditions to create a hybrid form to suit the needs of a new era. The structure of his speech follows the tripartite formula of classical jeremiads. He opens with an allusion to the promise of America as articulated in its founding documents: "We the people, in order to form a more perfect union....Our Constitution...had at its very core the ideal of equal citizenship under the law; a Constitution that promised its people liberty, and justice, and a union that could be and should be perfected over time." He notes that, even at the outset, there was a retreat from the promise, making his point about slavery with the use of familiar, shared Biblical language: "original sin." He expands on the retreat from the promise, detailing a litany of past racial injustices, the impact of which continues to be felt in Black communities today. He uses deductive reasoning (logos), anchoring his major claim in the long history of institutionalized racism and deeply entrenched structures of racial oppression in the United States. Given the constraints of time—this was a campaign speech, not, for instance, a lecture in a university hall—he skillfully paints a portrait of that history with broad strokes. The strength of this major premise is his logical, systematic accounting of historical facts. He establishes his minor claim by laying out the destructive effects of this past on the African American community today. He concludes by deducing the impact of this history on the pulpit oratory and public rhetoric of Reverend Wright—and on the consciousness and discourse of Blacks of Wright's generation.

On education: "Segregated schools were, and are, inferior schools; we still haven't fixed them, fifty years after *Brown v. Board of Education*, and the inferior education they provided, then and now, helps explain the pervasive achievement gap between today's black and white students."

On economic discrimination: "Blacks were prevented, often through violence, from owning property, or loans were not granted to African American business owners, or black homeowners could not access FHA mortgages, or blacks were excluded from unions, or the police force, or fire departments." The result: "Black families could not amass any meaningful wealth to bequeath to future generations. That history helps explain the wealth and income gap between black and white, and the concentrated pockets of poverty that persist in so many of today's urban and rural communities."

On the abandonment of Black neighborhoods: "The lack of basic services in so many urban black neighborhoods—parks for kids to play in, police walking the beat, regular garbage pick-up and building code enforcement—all helped create a cycle of violence, blight and neglect that continues to haunt us."

On the American Dream deferred: "For all those who scratched and clawed their way to get a piece of the American Dream, there were many who didn't make it—those who were ultimately defeated, in one way or another, by discrimination. That legacy of defeat was passed on to future generations—those young men and increasingly young women who we see standing on street corners or languishing in our prisons, without hope or prospects for the future."

On the impact on the Black psyche: "Even for those blacks who did make it, questions of race, and racism, continue to define their worldview in fundamental ways. For the men and women of Reverend Wright's generation, the memories of humiliation and doubt and fear have not gone away; nor has the anger and bitterness of those years...[The anger] find[s] voice in the barbershop or around the kitchen table....And occasionally it finds voice in the church on Sunday morning, in the pulpit and in the pews."

In characteristic jeremiadic fashion, Obama reaffirms his audience's belief in the promise of America, calling on both Blacks and Whites—all Americans—to rededicate themselves to the realization of America's destiny and the perfection of the union. "What we know—what we have seen—is that America can change. That is the true genius of this nation. What we have already achieved gives us hope—the audacity to hope—for what we can and must achieve tomorrow." Further, in keeping with the religious trappings of both the Black and the White American jeremiad, he links his call to action to global religious ideology: "What is called for is nothing more, and nothing less, than what all the world's great religions demand— that we do unto others as we would have them do unto us."

While the "Race Speech" taps into the basic structure of the Black jeremiad, in several significant ways it departs from that tradition. To begin with, Obama's rhetoric doesn't convey a sense of impending doom and destruction. Yes, failure to "come together" to talk about the common problems of education, employment, and health care that plague all citizens will impede the social change that most Americans are desperately clamoring for. But this line of reasoning conveys a very different emotional feeling than the fear engendered by predictions of imminent destruction and danger. This was the hallmark of the jeremiad in the Antislavery Movement as well as the racialized oratory of the twentieth century in which the jeremiad was often delivered to Black audiences, such as Malcolm X's "The Ballot or the Bullet" speech. And even King hinted at gloom and doom in his "I Have a Dream" speech, warning that there will be "neither rest nor tranquility" and "whirlwinds of revolt."

Obama's speech not only departs from the fiery zeal, the emotive language, and the biting, hard candor characteristic of the Black jeremiadic tradition, we also do not hear much of the rhythmic cadence of Tonal Semantics emblematic of the Black rhetorical style, nor more than a few vernacular tropes and phonological characteristics of African American Language.[44] None of this should be taken as a critique of this earlier style of Black protest oratory (or of Obama, for that matter). As a Curtis Mayfield twentieth-century people "movin on up" to self-realization after centuries of societally imposed inferiority; as a Black nation within the White nation in quest of a newfound sense of pride and self-determination; in a society that was blind to Black suffering and lacking in the courage and political will to address that suffering—given these concrete, historical conditions, a bold, caustic, agitational, Black Vernacular driven rhetoric was called for, as brilliantly argued in a pioneering work by Arthur Lee Smith (now Molefi Kete Asante) in *Rhetoric of Black Revolution* (1969).[45]

In the archetypal Black jeremiad, Whites are told what they need to do to redress Black grievances and thus revive America's promise. These instructions are often boldly stated, with the force of commanding, guilt-induced directives. Obama chooses not to go there, abandoning the rhetorical pathos of earlier Black jeremiads. Rather than using sweeping bombast and pulling rhetorical heartstrings, he proceeds with calm, deliberate reasoning, seeking to elicit rational, thoughtful understanding and action that will ultimately benefit the entire nation:

> In the white community, the path to a more perfect union means acknowledging that what ails the African American community does not just exist in the minds of black people; that the legacy of discrimination—and current incidents of discrimination, while less overt than in the past—are real and must be addressed. Not just with words, but with deeds—by investing in our schools and our communities; by enforcing our civil rights laws and ensuring fairness in our criminal justice system; by providing this generation with ladders of opportunity that were unavailable for previous generations.

It is not only Whites but also Blacks who have some work to do if America is to realize the promise and perfect the Union. Here is yet another example of Obama making a fundamental departure from the classic Black jeremiad where the message is usually directed solely at Whites and where there is no critique or exhortation for Black people to take a certain amount of personal responsibility for their condition. Or, rather, more accurately, the critique and exhortation are not voiced in the public sphere but reserved for intimate interactions in Black homes, mosques, churches, schools, community centers, and barber and beauty shops. In this racial uplift discourse, delivered "at home," the speaker may chastise Blacks for everything from lack of Black pride, disrespect of Black women, adoption of White cultural patterns and values, to eating "swine" and other foods believed to defile the Black body. In Obama's case, airing the race's dingy laundry was a decided rhetorical risk that an earlier generation of Black orators, speaking to a White or racially mixed audience, would not have taken. However, he correctly gauged that this national 2008 Black audience would be receptive. After all, many are living daily in communities rife with Black-on-Black crime, baby daddies and baby mommas, and an educational achievement gap spiraling out of control.

> For the African American community, that path [to the more perfect Union] means embracing the burdens of our past without becoming victims of our past.... And it means taking full responsibility for our own lives—by demanding more from our fathers, and spending more time with our children, and reading to them, and teaching them that while they may face challenges and discrimination in their own lives, they must never succumb to despair or cynicism; they must always believe that they can write their own destiny.

Then he goes one step further, to a place that would never have been heard in the classic Black jeremiad. He calls for Blacks to link our struggle against current economic and social injustices with that of Whites. "It also means binding our particular grievances—for better health care, and better schools, and better jobs—to the larger aspirations of all Americans: the white woman struggling to break the glass ceiling, the white man who's been laid off, the immigrant trying to feed his family." Those who listened closely heard that Barack Obama is asking Black people to link their struggle not only to that of struggling Whites but also to that of struggling immigrants. In the context of the shifting and sometimes tense relations involving Asian and Latino immigrants in historically Black communities, Obama presents yet another bridge we need to cross. While this may appear jarring to some Old Heads, it is logical to others who have always seen the political potential in building coalitions of folks, those who, knowing the particularly precarious position of Blacks, see allies everywhere.

Drawing on his personal character and credibility (ethos), Obama connects America's prophetic promise to his life's journey and his family history, establishing his identity and authenticity—again, an element not in the typical Black jeremiad, where the speaker generally eschews any presentation of his personal biography. Here the rhetorical strategy succeeds in not simply reintroducing him to the American public but more crucially, it displays the diverse, complex unfolding of the American promise—like Langston Hughes, he "too, sing[s] America":

> I am the son of a black man from Kenya and a white woman from Kansas. I was raised with the help of a white grandfather who survived a Depression to serve in Patton's Army during World War II and a white grandmother who worked on a bomber assembly line at Fort Leavenworth while he was overseas. I've

gone to some of the best schools in America and lived in one of
the world's poorest nations. I am married to a black American
who carries within her the blood of slaves and slaveowners....I
have brothers, sisters, nieces, nephews, uncles and cousins, of
every race and every hue, scattered across three continents, and
for as long as I live, I will never forget that in no other country
on Earth is my story even possible.

He continues with his personal disclosure, characterizing his relationship
with Reverend Dr. Wright. Here Obama uses inductive reasoning (logos),
citing several specific instances to establish his general argument about
the logic of his close association with Reverend Wright. He catalogues a
wide range of noble actions and services. Wright "helped introduce me
to my Christian faith...[he] spoke to me about our obligations to love
one another; to care for the sick and lift up the poor." He lauds Wright's
accomplishments in the Chicago urban community in his role as Pastor
of Trinity United Church of Christ as well as his leadership role in the
national Black community. Further, he knows Wright as a man who "not
once in my conversations with him have I heard him talk about any ethnic group in derogatory terms, or treat Whites with whom he interacted
with anything but courtesy and respect." Obama's powerful description
of a regular church service at Trinity, combined with a list of Wright's
good works, induces the audience to Obama's desired conclusion: Wright
is doing "God's work here on Earth," he uplifts the downtrodden, he has
an unfailing commitment to empowering the disempowered. At the same
time, Obama's personal ethos demands that he honestly acknowledge
Wright's "contradictions—the good and the bad," his "profoundly distorted
view of this country," and the "divisiveness" of his comments in the tele-
vised sermon excerpts.

This forthright characterization of Wright is juxtaposed with the candid
portrayal of Obama's White grandmother, "a woman who helped raise me,
a woman who sacrificed again and again for me, a woman who loves me as
much as she loves anything in this world." Yet she displays the same racial
prejudices and contradictions assigned to Wright: "a woman who once con-
fessed her fear of black men who passed by her on the street, and who on
more than one occasion has uttered racial or ethnic stereotypes that made
me cringe." The disclosure enhances his credibility as the audience is made
to understand both Wright and Toot (Obama's nickname for his grandmother; from Native Hawaiian *kupuna wahine*, or *kuku/tutu wahine*).[46] Both
figures provide a human face to the snapshot of the "racial stalemate" that
prevents society from moving forward. They vividly and sadly exemplify
the thought patterns of Blacks and Whites from another moment in time,

a time that Obama, though fully understanding it, makes every effort to distance himself from.

Symbolizing the unity that's needed in the country, the end of the speech rhetorically returns to its beginning, reiterating the charge to perfect the Union: "This union may never be perfect, but generation after generation has shown that it can always be perfected....As so many generations have come to realize over the course of the two-hundred and twenty-one years since a band of patriots signed that document in Philadelphia, that is where the perfection begins."

While the overall arc of the "Race Speech" is that of the Black jeremiad, Obama made significant departures from this tradition. Speaking from both a Black and a White (as well as a globally diverse) perspective on race, he displayed a depth of understanding of multiple racial perspectives and the past in which those perspectives are still mired—appropriately and symbolically quoting William Faulkner, that son of the South, whose Yoknapatawpha tales revealed to us that "the past isn't dead and buried. In fact, it isn't even past." This was the metaphorical backdrop that allowed him to portray and his audience to understand the persona of both Reverend Dr. Jeremiah Wright, who had been a surrogate father to him for two decades, and his beloved maternal grandmother, Toot, who had played a major part in bringing this Black boy to manhood. It is significant and a testimony to his power of understanding human nature that he did not disown either of them, nor did he throw them under the bus. Those who accused him of having done so were listening but didn't hear. Drawing on the courage and power of his love for and profound understanding of these elders of his and imbued with the "faith of the fathers," he allowed a national audience to view Wright and Toot through his eyes, presenting them in their symbolic glory and human limitations.

Conclusion: Searching for a New Discourse on Race

Ultimately, then, the genius of the "Race Speech" lies in the fact that Obama insightfully analyzed his Black and White audiences and selected a familiar cultural touchstone, the jeremiad, and core, shared values embodied in the American Dream and the prophetic tradition of Christianity. He framed it all in careful arguments that were both personal (*ethos*) and logical (*logos*). He remixed classical traditions in order to stamp his unique rhetorical imprint on American public speaking conventions, reinscribing old materials to chart a new and different trajectory for discussions of race in the twenty-first century. In many ways, though heavily influenced by the transformational figure of Malcolm X, he remixed the rhetoric of Malcolm and Martin in an effort to create a new discourse on race. As Robert Hinton of *H-AFRO-AM* commented, "He took Malcolm X's jeremiad and turned it inside out" and thus presented America "with an opportunity to act on its best principles."[47]

While there were critiques of the "Race Speech" from Blacks, Whites, and others across the racial (and political) spectrum, taken as a whole, the responses were generally laudatory. Notwithstanding some critical points of disagreement with aspects of Obama's analysis, what he received particular praise for was having publicly taken on the subject of race.[48] His open, bold, frank talk about race was, to some, the greatest legacy of the "Race Speech" because it "finally allowed our nation to begin to move forward in a way that we had been unable to before."[49] In just under 40 minutes, Obama laid out the complexities and contradictions of race in the United States. What we heard in this speech was not anywhere near the typical polarizing positions of the past—or present. It was an honest, reflective, thoughtful searching for a new discourse on race that provided us with a road map to begin the process of racial healing.[50] In much the same vein that Barack Obama remixes the White and Black jeremiadic traditions in order to speak to new people in a new time, he urges us to remix our race discourse in such a way that we are no longer locked into blindly reproducing the racial scripts of the past.[51] This way, our approach will articulate with an emerging postmodern, more ideologically flexible generation of Americans who never doubted the possibility of a Black president.

NOTES

1. From Dr. Martin Luther King Jr.'s speech, "Where Do We Go from Here?" delivered at the 11th Annual Southern Christian Leadership Conference in Atlanta, Georgia, in August 1967. The full text of this speech, as well as a wealth of resources on Dr. King, can be found at the Martin Luther King Jr. Research and Education Institute at Stanford University, directed by Professor Clayborne Carson. Get familiar: http://mlk-kpp01.stanford.edu/. Last accessed: 09-02-11.
2. From Barack Obama's "A More Perfect Union" speech, a.k.a. the "Race Speech," delivered on March 18, 2008, in Philadelphia, PA. For a full transcript of the speech, see T. Denean Sharpley-Whiting, ed., *The Speech: Race and Barack Obama's "A More Perfect Union"* (New York: Bloomsbury, 2009, 237–251). You can also catch it on YouTube: http://www.youtube.com/watch?v=zrp-v2tHaDo. Last accessed: 09-02-11.
3. Check out Joan Morgan's insightful essay and analysis, "Black Like Barack," in Sharpley-Whiting, ed. (2009), pages 55–68. In complicating Barack's "Blackness," Morgan provides an excellent example of the social construction of race and "Blackness" in particular.
4. From Barack Obama's "A More Perfect Union" speech, a.k.a. the "Race Speech."
5. From Keli Goff's "Living the Dream" in Sharpley-Whiting, ed. (2009), page 48.
6. Adam Mansbach runs down these events with incredible nuance in "The Audacity of Post-Racism" in Sharpley-Whiting, ed. (2009), pages 69–84.

7. Quoted in Derrick Z. Jackson, in Sharpley-Whiting, ed. (2009, 233). Jackson's "trifecta" serves as an excellent ground-level analysis of these events.

8. Hendricks Jr.'s chapter can be found in Sharpley-Whiting, ed. (2009), pages 155–183. This quote is from page 162.

9. Ibid., 163.

10. Ibid., 166.

11. Ibid., 164.

12. You can check out this sermon online at: http://binside.typepad.com/binside_tv/2008/03/reverend-jeremi.html. Last accessed: 09-02-11. It's followed by CNN contributor Roland Martin's analysis of the sermon versus the media's representation of it. The controversial sections of the sermon are reprinted in Wikipedia, "Jeremiah Wright Controversy," http://en.wikipedia.org/wiki/Jeremiah_Wright_controversy. Last accessed: 02-01-11.

13. Controversial sections of this sermon are reprinted in Wikipedia, "Jeremiah Wright Controversy," http://en.wikipedia.org/wiki/Jeremiah Wright controversy. Last accessed: 02-01-11. Check out Bill Moyer's interview (April 25, 2008) with Reverend Wright and his analysis of this sermon at: http://binside.typepad.com/binside_tv/reverend_jeremiah_wright/. Last accessed: 09-02-11.

14. In Hendricks, Jr. in Sharpley-Whiting, ed. (2009), page 169. Along similar lines, Randall Kennedy writes in *The Persistence of the Color Line* (New York: Pantheon, 2011) that Wright's statements contained "a useful message that was especially important to articulate after the 9/11 attack. Reverend Wright's message was that the United States, too, is tainted by worldly sin—its imperialism (the Mexican-American War, the conquest of the Philippines, the occupation of Haiti and Cuba); its dispossession of the Indians; its subordination of blacks; its use of atomic weapons; its misadventures in Vietnam, Chile, and Nicaragua; and still other misdeeds about which all too many Americans are ignorant or indifferent." (188).

15. Check Minister Paul Davis's full comments at: http://ezinearticles.com/?Obamas-Pastor-Jeremiah-Wright-Controversy-About-America—Rev-Wright-and-Obama-on-Race-and-Politics&id=1056014. Last accessed: 09-02-11.

16. Hendricks, Jr. in Sharpley-Whiting, ed. (2009), page 171.

17. In Keli Goff's "Living the Dream" in Sharpley-Whiting (2009), page 40.

18. *Neoenslavement* is a term used by a number of Black activists and intellectuals to indicate that nineteenth-century emancipation did not free America's enslaved African population. Rather, it simply reintroduced slavery in a different form—segregation laws and policies, employment discrimination, and so on. This period lasted from the end of Reconstruction in the late nineteenth century until the mid-twentieth century, with the passage of Civil Rights legislation and Supreme Court decisions such as the 1954 *Brown v. Board* decision declaring school segregation unconstitutional. However, there remain activists today who still use the term *neoenslavement* to indicate that African slave descendants are still not free, owing to the continuing existence of racism and discrimination in employment and other areas.

19. David Walker, who was legally free since African descendant children assumed the status of their mothers, is considered to have written the first uncompromising protest against enslavement. It was a bold and ultimately dangerous thing to do. A price was placed on his head by slaveholders, and he was found dead in his shop on June 28, 1830.

20. See Jackson's "Nuanced Genius" in Sharpley-Whiting, ed. (2009), page 118.

21. Born Stokely Carmichael in Trinidad in 1941, he grew up in New York City, attended New York's well-known Bronx High School of Science, and graduated from Howard University where he became active in the Civil Rights Movement. He was head of the Student Nonviolent Coordinating Committee (SNCC) and for a brief period held an honorary position in the Black Panther Party. Credited for thrusting the slogan "Black Power" into popular discourse, which he shouted out during a Civil Rights march in the South in 1966, he subsequently wrote a best-selling book by that title, coauthored

with Charles Hamilton. Though often vilified in the mainstream White media, Carmichael was immensely popular with Blacks, who saw him as a gifted, heroic orator, skilled in articulating their problems—and their promise. Internationally honored for his activism and commitment to social justice and freedom for African people, he was also widely celebrated for what was dubbed a "revolutionary union," his marriage to the late South African (then in exile) singer-activist Miriam Makeba. Founder of the All-African People's Revolutionary Party, Carmichael left America, became a citizen of Guinea, and in 1978 changed his name to Kwame Ture in recognition of the intellectual and political influence of his heroes and mentors, Kwame Nkrumah and Sekou Toure. Kwame Ture died in Guinea in 1998. His compelling autobiography, *Ready for Revolution* (with Ekwueme Michael Thelwell), was published posthumously in 2003.

22. *Benign neglect* of America's racial problem was a policy formulated by Daniel Patrick Moynihan, chief domestic adviser to Richard Nixon. In a secret memorandum to Nixon, Moynihan recommended nonenforcement of legislation on voting laws, laws prohibiting discrimination against Blacks and minorities in employment, laws outlawing school segregation and various other antidiscrimination laws that the federal government had clear legal powers to enforce. Although Black intellectuals and leaders denounced "benign neglect" as "criminal negligence," nonetheless, it prevailed.

   The "first" Reconstruction ended in 1877, with the federal government's abandonment of former slaves to southern governments, which promptly rolled back the freedmen's political gains, ushered in US-style apartheid and began an era of lynching and brutal assaults against Blacks which would not be redressed until the Black Freedom Struggle of the 1960s. Despite some economic, political, and educational gains in the 1960s and 1970s, the mission was incomplete. There followed a treacherous push back as the country shifted to a conservative climate of stagnation and dreams deferred—a move, according to the late Ronald Walters and other political theorists, that was solidified in 1980 by the election of Ronald Reagan and the subsequent Reagan-Bush years (1980–1992) in the White House. The year 1980 effectively marked the end of the "second" Reconstruction. See Ronald Walter's *Pan Africanism in the African Diaspora: The African American Linkage* (Detroit: Wayne State University Press, 1993).

23. A must-read on all of these issues is longtime Civil Rights advocate and legal scholar Michelle Alexander's *The New Jim Crow: Mass Incarceration in the Age of Colorblindness* (New York: The New Press, 2010). Alexander shows convincingly that, while explicit racial discrimination is now illegal, it continues through employment discrimination, denial of voting rights and public benefits, educational inequality, and so on, particularly for those labeled "felons."

24. While some Blacks may have questioned Obama's Blackness, Whites more often questioned his Americanness. Although Blacks are citizens of America, there is a lingering association, albeit implicit, that American = White. In an intriguing study conducted during the presidential campaign, psychologists Devos, Ma, and Gaffud (2008) posed the question, "Is Barack Obama American enough to be the next President?" Using San Diego State University students as their research population, which was "slightly polarized toward Democrats or liberals," the researchers asked the students to compare Barack Obama and Tony Blair in terms of the extent to which they perceived each as being American. When they focused on their racial identity, Blair was considered more American than Obama. However, when they focused on Obama's and Blair's personal identity, this association was reduced or in some cases altogether eradicated. The researchers concluded that while the "concept American was more strongly linked to the White target than to the Black target," when candidates are "construed as embodying the American identity, they are more likely to be actively supported."

25. In the "Race Speech," Barack Obama read a passage from page 294 of his book, *Dreams from My Father: A Story of Race and Inheritance* (New York: Crown Publishers, 1995, 2004). In the passage, Barack universalizes the Black struggle (and also helps others to perceive Black people's humanity). Describing his first service at Trinity,

he wrote: "And in that single note—hope!—I heard something else; at the foot of that cross, inside the thousands of churches across the city, I imagined the stories of ordinary black people merging with the stories of David and Goliath, Moses and Pharaoh, the Christians in the lion's den, Ezekiel's field of dry bones. Those stories— of survival, and freedom, and hope—became our story, my story; the blood that had spilled was our blood, the tears our tears; until this black church, on this bright day, seemed once more a vessel carrying the story of a people into future generations and into a larger world. Our trials and triumphs became at once unique and universal, black and more than black."

26. See Grace Sims Holt's chapter, "Stylin' outta the Black Pulpit" in Thomas Kochman, ed., *Rappin' and Stylin' Out: Communication in urban Black America* (Urbana, IL: University of Illinois Press, 1972, 189–204).

27. This term is used to characterize the organized mass movement for Black empowerment that began with the Montgomery, Alabama bus boycott, spearheaded by Rosa Parks's historic refusal to surrender her seat to a White man in 1955. The Black Freedom Struggle encompasses the Civil Rights Movement and the Black Power Movement. The decline of the Struggle by 1980 is generally attributed to attacks, assassinations, imprisonment, and the exile of Black leaders and activists, local as well as the more nationally known—King, Malcolm, Medgar Evers, Fred Hampton, Mark Clark, Angela Davis, Reverend Benjamin Chavis, Assata Shakur, and Eldridge Cleaver.

28. Born Hubert Brown in 1943 in Baton Rouge, Louisiana, he got his nickname Rap because of his oratorical ability, which, according to his political autobiography, *Die Nigger Die!* (1969), served him well growing up in the streets. He entered Southern University at the age of 15. Active in the Black Freedom Struggle, he chaired the Student Nonviolent Coordinating Committee (SNCC.). Although many activists of that era were under surveillance and attack by the FBI's COINTELPRO, Rap became a particular target because of his powerful, acerbic style of oratory, shot through with vernacular language and signifying discourse—perceived by government authorities as incendiary and capable of inciting violence. In summer 1967, he spoke from the rooftop of Detroit's old Dexter Theater to hundreds of Blacks assembled on the streets, in the aftermath of the worst of what the Kerner Report (1968) would come to call "civil disorders." Rap said, "Look what yall done did. Instead of calling this DEE-troit, uhma hafta call this DEE-stroyed." He converted to Islam and for more than 30 years has been Imam Jamil Abdullah Al-Amin. However, in 2002, he was convicted of the murder of a deputy sheriff and is currently serving life without parole—a conviction his supporters believe is unjustified, politically motivated retribution for his activism in another lifetime.

29 See Smitherman, Daniel, and Jeremiah's "'Makin a Way outta No Way': The Proverb Tradition in the Black Experience" in *Journal of Black Studies 17(4)*, June 1987, 482–508.

30. Ibid., 505.

31. In Barack Obama's *The Audacity of Hope: Thoughts on reclaiming the American dream* (New York: Crown Publishers, 2006, 245).

32. Multilingual societies characteristically employ a language that makes communication possible with those who live outside one's own hood. It's a language that allows a speaker to talk to a wider audience. In the United States, the LWC may be loosely equated with a variety of American English problematically referred to as Standard English. The troubling links between "standard" English, Whiteness, and articulateness are described throughout this book.

33. The theme of Black Language's "controversial" status runs throughout this book. Whether we're discussing specific linguistic features, nonverbal communication, or language education, Black Language continues to be monitored and maligned by dominant culture. Despite this, President Obama regularly articulates "Blackness" through the use of cultural tropes and symbols—it's part of his communicative M.O.

Time and again we see him giving subtle nods to his Black electorate, be it through cultural-linguistic symbols or rhetorical references to Black intellectual and philosophical traditions. Not only did his "making a way out of no way" reference the Black proverb tradition, he also recast one of Martin Luther King's famous observations that the great American paradox is that, as a nation of faith, we remain deeply segregated in our houses of worship. Obama explained that White America's surprise at Reverend Wright's anger was simply a reminder "of the old truism that the most segregated hour in American life occurs on Sunday morning." This "old truism" could be attributed to Martin Luther King's 1958 observations in *Stride toward Freedom: The Montgomery Story* (quoted in James M. Washington's edited collection, *A Testament of Hope: The Essential Writings and Speeches of Martin Luther King, Jr.*, New York: HarperCollins, 1991, 479): "Unfortunately, most of the major denominations still practice segregation in local churches, hospitals, schools, and other church institutions. It is appalling that the most segregated hour of Christian America is eleven o'clock on Sunday morning, the same hour when many are standing to sing: 'In Christ There Is No East Nor West.'" Although segregation is no longer legal, Obama and other Black Americans often recast King's observation to highlight the contradiction of "Christian" America's ongoing struggle with residential and social segregation.

34. This grand vision was rooted both in the Puritans' religious faith and in their enhanced sense of English nationalism. Whenever Native Americans died off—due to European diseases and warfare—the Puritans believed that it was God's will, paving the way for their establishment of the "city upon a hill." See, for example, Robert F. Berkhofer, Jr.'s *The White Man's Indian: Images of the American Indian from Columbus to the Present* (New York: Vintage Press, 1979) and Francis J. Bremer's, *John Winthrop: America's Forgotten Founding Father* (New York: Oxford University Press, 2003).

35. See Sacvan Bercovitch's *The American Jeremiad* (Madison: The University of Wisconsin Press, 1978, 11–12, 18).

36. Bercovitch (1978) writes: "What first attracted me to the study of the jeremiad was my astonishment, as a Canadian immigrant, at learning about the prophetic history of America. Not of North America, for the prophecies stopped short at the Canadian and Mexican borders, but of a country, that despite its arbitrary territorial limits, could read its destiny in its landscape, and a population that, despite its bewildering mixture of race and creed, could believe in something called an American mission, and could invest that patent fiction with all the emotional, spiritual, and intellectual appeal of a religious quest." (11).

37. See Bercovitch (1978) and David Howard-Pitney's *The African American Jeremiad: Appeals for Justice in America* (Philadelphia: Temple University Press, 2005).

38. Howard-Pitney (2005), pages 6–7.

39. Bercovitch (1978), pages 15–16, 84.

40. See William Jeremiah Moses's *Black Messiahs and Uncle Toms: Social and Literary Manipulations of a Religious Myth* (University Park: Pennsylvania State University, 1982, 31).

41. You can read the full text of Frederick Douglass's "The Meaning of July Fourth to the Negro" at: http://www.pbs.org/wgbh/aia/part4/4h2927t.html. Last accessed: 09-02-11. You might also wanna check out Philip S. Foner's five-volume set *The Life and Writings of Frederick Douglass* (New York: International Publishers, 1975).

42. According to Georgetown University professor and public intellectual Michael Eric Dyson in "A President-Preacher From Anaphora to Epistrophe," Obama's "audacity of hope" was first uttered by Dyson's late, beloved pastor Frederick Sampson and repeated by Jeremiah Wright in a sermon Obama heard (January 19, 2009). Dyson's article is available online at: http://www.smh.com.au/news/opinion/a-presidentp-reacher-from-anaphora-to-epistrophe/2009/01/18/1232213445525.html?page=2. Last accessed: 09-02-11.

43. The full text of Martin Luther King's "I Have A Dream" speech can be found at the Martin Luther King Jr. Research and Education Institute at Stanford University,

directed by Professor Clayborne Carson. Don't sleep on this: http://mlk-kpp01.stan-ford.edu/. Last accessed: 09-02-11.

44. Smitherman coined the term *Tonal Semantics* in *Talkin and Testifyin: The Language of Black America* (Boston: Houghton Mifflin, 1977) to refer to the use of speech rhythm, intonation, melodious repetition—that is, voice sound—to convey meaning in Black oratorical style. In the hands of a skillful rhetor, the sound becomes as important as and helps to convey the sense of the message.

    Of course, as we wrote in the opening chapter, when addressing primarily Black audiences, Obama draws heavily on the Black Oral Tradition, including the Oral Tra-dition of the Black Church, in particular. Even in the "Race Speech," while not deeply engaging in the Tradition's wide range of devices, Obama draws on what Michael Eric Dyson (2009) refers to as "anaphora," or "repeating the same word or phrase at the beginning of successive sentences." Dyson writes: "The complex signifying, ver-bal devices, oratorical talents and rhetorical mastery taken for granted in the black church, for instance, are largely unknown outside it. Yet a linguistic trace in Obama's speech leads straight to the black pulpit." (http://www.smh.com.au/news/opinion/a-presidentpreacher-from-anaphora-to-epistrophe/2009/01/18/1232213445525.html. Last accessed: 04-21-12).

45. Arthur L. Smith (Molefi Kete Asante). *Rhetoric of Black Revolution* (Boston: Allyn and Bacon, 1969).

46. According to Mary Kawena Pukui and Samuel H. Elbert's *Hawaiian Dictionary* (Hono-lulu: University of Hawai'i Press, 1986), *kuku* can refer to grandmother, grandfather, grandaunt, or any relative or close friend of a grandparent's generation. It is pro-nounced with the English *t* sound, *kuku >tutu*. They indicate that it is "apparently a new word as it has not been noted in legends and chants." (177).

47. *H-AFRO-AM* is a discussion network for scholars of African American Studies. Robert Hinton's comment was made on March 24, 2008.

48. Adam Mansbach captures the essence of the critique in his thought-provoking essay, "The Audacity of Post-Racism" in Sharpley-Whiting, ed. (2009) when he writes, from a White perspective: "I was with Obama until he let white people off the hook. Though I grasped the political necessity of the move, my expectations of this man were suffi-ciently high that it was disheartening to hear him fudge the difference between insti-tutional racism and white bitterness." (69). Mansbach's main issue with the speech is the false equation: "*Racism cuts in both directions. Anyone can be its victim, just as any-one can refuse to perpetrate it....* Obama's insights about white anger were salient, but to characterize ire at affirmative action and at *the thought that others might think them prejudiced* as 'similar' to the frustration felt by the victims of entrenched structural racism was disingenuous, and even irresponsible." (74–75). Mansbach concludes with thoughts on how Whites might interpret Obama's speech as "post-race": " 'Post-race' suggests, not without an air of self-congratulation, that we are moving toward an acceptance of the multifaceted nature of identity—learning to assimilate, for instance, the idea that a human being can be both Kenyan and Kansan. This may be true. The problem is that 'post-race' inevitably implies post-*racism*. To conflate the two ignores the very nature of oppression." (76).

    Randall Kennedy does not aim to deride the speech but was unimpressed and referred to much of the praise (quite derisively) as "Obamamania." Writing in *The Persistence of the Color Line* (New York: Pantheon, 2011), he states that while many have "lauded the speech for its intellectual ambitiousness," he doesn't see "what so impresses them." (119). He continues: "In neither its rhetoric nor its analysis nor its prescriptions did the speech offer much beyond a carefully calibrated effort to defuse a public-relations crisis....Much of what Obama had to say is, frankly, banal. To speak out loud now the sentences quoted above, removed from the fears and yearnings of March 2008, is to encounter rhetoric that should be seen as notably thin." (121). But that's precisely it—to lift the speech, any speech, out of its immediate politi-cal context would be a misreading of the speech. Kennedy's comments are striking, especially since in almost ever other case of his thought-provoking and well-argued book, he takes great pain to discuss particular events within the context of the racialized opposition to Barack Obama's presidency.

Though Kennedy takes Cornel West to task, perhaps he might agree with West on one point. As West commented, "As a speech given to a racially immature society, it was brilliant" (quoted in William Jelani Cobb's *Barack Obama and The Paradox of Progress* (Walker, 2010, 32). Like Mansbach, Kennedy and Cobb both point out moments of "false equivalence" in the speech, but as Cobb notes: "Those didn't matter much.…The speech was too slickly phrased and deftly argued for its flaws to register to many listeners." (30). In our view, Barack Obama sized up his audience masterfully by taking into account most Americans' intellectual "immaturity" in race matters and delivered a speech that could speak to Black and White audiences, both emotionally and rhetorically.

49. In Keli Goff's "Living the Dream" in Sharpley-Whiting, ed. (2009), page 53.

50. In terms of racial healing, note the perspective of Stanford University professor and former secretary of state Condoleeza Rice: "I think it was important that [Obama] gave [the Race Speech] for a whole host of reasons.…There is a paradox for this country and a contradiction of this country and we still haven't resolved it.…But what I would like understood as a black American is that black Americans loved and had faith in this country even when this country didn't love and have faith in them" (Reuters.com, March 29, 2008).

51. As we approach the 2012 elections, many wonder if Barack Obama can "show and prove" on race matters in the United States. As Michael Eric Dyson famously commented, Obama "runs from race like a Black man running from the police." However, as Randall Kennedy argues in *The Persistence of the Color Line* (New York: Pantheon, 2011), it is questionable, politically speaking, if Barack Obama should be more vocal on issues of race: "Given the antiblack racism that is so ingrained in American culture, Obama's reticence is probably the most realistic course of action under the circumstances.…On no topic is his caution more evident than race relations. Because that topic remains volatile and because his blackness makes him particularly vulnerable to demagoguery, Obama avoids confronting the American race question, thus underscoring its central but repressed and paradoxical presence in the political culture of the United States." (238–239).

4

"The Fist Bump Heard 'Round the World"

How Black Communication Becomes Controversial

I have to be greeted properly. Fist bump, please.[1]
—Michelle Obama

We wondered, were white folks really so ignorant,
our worlds so segregated, that they couldn't tell
what a good old-fashioned dap looked like?[2]
—Patrice Evans (www.theroot.com)

Certain types of African American speech are currently
being criticized, and to some extent, censured....Much of
the language being criticized is not understood by many
of those doing the criticizing....Controversial features
of African American verbal culture must be theorized
by those with the linguistic expertise to do so in order
to counteract the many misbegotten discussions and
analyses that are already in circulation.[3]
—Arthur Spears

On Tuesday night June 3, 2008, at a campaign rally in St. Paul, Minnesota, Senator Barack Hussein Obama sealed the Democratic nomination for president of the United States. In celebration of this historic victory, he and his wife, Michelle, hugged. Then Michelle extended her fist to give him a pound. Like any fluent Black Language speaker, Barack responded with a pound, extending his fist to meet hers. Used for decades all over African America, on the regular, the Obamas' pound sent shockwaves throughout mainstream White America. Unsure what to call this "exotic" Black gesture, White folks, both media playaz and everyday people, came up with all kinda labels—from

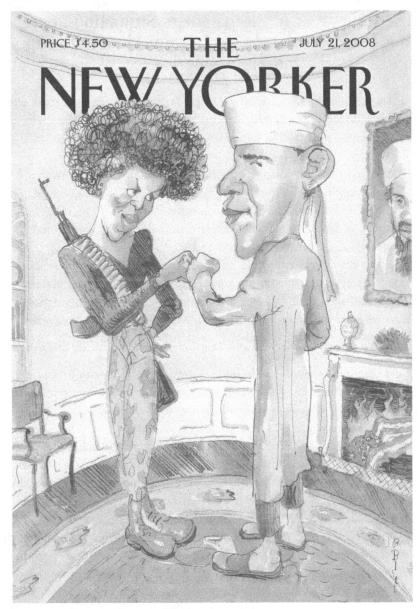

Figure 4.1 Barry Blitt, "The Politics of Fear," cover of the *New Yorker*, July 21, 2008.

"fist bump" (also "fist-bump"), "fist pump," "fist thump," "fist jab," "terrorist fist jab," "fist dap," "fist pound," "fist-to-fist thumbs up," and "closed-fist high five" to "knuckle bump," "knuckle buckle," "knuckle knot," "knocked knuckles"—and more. A *Washington Post* article referred to "the first couple" as "the fist couple" and announced that "it was the fist bump heard 'round the world."[4]

"Like a Bunch of Anthropologists Stumbling upon Some Aliens on Mars": The Cultural-Linguistic Gap between White and Black America

But first, y'all, before we go anotha fuhtha, let's git the nomenclature right. The correct term is *pound,* not *fist bump.* Chiding the media for using this term, the online journal *The Trickle-Down* posted:

> Please mainstream media workers and journalists and newscast-ers of America, it's not called a "fist bump," it's called giving dap or a pound....Where have you all been culturally for the last...40 years or so that you have never heard those terms? As presumably professionally trained journalists and media workers, who are sup-posedly covering nationwide cultural trends and events, has this really escaped your radar so long? "Fist bump"? That sounds ter-rible, in league with the terms "baby bump" and "bumping uglies." The term sounds like a bunch of anthropologists stumbling upon some aliens on Mars..."and they engaged in a 'fist bump.'"[5]

In Black Communication, The Pound is a gesture of solidarity and comrade-ship. It is also used in a celebratory sense and sometimes as a nuanced greeting among intimates and/or those with a shared social history. As previously noted, you might also refer to it as dap or givin dap. However, Black Vernacular purists only use dap to refer to fists touching in a verti-cal, not a horizontal position, and if you comin correct, you give dap twice in succession, the first time with one person's fist on top followed by a second time with the other person's fist on top.

Mainstream White America's unfamiliarity with The Pound—as well as many other aspects of Black communication—persists in this supposedly "postracial" twenty-first century. Scholarly work has shown that, both in its nonverbal and verbal forms, Black Language continues to be misunderstood by the White mainstream. In a study on the "dynamics of a Black audi-ence," scholar Annette Powell Williams concluded: "Cultural 'understanding' can only come about after a long period of involvement with a group. The subtle ways in which black people communicate with each other, unper-ceived by the outsider—or, if perceived, likely to be misinterpreted—are nevertheless the cues that make for effective communication."[6] Although Powell Williams's study was conducted four decades ago, her conclusion is dead on hit today. Unfortunately, White folks' confusion about and misin-terpretation of the Obamas' pound underscores the old adage, "the more things change, the more they remain the same." That is, despite the fact that we're living in a hi-tech media age, the cultural-linguistic gap between White and Black America remains because it is the consequence of the lack of a "long period of involvement" between the two groups.

There is a real structural barrier to cultural interpretation, no matter how many hours you sit in front of the "boob tube" swimming in Black Culture. We live in a country where residential segregation remains the order of the day, and more than half a century after *Brown vs. Board* found school segregation unconstitutional, all too few K-12 schools are racially integrated or racially balanced. As a minority in a White majority country, for survival sake, Blacks are forced to learn to be bicultural/bilingual. (Of course, not all succeed in mastering these two cultural-linguistic worlds.) Furthermore, other ethnic groups (Latinos, Asians, etc.) in the United States are also forced to learn to be bicultural/bilingual. The same societal pressure does not exist for many Whites, who unless they choose to go outta they way, may live and die and know little or nothing about the communicative culture of Blacks and other groups.

To be sure, racism yet plagues the republic as it moves into the second decade of the twenty-first century. While a good deal of racial bias can be attributable to just plain ignorance of the Other, racist perspectives are usually evident not in folks' inability to decode Black cultural signs but, rather, in the kinds of interpretations one makes when faced with the blank page of their own ignorance. With an infinite realm of possible explanations, the analyst is obligated to ask the question: Why *that* particular interpretation? White America's ambivalence toward Black modes of communication—be it a simple pound, an average nigga, or a bad muthafucka (all discussed in this chapter)—is ultimately best understood within a framework that considers language as a primary site of cultural struggle and as a proxy for multiple forms of discrimination. After all, as much linguistic and anthropological research has shown, how we feel about a given language, more often than not, reflects how we feel about its speakers. (Read that again.)

The "Hezbollah Fist-Jab" and Other Wild-Ass Verbal Assaults: (Mis)Understanding "Black Folks 2.0"

White ignorance was revealed not only in the misnaming of this Black cultural communicative gesture but also and, ultimately more importantly, in misunderstanding the meaning of the gesture. On the Internet, in the news media, and in everyday people's conversations, The Pound was characterized as symbolizing militancy, violence, and a terrorist Muslim ritual. On Fox News's *America's*

Pulse, television host E. D. Hill referred to the Obamas' gesture as a "terrorist fist jab."[7] Obama's mythical Muslim connection was symbolized by The Pound being dubbed a "Hezbollah fist-jab." The original source of this wild-ass verbal assault appears to have been a posting on HumanEvents.com whose home page bills it as "leading conservative media since 1944." In this posting, the reader commented that "Michelle is not as 'refined' as Obama at hiding her TRUE feelings about America—etc. Her Hezbollah style fist-jabbing."[8]

White folks was already mystified and confused by this presidential candidate with the "funny name" whose mother was White and whose father was a citizen of Kenya; who had grown up in an "exotic" place—Hawai'i (never mind that it is one of the "United" States and has been since 1959, albeit contentiously so)[9]; who had spent some of his childhood years in another "exotic" place—Indonesia; whose religion was believed to be Islam (never mind that he had, on numerous occasions, proclaimed his Christian faith and had spent some two decades as a member of Trinity United Church of Christ under the Pastorship of Reverend Dr. Jeremiah Wright). Now here the Black guy come comin up in the campaign with this weird "fist bump"—initiated, no less, by his slave descendant wife from the South Side Chi-Town ghetto, who might be a militant Black Nationalist holdover from the Black Power Movement. (White folks, we feel you; in retrospect, all of it may have been a bit much for y'all to process.) Thus the media and everyday conversations were rife with speculations about the Obamas' use of The Pound, at worst, as a symbol of solidarity with Islamic terrorists, or at best, as an expression of a Black American "hate Whitey" sentiment (echoing another White folks' myth that a tape existed of Michelle castigating "Whitey"; however, to date, nobody has ever produced the tape).

In contrast to the negative reactions in some White quarters, African Americans overwhelmingly applauded the Obamas' pound (at least initially). Sistas in beauty shops and hair-braiding salons everywhere high-fived and exchanged their own pounds of tribute to Michelle, "our brilliant, bad Sista," for taking the lead in initiating this gesture with her man. Many Blacks had been skeptical about what they referred to as Obama's "Blackness" (after all, he is "half-White," as many Black folk put it, and not the descendant of enslaved Africans and the neoenslavement experience like millions of other African Americans). For these sistas and brothas, The Pound indicated that at last the "boy is showing his Black-hand side" (as one Baptist church deacon put it). Black author and public intellectual Ta-Nehisi Coates said that "it thrilled a lot of black folks," noting that previous generations of Blacks suppressed this kind of Black communication for fear of "looking *too* black" in mainstream settings. Coates concluded that "it's liberating to be able to run for president as a black man....Barack is like Black Folks 2.0."[10] Even boojie Blacks raved about the Obamas' pound. On JackAndJillPolitics.com, whose home page bills it as "a black bourgeoisie perspective on U.S. politics," one reader commented: "When I saw them give each other dap, I was like 'Hell yeah!'"[11]

Notwithstanding the negativity and disturbing reactions in some White quarters, there were others who celebrated the event. As one writer commented:

> The Obama pound, exchanged between Michelle and Barack on Tuesday night, marked a historic moment. Yeah, there's that whole first black nominee for president thing. But more significant is the fact that the greeting which has been described by confused white journalists as a "fist bump," "a frat-tastic fist bump," and a "Hezbollah style fist-jabbing" is finally being introduced to mainstream culture. The introduction of "The Pound" into our national vocabulary will have ripple effects....People previously unfamiliar with "The Pound" are seeing the world in a whole new way.[12]

David Givens, Director of the Center for Nonverbal Studies in Spokane, Washington, found the Obamas' pound "very touching. It was an elegant little nonverbal moment and it gave us a view into their relationship."[13] Karen Bradley, researcher and at the time visiting professor at the University of Maryland, told the *Washington Post* that the "fist bump" seemed more "spontaneous and authentic than the hug" and went on to note: "He's looking right at her, she's looking right at him—it's a partnership, it's 'We did it.'"[14] Rachel Sklar (Huffington Post) indicated that she and viewers were "happy to see that kind of genuine, affectionate moment between the nation's fastest-rising power couple."[15] Borrowing the phrase "fist bump of hope" from an Internet posting, the *NY Daily News* penned the article, "Barack and Michelle Obama's 'Fist Bump of Hope' Shows Them Silly in Love." The article quotes psychologist Drew Western, author of *The Political Brain: The Role of Emotion in Deciding the Fate of the Nation*: "People saw their willingness to display their affection in the way they really do—at home, or in private moments." The article also quotes psychologist Judy Kuriansky, who stated that "America wants to see what's going on in the relationship....[It] was very hip, very cool, an 'I'm-with-it' move. It's almost cocky."[16]

National and World Fist Bump Day: The "Fist Bump" Goes Global (and Viral)

The news media and White mainstream folks might not have been in the know on June 3, 2008, but they got busy wit a quickness. Articles, pictures on the Internet, and commentaries about The Pound started sprouting up everywhere, showing Whites in a variety of situations and activities using the gesture—playing golf, kayaking. Several schools in Hawai'i, concerned about the H1N1 virus, changed the traditional graduation handshake to The Pound.[17] Writing in the *New York Times* on June 11, 2008, journalist Jim Rutenberg noted:

> Um, people. This is a common gesture, and its use is not lim- ited to Democrats with unusual names. In 2001 it was used by Carleton S. Fiorina, the former Hewlett-Packard chief executive— now advising Senator John McCain—and Michael D. Capellas, then the Compaq chief executive, to salute the completion of their merger. And in 2006, former President George Bush shared a fist bump with Anna Kournikova at a celebrity tennis event— and he was 82 at the time.[18]

According to Frank Rich of the *New York Times* (July 27, 2008), *USA Today* noted that fist bumps had become the rage among "young (nonterrorist) American businessmen."[19] A YouTube video demonstrated instructions for The Pound in four moves, the first of which is to bend your elbow at an 82-degree angle![20] On *Reliable Sources* the Sunday after the Obamas' cel- ebrated pound, the program host brought up the subject of what he referred to as the "knuckle bump." He then ended the show by giving a pound to one of the guests (a White male), who accompanied his pound with "Word."[21] And at least one foreign head of state got in on The Pound frenzy. A *New York Times* photo captured what wound up being an awkward moment when then-French president Nicolas Sarkozy attempted to execute The Pound with an unsuspecting Obama, who had anticipated a handshake and extended his palm instead.[22]

And, of course, with our hyperracial lenses on, Obama was taken to task on Internet blogs and cable news networks for "refusing" to give a pound to an elementary school White boy who had requested it—or so it was thought. A closer viewing of the classroom setting where the alleged slight of this young White boy occurred revealed that the kid had asked Obama to "sign my hand" and raised his fist for Obama to sign it. Obama then said that his mother might not like that—"She'll be like, 'What is the dirt on your hand ?" He then autographed pictures the children had been drawing.[23] Despite the initial drama of misunderstanding and misinter- pretation that prevailed in White mainstream culture about the so-called "fist bump", in the final analysis it seem like everybody and they momma wanted to be down.

All the hoopla about the Obamas' pound led to a call to establish National Fist Bump Day on June 3 each year and to a more global movement to establish World Fist Bump Day each July 7. On the former, organizers posted the following on NationalFistBumpDay.com in 2009:

> On June 3rd, 2008, Barack Obama and his wife Michelle took part in what immediately became known as "the fist bump heard 'round the world." Though it was an intensely personal and affectionate gesture of love and respect at a pivotal moment in Obama's presidential campaign, it firmly placed the fist bump on the national stage. In the following days and weeks, the fist bump took the country by storm. Though the "knuckle bump" had been used for years, it had never been used so publicly, or by such an important figure....Nearly a year later, a group of like-minded people got together to commemorate Obama's grand gesture, but also to take the fist bump to a higher level, one above partisan politics and social divides. For one day we call for Americans, and perhaps even global citizens, to put aside their differences—be they class, race, religion or values—and show their respect with a little bump. Sometimes all the world needs is a little human touch, a little flesh to flesh action, and a little understanding.

> SO THIS JUNE 3RD, SHOW THE WORLD SOME LOVE
> AND BUMP IT!

> AND WHILE YOU'RE AT IT, CHECK OUT OUR STORE FOR SOME
> GREAT NATIONAL FIST BUMP DAY™ GEAR.[24]

The founder of the movement for World Fist Bump Day is Thomas Sandberg, who says he is "a Norwegian living in USA...an artist and an author" and that he had "tried to raise the issue [of the Fist Bump] 3 years ago" but to no avail. However, he is now "giving it a second try" since "even the president seems to buy into this, plus many celebrities and others." Unlike National Fist Bump Day organizers, the bottom line rationale in Sandberg's call for an alternative to the handshake is not so much reppin for peace and brotherhood (and tryna make an extra dollar!) as for hygiene and health:

> More and more people are bumping fists as a form of greeting. I think time has come to make the Fist Bump an acceptable alternative to the handshake. The main reason I started this movement is not related to politics or any deeper meaning of the Fist

Bump or its origin. I'm concerned with the health aspect of a handshake. It's been proven beyond doubt that germs swapped in a handshake is one of the main ways people contract a wide range of viruses...[A] Fist Bump...is a fine gesture between two people. You're still acknowledging and focusing on giving sole attention to the other person and by timing it right with the proper touch it can still be a special moment.[25]

If a National Fist Bump Day and a World Fist Bump Day wasn't enough, there's even something for folks who spend their days and nights out there in the blogosphere. We now have a World #tweetbump Day! (Tellin you, can't make this shit up). Founded by public relations and media consultant Sarah Evans, World #tweetbump Day "is inspired by President Obama's public fist bump" and is a day "dedicated to putting aside differences, embracing one another as human beings and spreading some good cheer." Evans explains: "While National Fist Bump Day is great for face-to-face interactions, it leaves those of us in the virtual world a bit 'bumpless.' Therefore I'm unofficially partnering with National Fist Bump Day and declaring June 3, 2009 World #tweetbump Day on Twitter."[26]

It's unclear how the movement for National, World, or Twitterverse Fist Bump Day is doing at this stage (the national group posted a "Happy Fist Bump Day" for June 3, 2010). But mos def, the Obamas' pound was the "fist bump heard 'round the world."

Michelle Obama: Pound for Pound Barack's Biggest Fan

For their part, the Obamas seemed to take the "mass hysteria" about their Black communicative gesture in stride. Then-candidate Barack, ever Mr. Cool, appeared unfazed and oblivious to all the drama about their use of a gesture that can be witnessed countless times every day in Black communities across the nation. Crediting Michelle with the impetus for their special historic moment, he said that "it captures what I love about my wife. There's an irreverence about her and sense that for all the hoopla, I'm her husband and sometimes we'll do silly things."[27]

In Michelle's case, her response to the mania over The Pound contributed greatly to the redemption of her image at the time, muting conservative attempts to paint her as an anti-American militant. The criticism stemmed from a convoluted misinterpretation of a comment she had made early on in the campaign, in which she noted that for the first time she was proud of her country—that is, for assessing Barack the man, not Barack the *Black* man. It was actually intended as a compliment acknowledging the developing sophistication of some American voters for realizing King's vision of looking beyond color to the "content of [a person's] character."

Ever comfortable with who and why she is, Michelle launched her redemption-by-pound on June 18, 2008, when she cohosted the popular daytime show *The View*. From Jump, she told her female cohosts: "I have to be greeted properly. Fist bump, please." As they exchanged pounds all around, she noted that this is now "my signature bump. But let me tell you, I'm not that hip. I got that from the young staff. That's the new high-five." Entertainer and actress Whoopi Goldberg, one of the regular cohosts on *The View*, in her own inimitable comedic way, lambasted the foolish hysteria over the Obamas' pound. After all the women had greeted Michelle "properly," Whoopi mocked the negativity: "I'm sorry, what did that mean? Should I be worried about doing that with you?" By immediately calling lighthearted and positive attention to The Bump and describing herself as unhip (read: harmless), Michelle, with the help of Whoopi, took the air out of any further negative criticism that could have possibly been directed at her. With this move, Michelle scored points on both the political and personal levels. On a personal level, as Maureen Dowd concluded, Michelle "scored a pre-emptive hit both with her chic style…and with her playful fist pump [sic]….The dap or pound, as it's also called, was a natural and beguiling moment that showed the country that, even though she started out as her husband's boss and has a resume that matches his, she likes him and is rooting for him."[28]

Crossin over Like Allen Iverson: Black Communication in the Public Sphere

The Pound was first introduced into mainstream Black Culture in the late 1970s/early1980s as Hip Hop Culture spread out from its New York home to Blacks all across the country. Like Hip Hop, The Pound was also adopted by many multiracial urban youths. The dap preceded The Pound, having been introduced into Black Culture in the 1960s by African American soldiers fighting in The Nam.

In these days when The Pound and the high-five have gone global, it's well to remember that Black nonverbal (and verbal) communication has always had an ambivalent status in White mainstream culture. What White mainstream media once referred to as "palm slapping" among Blacks has evolved into the high-five and spread out from its Black Culture roots. It was once perceived of as the province of "street" Blacks hangin out on the corners of Harlem, South Side Chicago, Black Bottom Detroit, and other urban centers peopled by the Great Migration of Blacks from the rural South in the first half of the twentieth century. Yet the gesture of what Blacks called "givin skin" and "givin five" was not the sole province of street people in those urban centers, nor did it originate there. Rather, givin skin/givin five was widely used by all groups throughout Black speech communities (although it was sometimes frowned on if used by females when males were around). Further, the gesture reflects the carryover of African communication styles used among such West African ethnic groups as the Mandingo.[29]

The Black Liberation Movement of the 1960s and 1970s accelerated the adoption ("crossover") of Black Popular Culture, like the high-five. By August 1991, *Ebony* magazine was referring to this cultural adoption as the "high-five revolution." With a photo of President George Bush (the elder) giving an Air Force Academy cadet a high-five instead of the customary salute, *Ebony* declared: "The high-five congratulatory hand slap has moved from the urban basketball court to the sports arena and corporate settings. Even President George Bush has given a high-five in a moment of elation."[30]

Among the originators of the high-five, though, the high-five wasn't always high. In the decades before 1990, givin skin/five was done by extending the palms from waist level, and there were several different variations to convey diverse meanings. Using field research conducted in 1968 and 1969, African American scholar Benjamin Cooke developed a schema for classifying the complex system of givin and gettin skin. In addition to givin and gettin skin as "gestures of greeting or parting," he noted that there was "agreement skin," "complimentary skin," "emphatic skin," and "five on the sly." Cooke concluded that there were more than 28 combinations of givin/gettin skin possible in social situations in the Black community. He thus cautioned against misinterpretation: "One look at this variety of meanings associated with the kinemes of giving and getting skin is enough to indicate that the only way to interpret the act in any one situation would be to analyze the entire communicative event."[31]

In today's world, both nonverbal and verbal Black communication can be observed in the White public sphere. While the "crossover" label is new, the process is as old as the African Holocaust.[32] Late linguist J. L. Dillard's history of African American Language traced young White Americans' borrowings from the speech of Africans during and after the enslavement period.[33] In the Harlem Renaissance era of the 1920s—a period in which the Negro was "in vogue"—Whites flocked uptown to Harlem clubs and cabarets to immerse themselves in the language, music, and culture of the "New Negro." In 1957, White American writer Norman Mailer noted in his historic essay "The White Negro" that:

In certain cities...New York...New Orleans...Chicago...San Francisco, and Los Angeles...this particular part of a generation [of Whites] was attracted to what the Negro had to offer....And in this wedding of the white and the black it was the Negro who brought the cultural dowry....So there was a new breed of adventurers, urban adventurers who drifted out at night looking for action with a black man's code to fit their facts. The hipster had absorbed the existentialist synapses of the Negro, and for practical purposes could be considered a white Negro.[34]

Mailer's piece created widespread controversy, but he had simply set out in the public sphere what many African American writers, intellectuals, and cultural theorists had been saying privately for decades. As Langston Hughes bemoaned in the aftermath of the Harlem Renaissance, "they done taken my blues and gone."

Cornel West has called this crossover the "AfroAmericanization of youth," but it's broader than that. Adults of varying ages and class groups throughout the global village have also become AfroAmericanized. Crossing over is writ large in fashion, music, attitude, dance, and even in what used to be Black children's games. White women have now picked up Double Dutch, the jump rope game young sistas done been playin for years on the streets of the Bronx, Motown, South Central, Chi-Town, the ATL, the Illadelph, and other urban hoods. Journalist Elizabeth Ahlin, writing about the group Double Dutchess, noted: "White and in their 20s, the women of Double Dutchess are bringing a new look to a pastime long considered the province of young African American girls."[35]

On the linguistic front, we are witnessing the "Africanization of American English."[36] While much more pervasive today, this phenomenon was also documented by Mailer back in 1957: "The child [in the cultural marriage of White and Black] was the language of Hip, for its argot gave expression to abstract states of feeling which all could share....The language of Hip is a language of energy....The nuance of the voice uses the nuance of the situation to convey the subtle contextual difference." He lists "perhaps a dozen words...most in use and most likely to last with the minimum of variation: man, go, put down, make, beat, cool, swing, with it, crazy, dig, flip, creep, hip, square."[37] More than five decades later, Mailer's word list has undergone some modification, but his conceptual point still holds. Black linguistic innovations have continued unabated in our postmodern, high-tech, cyberspace, media-driven world as the Africanization of American English moves fast and furious throughout the globe. Nonetheless, as the Obamas' "fist bump" has demonstrated, even with a Black man in the White House, there are dimensions of Black Language and Culture that remain unknown and/or misunderstood by the White mainstream. This cultural-linguistic gap is even more striking in the case of verbal communication, which makes it imperative for speakers to know the answer to what late linguistic anthropologist Dell Hymes referred to as the fundamental question of all communication in any language, wherever it occurs: Who can say what to whom under what conditions?[38]

Understanding the Rules of Engagement: Different Linguistic Strokes for Different Folks

The answer to the Hymesian question is not the same for Black folks as it is for White folks. Of course, there are many areas of shared communication between the two groups. However, there are also many areas where the rules of linguistic engagement differ and become glaring as Black insider talk moves out into the White public sphere—in the media, on the Internet, in Hip Hop, sports, and entertainment. While this difference is most often noted with the so-called "N-word" (more on that in a few), it also pops up in the case of seemingly less controversial verbal and nonverbal forms of Black communication.

The phrase "Just throw yo hands in the air, and wave 'em like you just don't care!" is a common invocation used by Hip Hop artists and DJs in da club to get the party started. This same hand waving in the air is a common gesture in the Black Church. It is used to convey approval as a response to what the preacher or someone in the congregation has said. Or the waving hand can be used to express a spirit-filled moment, in which case the gesture substitutes for talk. As church folks chant, "If I couldn't say nothin, I'd just wave my hand." Cultural outsiders are mystified by the use of the same nonverbal gesture in two different contexts, one sacred, the other secular. However, in Black Culture there is really no sharp division, no dichotomy between sacred and secular. Rather, in keeping with the African World View, there is a continuum of the sacred and profane. This sacred-secular continuum accounts for Black musical artists with ties to and performances in both the Black Church and pop worlds, such as Hip Hop/R&B artist Faith Evans and Queen of Soul Aretha Franklin. It also accounts for the much-applauded performance style of the late James Brown, Godfather of Soul, who would go offstage and return wearing a black cape symbolizing the preacher's robe. He would continue to sing and shout (as in church) until he got the Spirit and had to be pulled away from the stage. Similarly some church folk "git happy" (also referred to as "catch the Holy Ghost") and have to be attended to by the church's nurses.

In the verbal realm, consider the label *nappy*, a term that simply refers to the tightly curled natural state of African American hair. Ha, not so fast. Yes, it's true that we have had a celebration of natural/nappy Black hair since the Black Liberation Movement of the 1960s and 1970s. Yes, we now have the upbeat oft-used slogan, "Happy to be nappy" (also found on T-shirts). And the children's book *Nappy Hair* by African American writer-professor Carolivia Herron celebrates the symbolic value of Black women's natural hair. Yet *nappy*, a term that can have either a positive or negative meaning, can only be used by Blacks with Blacks in Black social contexts. In this linguistic case, that's the answer to the Hymesian question.

Some years ago the nation witnessed the violation of this communication rule when a White teacher in Brooklyn, New York, used Herron's book with her African American students. All hell broke loose: Black parents protested, accused the teacher of racism and/or poor pedagogical judgment, and the teacher requested a transfer to another school. Economist and former President of the HBCU Bennett College for Women, Dr. Julianne Malveaux, a self-described nappy-headed sista, called this a "nappy misunderstanding...[that] turned a classroom misunderstanding into a national incident."[39]

More recently in 2007, nationally syndicated White radio host Don Imus caught hell over his decision to call the women of the Rutgers University basketball team "some nappy-headed hos." The response to Imus's suspension showed how deeply divided the country was and is along racial lines. While many Whites (from conservative Republican Pat Buchanan to liberal comedians Bill Maher and Rosie O'Donnell) claimed Imus was protected by freedom of speech or that his apology should be enough, most Blacks viewed the comment as both racist and sexist coming from a White male in a society that routinely denigrates Black women. To make matters worse, many Whites then turned around and accused Black folks such as Al Sharpton and Jesse Jackson, who were most vocal throughout the controversy, of seeking to profit by creating racial division. These responses showed, again, that rather than "postracial," America was and is a hyperracial society. The national reaction also underscored the fact that, even though Blacks and Whites appear to be speaking the same language, the meanings and rules of engagement for using that language differ significantly. This is glaringly obvious in the case of ritualized language traditions, such as snappin, and in the semantic inversion of common English words, such as *muthafucka* and *nigga*.

The tradition of snappin, a.k.a. signifyin and playin the Dozens in Old School lingo, is a style of verbal communication that incorporates double meaning and humor to comment on an individual, event, or situation. Snappin can be in the form of playful commentary or serious social critique couched as verbal play. It involves rhetorical hyperbole,

irony, indirection, metaphor, and deployment of the semantically or logi-
cally unexpected. Most importantly, the signifyin must be funny. There
are double—and sometimes multiple—layers of meaning. Although signifyin and playin the Dozens ("yo momma" verbal taunts) is tantamount to
a dis, it's acceptable in Black communication because those in the social
context recognize it as a longstanding form of Black Culture, with socially
defined rules and linguistic norms shared by those born under the lash.
Until the global explosion of Hip Hop Culture, this verbal tradition was
rarely heard outside the confines of the Black community. Still today,
the language forms used in this style of Black verbal communication are
associated with and believed to be used only by Black males, particularly brothas who are young Hip Hop headz. Not so. Snappin and the raw
language involved in this communicative style is used by males and females,
young and old, lower and upper classes and this cultural form was in use
long before most Hip Hop heads were even born. This erroneous association reflects the generational and class divide in Black America that has
arisen over the past two decades.

Smitherman's study, "If I'm Lyin, I'm Flyin: The Game of Insult in Black
Language," describes several conversations in which sistas engage in snappin,
including incorporating raw language. For example, this exchange between
two 30-something sistas:

LINDA: Girl, what up with that head? [referring to her friend's
hairstyle]
BETTY: Ask yo momma.
LINDA: Oh, so you going there, huh? Well, I did ask my momma
and she said, "Can't you see that Betty look like her momma
spit her out!"

And this from some older, middle-aged sistas:

ARLENE: No, un-unh, I don't think I know any of that stuff
[responding to Smitherman's query, asking if they knew how
to play the Dozens].
RENEE: I remember something like, uh, I don't play the Dozens
cause the dozens is bad.
BARBARA: But, Arlene, I can tell you how many dicks yo momma
had.
ARLENE: Well, I hate to talk about yo momma, Barbara, cause
she's a good old soul.
RENEE: Aw, nah, heifer, thought you didn't know any of that
stuff.

ARLENE: [Finishing the rhyme she started above]...she got a two-ton pussy and a rubber ass hole.[40]

In all-female contexts, the sistas can come real and raw, and their snappin can rival even the most highly criticized Black male Hip Hop artist whose lyrics have been deemed vulgar or offensive. In Spike Lee's 1991 film, *Jungle Fever*, there is a scene in which the women gather to commiserate with Drew over her husband's unfaithfulness. Described as the "War Council," this scene in the film was not scripted. The sistas, all professional, college-educated women, freestyled, reflecting the authentic verbally rich skills of Black women steeped in the rules, norms and rituals of snappin and other forms of Black Language:

INEZ: Deal with the Black man for a minute. There's a lot of self-hate goin on when he can't deal with a sista.

DREW: Yeah, Inez, how would you know? You won't deal with a Black man.

INEZ: Oh yes, I *do* date Black men, but I also date Chinese, Latino, Jewish, the full spectrum....I know you think I should date Black men, but I'm going to date who I like. Give me a man, regardless of the color of his skin, who is nice to me, who is sweet to me, and who I strongly believe loves me.

DREW: Inez, I am not the rainbow-fucking kind.

INEZ: Drew, if it will make you happy, honey, I will make a pilgrimage to Africa...and find myself a true tribesman.

VERA: A true Asiatic Black man.

INEZ: With a dick down to his knees to keep me happy for days.

NILDA: Oooh, Zulu dick.

INEZ: That's right, girl. Ima get me some serious Zulu dick in the bush....

NILDA: Most of the Brothas who have made it got White women on their arms. Their responsibility level isn't the same as ours.

VERA: It isn't a question of responsibility. It's just a fundamental disrespect...for women.

NILDA: I don't care, the best man, it's hard for him to say no, some pussy staring him in the face....I don't know the man that's been born, that's gon say no....He gon look around, ain nobody looking, he gon fuck the pussy. If you are in a committed relationship, you are supposed to be able to say "No."...You gon get turned on...you gon see somebody you want to fuck. But your mind supposed to tell you, "I have a committed relationship here. I have a wife, whatever," and tell the dick to shut the fuck up. Tell the dick to get down, strap that muthafucka down.

More recently, as we've seen with the young sistas from the San Francisco Bay Area in Alim's work, the tradition of signifyin is goin strong, even reinvented within verbal duels where these youth try to put each other on hush mode (using their wit to leave opponents speechless, without a response).[41]

The Logic of *Niggaz* and *Muthafuckaz*: The Uncensored Mode in Black Communication

It's been said that the two most popular words in African American Language are *muthafucka* and *nigga*. Both exemplify the semantic inversion characteristic of Black communication that extends the meaning of words on multiple levels. These forms have enjoyed longstanding use throughout the Black community and by Blacks from all walks of life for generations. Though not used by everyone, these terms have endured for many reasons, not the least of which is the pleasure Black folks get outta playin wit the semantic ambiguity, inventing new meanings, spellings, and contexts of use. Their use today is by no means a new phenomenon. What is new is the widespread use of these terms outside Black community contexts—in Hip Hop, at Black comedy shows, on the Internet, and in other arenas of the public sphere.

African American linguist Arthur Spears has coined two useful concepts for analyzing these widely spoken language forms: uncensored mode and normalization. Rather than refer to such terms as *nigga* and *muthafucka* as taboo language or obscenities, he proposes that we use the phrase "uncensored mode":

> The term *uncensored mode* has been coined in recognition that individuals operate effectively within different evaluative language norm contexts—which is true of language users worldwide....In this mode, expressions that in censored contexts are considered obscene or evaluatively negative are used in an almost or completely evaluatively neutral way. Among *censored contexts*, I include church services and other contexts in which persons of high, mainstream-supported respect are present, e.g., ministers, elderly relatives, etc. Thus we could say that in locker rooms, almost invariably uncensored mode (hereafter UM) speech is used, whereas in church, we would expect censored speech.[42]

As a consequence of UM language use, terms that were once considered taboo have become "normalized." Spears explains:

> What is new...is...*normalization*, the use of uncensored expressions by some types of people in most social settings in an evaluatively neutral way, i.e., the expressions are not inherently negative or positive...they are neutralized: they are negative, positive, or neutral in force depending on how they are used. Many people who function exclusively or primarily in mainstream settings are not aware of this.[43]

Rather than referring to "obscenity" or "taboo words," the advantage of the concepts UM and normalization is that they call for linguistic analysis to confirm what's being communicated before we pass judgment on speakers and their language. To consult Spears again:

> [Rather than obscene language], I prefer to use the term *uncensored speech* in order not to prejudge the actions of the users of such speech. My wish not to prejudge is not the result of unreflexive liberal humanism; rather, it reflects one of the major conclusions presented...namely, in many cases, rigorous analysis of form, meaning, and communicative behavior is required before one can pass judgment on the speech of members of communities other than one's own, where the term *community membership* is determined by age, socioeconomic class, ethnicity, gender, and other variables.[44]

If we heed Spears's call for "rigorous analysis," we can see that *nigga* and *muthafucka* each allow for a multiplicity of meanings and a range of evaluations. Smitherman first documented this phenomenon more than three decades ago in her *Talkin and Testifyin: The Language of Black America*. She explained that "we are talking about terms rooted in the Black cultural experience" and that the "semantics...depend not only on the immediate linguistic context but on the sociohistorical context as well." She also added:

> When White English words are given a Black Semantic interpretation, their range of referents increases...on one level a word's referent is the same for Blacks and Whites. But since Blacks also share a linguistic subculture outside the White mainstream, on...the Black Semantic level the same word has multiple meanings and associations....One dude said to another, noticing how he

was dressed. "You sho got on some bad shit," which means he got
on good shit, which means he's attractively dressed.[45]

Yet, following Spears, some terms are censored in the presence of
elderly relatives, ministers, teachers, and others. Thus Black speakers
shift styles based on unwritten rules of engagement, varying their use
from context to context, moment to moment. This linguistic styleshifting applies in the case of Black Language's most (in)famous widely used
term: *nigga*.

In *Talkin and Testifyin*, Smitherman called attention to what in those
years she was representing as *nigguh*: "Whereas to Whites it is simply a way
of callin a Black person outta they name, to Blacks it has at least four different meanings as well as a different pronunciation: *nigguh*"[46] (reflecting
the general pattern of postvocalic *r*-lessness [no "r" after a vowel] in
some varieties of African American Language). Despite the range of
meanings in the term, there have been a number of efforts, both individual and organized, to discourage the use of *nigga*, if not to ban it
from the Black speech community altogether. At the 2007 annual convention of the National Association for the Advancement of Colored
People (NAACP), the group gave *nigga* a formal funeral and burial,
complete with a casket and other funeral trappings, at Hart Plaza on
Detroit's riverfront. (Yeah, y'all, this actually happened.) Nonetheless,
despite its rocky journey, today in 2012 *nigga* is alive and well—and has
even been used by some of those same leaders who object to it. (More
on this in a few.)

Not only is *nigga* still omnipresent, since 1977 it has taken on expanded
uses and meanings. In both editions of Smitherman's *Black Talk* dictionaries,
she notes these semantic expansions, and by the publication of her *Word from
the Mother* in 2006, *nigga* had acquired at least eight different meanings, and
it had taken on the twenty-first-century Hip Hop spelling, "nigga":

1. Close friend, someone who got yo back, yo "main nigga."
2. Rooted in Blackness and the Black experience. From a middle-aged
social worker: "That Brotha ain like dem ol e-lights, he real, he a
shonuff nigga."
3. Generic, neutral reference to African Americans. From a
30-something college-educated Sista: "The party was live, it was
wall-to-wall niggaz there."
4. A sista's man/lover/partner. From the beauty shop: "Guess
we ain gon be seein too much of girlfriend no mo since she got
herself a new nigga." From Hip Hop artist Foxy Brown, "Ain no
nigga like the one I got."

5. Rebellious, fearless, unconventional, in-yo-face Black man. From former NBA superstar Charles Barkley, "Nineties niggas... *The DailyNews, The Inquirer* has been on my back.... They want their Black athletes to be Uncle Toms. I told you white boys you've never heard of a 90s nigga. We do what we want to do" (quoted in *The Source*, December 1992).

6. Vulgar, disrespectful Black person, antisocial, conforming to negative stereotype of African Americans. From former Hip Hop group Arrested Development, in their best-selling song, "People Everyday" (1992): "A Black man actin like a nigga... got stomped by an African."

7. A cool, down person, rooted in Hip Hop and Black Culture, regardless of race, used today by non-Blacks to refer to other non-Blacks.

8. Anyone engaged in inappropriate, negative behavior; in this sense, Blacks may even apply the term to White folk. According to African American scholar Clarence Major's *From Juba to Jive*, Queen Latifah was quoted in *Newsweek* as criticizing the US government with these words: "Those niggers don't know what the fuck they doing" (1994:320).[47]

Although we are here focused on *nigga*, we should note that there are actually three so-called "N-words": *nigger, nigga,* and *Negro*. All three have the same origin. They came into English by way of Latin (*niger/nigra/nigrum,* "black or dark colored"), Spanish and Portuguese (*negro,* "black"). While *nigger* is the racial slur and is used only in a negative sense, *nigga* is the Black pronunciation and can be used negatively, positively, or neutrally. *Negro* was for decades a perfectly acceptable label for the race. Even the fiery radical W.E.B. Du Bois not only used the term but also campaigned to have it capitalized in the 1920s. This racial label fell out of favor in the Black Liberation Movement of the 1960s and '70s and was used for Blacks who weren't down with the Black Struggle and/or had low racial self-esteem.

In the twenty-first century, *Negro* has been reclaimed as a euphemism for *nigga* in the neutral sense and is used in contexts where the speaker feels *nigga* would be inappropriate. Check out this example where a sista was extolling the culinary talents of Black cooks at an outdoor, multiracial festival: "Girl, those Negroes know they was throwin down!" Or P. Diddy's 2004 *Vibe* magazine interview conducted when he was playing Walter Lee Younger in the late Lorraine Hansberry's 1959 play *Raisin in the Sun*. Referring to the photo of O. J. Simpson on the wall of his dressing room, Diddy said: "I've been right at that place.... It's a constant reminder of what they can do to you if you ever get too comfortable. I'm one of those Negroes that's allowed into certain parties, but if I start believing the hype, like I'm the 'special Negro,' then I could end up just like that."[48]

Dismantling the Master's House: Black Youth's Project of Linguistic Reclamation

While most people probably never expect to utter Humpty Dumpty and Hip Hop in the same breath (unless they talkin bout that Oaktown playa Humpty from Digital Underground!), these two debates over semantics and pragmatics, or how we use and make meaning in language, force us to call the Question: In this social struggle over language, who is to be master? The response from the Hip Hop Nation, both those in Public Enemy's generation of the 1980s and 1990s and younger, twenty-first-century Hip Hop headz, is that they are the masters of the Black Word. In their language reclamation project, they are asserting that *nigga* belongs to the speakers of Black Language. It is theirs to reshape, to redefine, and if they so choose, to circumscribe its use. While this might strike some as racial and/or youthful arrogance, history is instructive.

For centuries, *nigger* was used in a neutral sense, simply as an identifying label for African and African descent people. It was not a way of calling a Black person outta they name but used simply as a way of referring to a person who was racially Black. The precise historical moment when *nigger* became a term of racial disrespect in White American discourse is unknown. One possibility is that the semantic negativity emerged during the beginning of the "separate but equal" Jim Crow era (roughly 1877, end of Reconstruction) and the backlash against the all-too-quickly-aborted movement for political and economic empowerment of America's formerly enslaved Africans. Throughout the nineteenth century and even during the Civil War, the question had persisted: What should America do with its enslaved African population? Resettle them in Africa? Make them citizens of the American state? If so, they don't have anything but the clothes on their backs. What reparations are they due? "Forty acres and a mule"? The issue of what to do with the freedmen became a question that was ultimately never settled. The period following the end of the Civil War—the Reconstruction Era—brought with it the (threatening?) possibility of millions of freed Africans, working and living among the White population. In this sociopolitical context, the previously neutral racial label *nigger* would have

Table 4.1 **Dismantling the master's house with language: Humpty Dumpty and Pharcyde break it down**

"I don't know what you mean by 'glory,'" Alice said.	Booty Brown: There's more than just one definition for words! We talk in slang. We always talk basically in slang. We don't use the English dictionary for every sentence and every phrase that we talk!
Humpty Dumpty smiled contemptuously. "Of course you don't—till I tell you. I meant 'there's a nice knock-down argument for you.'"	
"But 'glory' doesn't mean 'a nice knock-down argument,'" Alice objected.	Pharcyde: No, there's a lot of words out of the words that you just said which all...
"When *I* use a word," Humpty Dumpty said, in a rather scornful tone, "it means just what I choose it to mean—neither more nor less."	Booty Brown: Yeah, but the way I'm talking is not the English language....We're not using that definition....We're making our own....Just like they use any other word as a slang, *my brotha*! Anything. I'm not really your brother. Me and your blood aren't the same, but I'm your brother because we're brothas....I mean, it depends whose definition you glorify, okay? That's what I'm saying. Whose definition are you glorifying?[50]
"The question is," said Alice, "whether you *can* make words mean so many different things."	
"The question is," said Humpty Dumpty, "which is to be master—that's all."[49]	
—From Lewis Carroll, *Through the Looking-Glass, and What Alice Found There* (1871)	—Members of Hip Hop group Tha Pharcyde

been recast as a term to linguistically re-enslave African slave descendants (or at the very least, to keep them from goin buck wild). In any event, by the time of the Harlem Renaissance of the 1920s, when a "new negro" was born (albeit still lowercased!), *nigger* had become a name-calling word.

On the other hand, the term has always been owned by the Black speech community, for only Blacks have had access to its multiple meanings. Many older Blacks have childhood memories of hearing folk ditties like "You my nigga if you don't git no bigger, and if you get bigger, you gon be my bigger nigga."[51] In the 1960s, lyrical activists The Last Poets used *nigga* (then spelled "nigger") in semantic solidarity with their people, rappin: "I love niggers / I love niggers / I love niggers / Because niggers are me / And I should only love that which is me."[52] In the twenty-first century, cofounder of the West Coast Hip Hop group Niggaz Wit Attitude and now actor/producer, Ice Cube said: "We take this word that's been a burden to us...digest it, spit it back out as...a badge of honor."[53] Writer J. Clinton Brown put it this way: "I have heard the word "niggah" (note the spelling, dig the sound) all of my life. Many of my elders and friends use it with phenomenal eloquence.... These people are very much about being themselves—proudly, intensely, sometimes loudly."[54]

There is a certain sense of linguistic mastery here, a sense of Black identity and bonding, fully understood only by those who have endured— and lived—the Black Experience, both the bitter and the sweetmeat parts. Building on this linguistic history, Hip Hop headz are pushing the linguistic envelope. As Hip Hop has expanded its cultural imprint in the past two decades, part of that expansion has been a conscious rhetorical effort to reclaim and redefine the "N-word." For Hip Hop headz, positive *nigga* can be used to speak to a profound connection, a relationship beyond friendship, a ride-or-die allegiance. Thus late Hip Hop artist Tupac Shakur rapped about a sista, "I don't wanna be her man / I wanna be her nigga."[55] Co-signing Pac, Hip Hop artist DMX said about his wife: "I tell my wife shit I don't tell nobody. She's like everything to me.... That's my nigga."[56]

Whereas *nigga* has a long history of use within the confines of the Black community, a new generation has boldly made this language reclamation project a matter of public record, which is the source of the generational conflict around this as well as other Black Language forms—although none so problematic as *nigga*. Few, if any Blacks, regardless of age or social station, would claim that the term has not been widely used in Black social contexts. Their objection is that a new generation has taken the community's term to the public, in prime time, and to the farthest corners of the globe. Sometimes, though, this new generation gets linguistic vindication. This has occurred on those rare occasions when older Blacks have also gone public with *nigga*.

Caught with Their Linguistic Pants on the Ground: Generational Conflict When *Niggaz* Go Public

One such event occurred on the Michigan Supreme Court on May 10, 2006. The court's only Black member, Justice Robert Young Jr., a middle-aged Republican from an affluent Detroit suburb, used *nigga* during the court's discussion of commissioner report cases. This was not revealed to the public until the fall 2010 elections in a transcript of a recording of that discussion provided by retired Justice Elizabeth A. Weaver. The transcript was posted on delayedjustice.com, on Weaver's private website, and also referred to in a speech she gave during the fall election campaign (statement by Justice Weaver, October 25, 2010). Young is reported to have said: "Watch out for those niggas out there. (Laughter) Really." Justice Young acknowledged to a reporter that he had used *nigga* but attempted to justify his use of this "*N*-word" in the public setting of Michigan Supreme Court deliberations by declaring that he had been making an "impassioned plea" to emphasize how a person was being treated "without rights, without dignity....That's why I used the word. I remember the heat and the purpose for using it." However, when he was pressed for details he couldn't recall any particulars of this case about which he had been "very hot."[57]

Some citizens questioned Weaver's motives for recording the court's meeting back in 2006 and releasing the transcript during the 2010 campaign (she was not up for re-election). However others did not allow this question to obscure the fact that a Black state supreme court justice had not only used *nigga* in the public sphere but had added insult to injury with his "untruthful" statement about it, as Philip posted in "No, Mr. Justice, not according to her transcript":

> The transcripts that Justice Weaver has supplied show that Justice Young was untruthful in his statement to the reporter—plain and simple. No one can justify what Justice Young said....It was cavalier, unprofessional, vulgar, and a violation of judicial decorum. Instead, Justice Young's supporters try to deflect the fact of what he said by trying to impugn the motives of Justice Weaver. Obviously, Justice Weaver felt the need to record Justice Young because she knew that he and his supporters...would otherwise question her credibility in addition to her motives.[58]

The website attorneybutler.net posted the following:

> In the aftermath of the revelation that Michigan Supreme Court Justice Robert Young used the "N" word during a Supreme Court conference, I was reminded of an instructional video, shown below, from HowCast, showing how to Backpedal, Spin and Dodge. It appears Justice Young may have indeed studied that video before responding to the AP reporter. He used many of the video's tactics. He blamed someone else: Justice Weaver. Justice Young expected his use of the word to remain private and secret....He tried to make himself the victim. Justice Weaver had never been called the "N" word, though he and his family had....For a "rule

of law" "textualist," who only goes by the plain meaning of the words he encounters in his work, he certainly has an "activist" explanation for his words in this instance. What a surprise.[59]

The other public use of *nigga* by an older African American occurred on the national scene during the Obama presidential campaign. On July 6, 2008, Reverend Jesse Jackson was taking a break from taping a television interview for *Fox & Friends* news show. Unaware that his mic was still on, Reverend Jackson began complaining that Obama was "talking down" to Blacks in a speech where he took Black men to task for not fulfilling their role as fathers in their children's lives. He said that Obama was telling "niggaz how to behave." (He also, by the way, said that he wanted to "cut [Obama's] nuts off.") Jackson apologized profusely for what he called his "hurtful words," stating that he was "deeply saddened and distressed by the pain and sorrow that I have caused as a result of my hurtful words. I apologize again to Senator Barack Obama, Michelle Obama, their children as well as to the American public...I hope that the Obama family and the American public will forgive me." This was the same Jesse Jackson who had made national appeals to Hip Hop artists, entertainers, actors, and others to stop using *nigga* and who had supported the NAACP's funeral and burial of *nigga* at its national convention in Detroit less than one year before.

The range of responses to Reverend Jackson's remarks raised the issue of his choice of words and his relevance to the Struggle today. One reader of Slava Kuperstein's "Jesse Jackson Reportedly Used N-Word in Tirade" responded:

> Jesse has proved himself to be nothing more than a big hypocrite with this one. He said all these terrible things once he THOUGHT the camera was off so these were his TRUE feelings coming out. I wonder if he is upset that Obama is closer to being President than he was back in '88? How can you advocate banning the N word and you're still ABUSING it....Damn Jesse, you used to be one of my heroes back in the day...it's a new day now.[60]

Hip Hop artist Nas and filmmaker Spike Lee each made similar points. Spike Lee said:

> I'm very disappointed in Jesse Jackson. These old heads. I don't know why they're doing this stuff....I think jealousy has to be somewhere in there....I think it's really making Jesse look bad....In life, sometimes you have your moment....You have your window that lies upon you and then it leaves. This is not

Jesse's time right now. This is Barack Obama's time, and I think he's having a problem with that.[61]

Nas, perhaps one of the most critically acclaimed and politically conscious lyricists in Hip Hop, had this to say:

I think Jesse Jackson, he's the biggest playa hata. His time is up. All you old niggas, time is up. We heard your voice, we saw your marching, we heard your sermons. We don't wanna hear that shit no mo. It's a new day. It's a new voice. I'm here now. We don't need Jesse. I'm here. I got this. We got Barack....We're the voice now....No more Jesse....You ain't helping nobody in the hood. That's the bottom line. Goodbye, Jesse, Bye!"[62]

If Nas's comments appear harsh, it's probably because he had been embroiled in his own *N*-word controversy with Jesse Jackson just a year before Jesse's *nigga* went public. Nas had planned to release his ninth studio album under the title *Nigger*. And while most Hip Hop artists supported his decision, the NAACP put out an official statement denouncing Nas's album title and Jesse Jackson appeared on Fox News to condemn Nas. Al Sharpton went so far as to say that Nas, rather than taking the power away from White folks, was actually "helping out the racists."[63] Speaking to MTV News, Nas explained:

We're taking power away from the word....No disrespect to none of them who were part of the civil-rights movement, but some of my niggas in the streets don't know who [civil-rights activist] Medgar Evers was. I love Medgar Evers, but some of the niggas in the streets don't know Medgar Evers, they know who Nas is. And to my older people who don't now who Nas is and who don't know what a street disciple is, stay outta this muthafuckin conversation. We'll talk to you when we're ready. Right now, we're on a whole new movement. We're taking power [away] from that word.[64]

Responding directly to Jesse Jackson's derisive comments about his album title and pointing out his generationalism and possible classism, Nas added: "If Cornel West was making an album called *Nigger,* they would know he's got something intellectual to say....To think I'm gonna say something that's not intellectual is calling *me* a nigger, and to be called a nigger by Jesse Jackson and the NAACP is counterproductive, counter-revolutionary."[65] Like many Hip Hop artists have argued in the past, Nas continued to insist that elders in the Black community who may have legitimate concerns with his music should talk to him first rather than "acting like you know what my album is about."[66] Then in an incredible moment of foreshadowing, he cautioned Jesse about Fox News: "Whether you in the NAACP or you Jesse Jackson. I respect all of them....I just want them to know: Never fall victim to Fox. Never fall victim to the shit they do."[67] Ironically, a year later, it was *Fox & Friends* that recorded Jackson's private *nigga* and took it public. As the old saying goes, "with friends like these..."

While the negative reactions dominated, including some from Jesse Jackson's own son, a few reminded us that Jesse was and is a race man and that he has contributed to the Struggle. These sympathizers called for understanding how Reverend Jackson might have "misspoke" or perhaps that he had taken Obama's comments too much to heart "since he himself has fathered a child (or children) out of wedlock."[68]

The fact that Jackson and Young, both older, elite, respected African Americans, used Black Language's highly "controversial" word, *nigga*, should not have come as a surprise to anyone. The term is a household word in Black communities, easily rolling off many Black folks' tongues in private Black social settings and contexts. For some Blacks, that's the "under what conditions" answer to the Hymesian question of who can say what to whom under what conditions when it comes to *nigga*. The irony is that, unlike Hip Hop headz and other young Blacks who have boldly insisted on their right to use *nigga* when and wherever they please, neither Jackson nor Young anticipated that their *niggas* would go public. They were, one could say, caught with their linguistic pants on the ground.

Deeper Than a *Muthafucka*: The Implications of Black Language in White Public Space

The term *muthafucka* sits right alongside *nigga* as one of Black Language's most popular and "controversial" words. Smitherman previously described the Black semantic interpretation of *muthafucka* (and its euphemistic representations, *M.F., Marilyn Farmer, Mister Franklin, motor scotor, monster, mutha, mamma jamma*) in these terms:

> The word is used in both negative and positive ways and sometimes just as a filler with no meaning at all. Here are some examples:
>
> 1) In an urban ghetto, a Brother described a Cadillac Eldorado as a "bad muthafucka." Here the speaker was obviously expressing approval. Possible translation: "beautiful car."

2) One middle-class Black female commented to another, concerning her man who she'd just discovered was going around with someone else: "That no-good muthafucka." Here the speaker is obviously expressing disapproval. Possible translation: "deceitful man."

3) One Black middle-class male says to another, in a barber shop, "You muthafuckin right I wasn't gon let him do that." Here the speaker is simply emphasizing how correct the listener's assessment is, using the "obscenity" as a grammatical intensifier, modifying "right."

...The whole point, of course, is that in none of these statements does the speaker refer to the act of sex with anybody's mother.[69]

The same intensifying use of *muthafucka* in statement (3) is what we find in the recent Hip Hop song/YouTube video "Baracka Flacka Flames—Head of the State."[70] Using Atlanta Hip Hop artist Waka Flocka Flame's "Hard in Da Paint" for its musical framework, "Head of the State" is a parody of both President Obama and Hip Hop Culture. Performed by Black comedian James Davis, in the persona of President Obama, the piece opens with the lyrical refrain, "I'm the head of the muthafuckin State, nigga."[71] As with Smitherman's 1977 example quoted in the third statement there clearly is no obscene—lewd, indecent—meaning conveyed by this 2010 Hip Hop use of *muthafucka*. Rather, again, this is an instance of *muthafucka* used as a grammatical intensifier. Like, "I, Barack Obama, am the head of not just some corporation or organization. I am the head of not just any old state in the world. I'm the head of the Supreme State, the one and only Superpower State in the world. I'm the head of the only state in this global world that could be called the 'muthafuckin State.'" Nonetheless, there have been plenty of objections to the song and video, mainly from those who don't roll with the uncensored mode's linguistic rules and norms. (Despite these objections, as of April 2012, this YouTube video's gotten almost eight million muthafuckin hits, nigga!)

In linking the Obamas' seemingly harmless pound—performed between two adults happily in love—with some of what are perceived as the most "controversial" features of Black verbal culture, our focus is not on the specific gestures or words but rather on the social process of how Black communication **becomes** controversial. *Becomes* is highlighted to indicate the fact that nothing is inherently controversial. Rather, through social processes of valuation and devaluation, controversies are of our own making. Thus, what **becomes** controversial in any given society over time—as we saw with the changing meanings of the *N*-words—often reveals the nature of social relations between groups, attempts at social control, and the struggle for power. As social phenomena, languages are tied up in a world of unequal power relations, gaining or losing status not based on technical linguistic grounds but on social judgments, biases, and stereotypes that are based on the status of their speakers. As such, we argue that White America's love-hate relationship with Black modes of communication can only be interpreted within a framework that considers language as a primary site of cultural contestation. It should be clear by now that it's about more than a *muthafucka*, right? Our analysis of Black Language forms that the dominant culture considers inflammatory, controversial, or stigmatized allows us to make several crucial observations.

First, building off what anthropologist and linguist Arthur Spears noted in his discussion of uncensored speech, Black verbal culture, like all cultures, is "a complex network of predispositions, values, behaviors, expectations, and routines."[72] Language practices, in their varying sociocultural contexts, can only be understood if read within the full range of the community's speech activities, and that requires rigorous ethnographic research and analysis. Second, the community's beliefs and ideas about language—its language ideologies—should be the primary point of departure for investigation and interpretation. When it comes to *muthafucka*, for example, we should consider not only that some speakers experience the pleasure of the poetics of the term, using it in all its variations, with all its nuances, and within verbal routines that require clever wit and sophistication: Who can forget Rudy Ray Moore's artful use of the term in "Dolemite" or, not too long ago, the way D'Angelo sang it so smoov and soulful, "Shit...damn...*muthafucka*"? But we should also consider folk theories about the politics of *muthafucka*. Two examples come to mind, each levying sociopolitical critiques at mainstream America.

Black folk etymological theory posits that *motherfucker* was a term developed by the children of enslaved Africans in the United States. According to this theory, the neologism was invented by these children as the best way to refer to White slavemasters, who enacted a particularly savage form of physical and sexual abuse on the bodies and spirits of Black women. To make it painfully plain: It was used to describe White men who raped your mother in order to break the Black family down, physically and psychologically, and as a means to avoid calling your slavemaster your "father." Muthafucka, as the theory goes, then became the worst thing you could call somebody, next to an Uncle Tom (someone who betrayed the race). In historicizing the use of the word in the sociopolitical context of enslavement, this theory provides a sociopolitical critique by positing the word's use as having stemmed from the inhumane and horrific treatment of Black folks. Over time, through the linguistic process of semantic inversion and as a result of the changing material conditions of Black life, the word took on additional meanings, even nuancing positive characterizations of people, objects, and events.

Our second example references specific moments when Black speakers, such as Hip Hop artists, come under attack for their use of the word in public. One of these high profile moments came in 1993 during the filming of *Poetic Justice*, which starred Janet Jackson and Tupac Shakur. When asked if there was a point in the film when he thought there was just a little too much "muthafuckin" in there, Pac responded: "I fought to have all the muthafuckas and more of them."[73] Not only did Pac not shy away from them *muthafuckaz*, but while there was the usual conservative clamor about "preserving the image of the race" (albeit no call to alleviate the material conditions of the race), he displayed a particular kind of double irreverence for the White gaze *and* those African Americans who fashion themselves as the arbiters of respectability.

Tupac hung out in the streets in order to get an ethnographic feel for the specific setting of the film. "I just threw myself around that L.A. crowd. Learned the language. Learned the culture."[74] He insisted on remaining faithful to the language and culture of the streets because he wanted to display the multidimensionality of Black men with all of its complexity and contradictions. "I took that signal from my brothers, put it in the movie very loud."[75] For Tupac, there was a practical reason for maintaining faithfulness to the language and culture of the Black men whose lives he portrayed: "I fought to have all that shit in there so people could see it and go, 'Oh yeah. That's how we do it. Oh shit! Damn, maybe that's how she feels when I be calling her [bitch]....But if I'm not talkin the language they talkin, they won't even see themselves....So, I'm fitna give y'all this whole big picture. I want everybody to see the details."[76]

Pac's philosophical take on *muthafucka* is crucial. He recognizes that a particular variety of Black Language comes from the streets, from those locked out of participation in mainstream society. Rather than acquiesce to demands to "clean up" his language, he insisted that society "clean up" the mess that is the plight of many urban communities. Pac made a conscious decision to highlight the problem of Black folks' social marginality, rather than covering it up with inauthentic dialogue or trying to sweep it under the rug. In short, it was about much more than censoring a *muthafucka*. It was about the censoring of the working-class, Black poor from America's narrative and the erasure of White folks' responsibility for creating what sociologists refer to as the "Black underclass" and what Smitherman once referred to as the "UN-working class."[77] Whether empirically verifiable or not, the Black folk etymology and Tupac's observation about *muthafucka* flip the script on dominant culture by pointing out the tragically absurd: Some folks' moral panic over a *pound*, a *nigga*, and a *muthafucka* eclipses their moral panic over the poverty created by centuries of oppression and injustice.

Importantly, as Spears notes, it is not at all useful for African Americans to "turn automatically apologetic when African American cultural behaviors have a negative value within a White mainstream context, even though they have a positive or neutral value within the context of the African American community."[78] The kind of irreverence displayed by Tupac and advocated by Spears here is certainly part of what Barack Obama appreciated about Michelle's public pound and what Black folks more generally appreciated about Barack's reciprocating The Pound. Their communicative behavior takes on great importance not solely because they are now President and First Lady of the United States, but because it usually occurs in spaces where White mainstream culture and language are expected to prevail. In these same spaces, Black Language and Culture are not only made highly visible but are highly monitored, policed, and scrutinized for anything that might be considered "problematic" or as further signs of Black folks' "deficiency," "inadequacy," or "incompetence." Recognizing this particular type of racializing hegemony brings us to yet another fundamental concern in relation to Black speech: "On what basis is speech to be judged negative, positive, or neutral? On whose norms is such an evaluation based?...In all cases, scientific analysis is required before we dismiss behaviors with negative value judgments, especially when those negative judgments are based on imposed values of an oppressive outside culture."[79] Or as Spears put it more succinctly: "If *muthafucka* is not an obscene word for me but it is for you, whose norm should prevail?"[80]

While most Black folks are happy about the expression of Black Culture that The Pound symbolized, many also question White America's embrace of the gesture. Their skepticism arises for many reasons, not the least of which is the observation that in the supposedly even cultural exchange between groups, White folks emerge enriched while Black folks leave empty handed. Folks that are hip to the history know that White participation in Black cultural forms has almost always been preceded by White abhorrence of the forms, followed by White appropriation (theft, as some call it). This process is completed (at least for the time being) when Black folks finally forfeit the form and invent something altogether new. Like, "Okay, you want that? It's all yours. We're on to something else anyway."

In light of that, it's easy to see why some Black folks are not so thrilled about White mainstream culture's embrace of Michelle and Barack Obama's pound. Their gesture has taken on a life of its own, as a "fist bump," a label that Blacks look at sideways. The Pound, reinvented (stolen?) as the White folks' fist bump, has been lifted up out of its Black cultural context and carried to some far out and unexpected places. Further, for many Black folks, to paraphrase De La Soul, the stakes is even higher because language and culture are some of the few things they actually own in a context in which Blacks are often culturally rich but materially dispossessed. As Ta-Nehisi Coates humorously lamented about this unauthorized transfer of cultural ownership:

> It's funny the stuff that some white people want to take owner-ship of. I mean, can't we have shit??? We had to concede basket-ball after the Argentine team won the gold medal, then sprinting after Jeremy Wariner, and even Paul Wall wears diamond fronts. (Can't claim golf, cause Tiger says he's not black.) Now we got to concede giving people a pound? What's next...the black hand-shake, too? Damn, I guess at least we can still have locs, cocoa and shea butter, barbeque (I had to check on this and Wikipedia says it traces back to the Taino Indians, whew) the inner city, goo macaroni and cheese, and of course, the Black church! And of course if nothing else we keep the correct name—that would be "dap" or "pound"...because if it's now a "fist bump," we won't be doing it anymore anyway![81]

For now, given that the process of cultural crossover in the United States often takes place within the broader context of the marginalization of Black people, it's difficult for Blacks to see genuine, well-intentioned White participation as a nonthreatening sign of cultural appreciation.[82] This is especially true when the overwhelming collective pattern of cultural inter-action suggests that White folks—like most other dominating groups in postcolonial or postenslavement societies—are complex enough to find a way to love the culture and yet hate on its creators (Well, *complex* is one word for it). Black Communication **becomes** controversial only in a society that deprecates Blackness. If people continually deny this racially discrimi-natory context, mutual respect will prove to be elusive as a *muthafucka*.

NOTES

1. This was Michelle Obama's greeting to the cast of the popular daytime show *The View*, only days after the "fist bump" firestorm. Check the video: http://www.youtube.com/watch?v=59twO1fJwtQ. Last accessed: 09-14-11.
2. See Patrice Evans's article, "The Bump Heard 'Round the World: Why You Should Be Celebrating the Anniversary of President Obama's Famous Dap for the Democratic Nomination," posted June 2, 2009, at: http://www.theroot.com/views/bump-heard-round-world. Last accessed: 09-14-11.
3. From pages 239–240 of Arthur Spears's chapter, "African-American Language Use: Ideology and So-Called Obscenity," in Salikoko Mufwene, John R. Rickford, Guy Bai-

ley, and John Baugh (eds.) *African-American English: Structure, History, and Use* (New York: Routledge, 1998).

4. See Amy Argetsinger and Roxanne Roberts's article, "The Fist Couple: Giving a Big Bump to Authenticity" posted on June 5, 2008, at: http://www.washingtonpost.com/wp-dyn/content/article/2008/06/04/AR2008060404521.html.   Last   accessed: 09-14-11.

5. Check the full article at: http://trickledown.wordpress.com/2008/06/06/the-obama-fist-bump-its-called-giving-dappound/. Last accessed: 09-14-11.

6. Annette Powell Williams, "Dynamics of a Black Audience," in Thomas Kochman (ed.) *Rappin' and Stylin' Out: Communication in Urban Black America* (Urbana: University of Illinois Press, 1972, 106).

7. See: http://mediamatters.org/mmtv/200806060007. Last accessed: 09-14-11.

8. See: http://www.dailykos.com/story/2008/07/15/552233/-Cal-Thomas,-Terrorist-Fist-Jab,-and-MiniTruth.

9. We say "contentiously so" here because, from the perspective of many Native Hawaiian sovereignty movements, Hawai'i's statehood process was an invasion, annexation, and colonization. To those Indigenous Hawaiians who resisted the annexation of their land, the statehood process was riddled with intentional perversions of the truth and shady voting practices that excluded those who refused to accept the imposed American citizenship. And since most high school history teachers never teach about the contentious process of how Hawai'i became US property, check out Noenoe K. Silva's *Aloha Betrayed: Native Hawaiian Resistance to Colonialism* (Durham, NC: Duke University Press, 2004) for an excellent account of this silenced narrative. Crucially, Silva goes beyond English-language sources and relies on thousands of archival sources written in the language of Native Hawaiians in order to challenge conventional histories.

10. Quoted in Amy Argetsinger and Roxanne Roberts (June 5, 2008). See link in note 4.

11. Check   also: http://superbeesphilosophy.blogspot.com/2008/06/thats-it-im-in.html. Last accessed: 09-14-11.

12. See Katie Halper's article, "In Historic Moment, White People Exposed to 'Fist Bump' for First Time," first posted on June 6, 2008, at: http://www.alternet.org/election08/87230. Last accessed: 09-14-11.

13. Quoted in M. J. Stephy's article, "A Brief History of the Fist Bump," first posted on June 5, 2008, at Time.com: http://www.time.com/time/nation/article/0,8599,1812102,00.html. Last accessed: 09-14-11.

14. Quoted in Amy Argetsinger and Roxanne Roberts (June 5, 2008). See link in note 4.

15. Rachel Sklar (2008). See link in note 7.

16. See: http://articles.nydailynews.com/2008–06-05/news/17899960_1_michelle-obama-bump-barack-obama. Last accessed: 09-14-11.

17. See, "Fist Bump in the News" on worldfistbumpday.org. Last accessed January 2011.

18. See Jim Rutenberg's article, "THE NEWS MEDIA; Deconstructing the Bump," posted on June 11, 2008, at: http://query.nytimes.com/gst/fullpage.html?res=9A04E7D81138 F932A25755C0A96E9C8B63. Last accessed: 09-14-11.

19. See Frank Rich's *New York Times* op-ed at: http://www.nytimes.com/2008/07/27/opinion/27rich.html?hp. Last accessed: 09-15-11.

20. See: "J. Peder Zane: Fist Bumping," posted on June 9, 2008, at: http://www.youtube.com/watch?v=9ixVBlA6zFk. Last accessed: 09-15-11.

21. See this site for a discussion of this moment: http://www.newsbusters.org/blogs/noel-sheppard/2008/06/08/medias-fist-bump-focus-shows-theyre-obama-fixated-out-touch. Last accessed: 09-15-11.

22. Check the photo and the broader context here: http://sociologistsforobama.blogspot.com/2008/07/franceand-obama-hit-it-off.html. Last accessed: 09-15-11.

23. Check James Gerber's July 2, 2008, article, "Obama Fist Bump Refusal? Not So Fast," at: http://abcnews.go.com/blogs/political-radar. Last accessed: 10-31-11. Check

the video at: http://abcnews.go.com/Video/playerIndex?id=5294981. Last accessed: 10-31-11.

24. Can't make this shit up, y'all. On http://www.nationalfistbumpday.com/store/ you can actually purchase different T-shirt designs celebrating the "fist bump." This is the commodification of Black Culture and Communication at one of its most absurd moments. Fist bump gear? *Get* the hell outta here.

25. Check: http://worldfistbumpday.org. Last accessed January 2011.

26. Check out World #tweetbump Day at: http://prsarahevans.com/2009/05/29/world-tweetbump-day-is-coming-on-june-3/. Last accessed: 09-15-11.

27. In M. J. Stephy (June 5, 2008). See note 13. Last accessed: 09-14-11.

28. See Maureen Dowd's article, "Mincing up Michelle," here: http://www.nytimes.com/2008/06/11/opinion/11dowd.html. Last accessed: 09-15-11. As William Jelani Cobb put it in *The Substance of Hope: Barack Obama and the Paradox of Progress* (New York: Walker and Company, 2010): "[The fist bump] said to those arrayed around a massive flatscreen—and to those watching around the world—that Michelle Obama was not only his wife but also his teammate and collaborator, his homegirl." (85).

29. D. Dalby's work has shed light on Africanisms in African American (and broader American) culture. Check out his July 19, 1969, *New York Times* piece, "Americanisms that May Have Once Been Africanisms." Also, see his "The African Element in American English," in Thomas Kochman (ed.) *Rappin' and Stylin' Out: Communication in Urban Black America* (Urbana: University of Illinois Press, 1972, pages 170–186).

30. Renee D. Turner's article from *Ebony* magazine can be found online at: http://findarticles.com/p/articles/mi_m1077/is_n10_v46/ai_11098726/. Last accessed: 09-15-11.

31. Benjamin Cooke, "Nonverbal Communication among Afro-Americans: An Initial Classification," in Kochman, ed., (1972), page 42. Also, for an update on how Black youth view Cooke's classification, see Deric M. Green and Felicia R. Stewart's article, "African American Students' Reactions to Benjamin Cooke's 'Nonverbal Communication among Afro-Americans: An Initial Classification'," in *Journal of Black Studies* April, 2011, 42(3): pages 389–401. According to the authors, Black youth noted some "differences and variations" in contemporary Black nonverbal communication, yet there "remains a similarity in the cultural significance and motivation behind the displays" (389).

32. *African Holocaust* is a term used by Black writers, rappers, activists and others to refer to the enslavement of African people in the United States and throughout the Diaspora. The term captures the experience of the wholesale disruption of African communities in the European slave trade, during which it is estimated that as many as 100 million Africans were forcibly removed from their native lands, not all of whom reached the "New World." Millions perished as a result of torture, disease, and the horrendous Middle Passage across the Atlantic Ocean. A number of contemporary Black historians and scholars have argued that the consequences of this mass terror against Africans and its impact on present-day Black communities have yet to be fully assessed.

33. See J. L. Dillard's *Black English* (New York: Random House, 1972).

34. See Norman Mailer's 1957 article, "The White Negro," in *Dissent*, reprinted in San Francisco by City Lights Books in 1969.

35. Check Elizabeth Ahlin's article in the *New York Times*: http://www.nytimes.com/2004/08/16/national/16dutch.html. Last accessed: 09-15-11.

36. See Geneva Smitherman, "From Dead Presidents to the Benjamins: The Africanization of American English," in Smitherman, *Black Talk: Words and Phrases from the Hood to the Amen Corner* (Boston: Houghton Mifflin, 2000).

37. Mailer (1957), page 11. See note 34.

38. Check out Dell Hymes's *Foundations in Sociolinguistics* (Philadelphia: University of Pennsylvania Press, 1974). We'll refer to the question of "Who can say what to whom under what conditions" as the Hymesian question.

39. See Julianne Malveaux's December 24,1998, article, "Just a Nappy-Headed Sister with the PC Blues," in *Black Issues in Higher Education*, 15(22): page 30.

40. In Smitherman's *Talkin That Talk* (New York: Routledge, 2000, pages 226–228).

41. See Alim's *You Know My Steez: An Ethnographic and Sociolinguistic Study of Styleshifting in a Black American Speech Community* (Durham, NC: Duke University Press, 2004). Also, we discuss the educational implications of this verbal art and dueling in chapter 6.

42. From Arthur Spears, "African-American Language Use: Ideology and So-Called Obscenity," in Mufwene, et al.,eds., pages 232–233. See note 3.

43. Ibid.

44. Ibid, page 226.

45. Check Geneva Smitherman's *Talkin and Testifyin: The Language of Black America* (Boston: Houghton Mifflin, 1977, reissued with revisions, Detroit: Wayne State University Press, 1986, pages 59–62).

46. Ibid., page 62.

47. Check Geneva Smitherman's "Word from the Mother: Language and African Americans" (Routledge: New York, 2006, page 52). Also see both editions of Smitherman's *Black Talk: Words and Phrases from the Hood to the Amen Corner* (New York: Houghton Mifflin, 1994, revised 2000).

48. Diddy was quoted in L. Ogunnaike's article, "The Passion of Puff," in *Vibe* magazine, August, 2004, pages 88–100.

49. That's your boy Humpty Dumpty in Lewis Carroll's *Through the Looking-Glass, and What Alice Found there*, way back in 1871.

50. Them's your boys Tha Pharcyde. Check the full interview in James G. Spady, H. Samy Alim & Charles G. Lee's *Street Conscious Rap* (Philadelphia: Black History Museum, 1999), page xix.

51. Most folks don't know that the San Francisco Bay Area's Hip Hop legend JT the Bigga Figga gets his name from that old ditty. See interviews with JT the Bigga Figga in James G. Spady, H. Samy Alim & Samir Meghelli's *Tha Global Cipha: Hip Hop Culture and Consciousness* (Philadelphia: Black History Museum, 2006, 209–236, 404–40.

52. These lyrics are from the Last Poets's well-known poem, "Niggers Are Scared of Revolution." Check their self-titled album, "The Last Poets" (Harlem, New York: East Wind Associates, 1970).

53. Cube was quoted in the *Detroit Free Press* on June 14, 2004, page 2E.

54. See J. Clinton Brown's article, "In Defense of the N Word," in *Essence* magazine, June, 1993, page 138.

55. Pac rapped this along with Richie Rich on "Ratha Be Ya Nigga," from the album *All Eyez on Me* (Death Row/Interscope, 1996).

56. DMX was quoted in an interview with *The Source* in February 2000, page 170.

57. See the Associated Press article, "Up for Re-Election, Michigan Supreme Court Justice Robert Young Jr. Explains Use of N-Word," October 23, 2010, updated October 29, 2010: http://www.mlive.com/politics/index.ssf/2010/10/up_for_re-election_michigan_su.html. Last accessed: 09-19-11.

58. Posted on November 9, 2010, on: www.mymicourt.com. Last accessed: 09-19-11.

59. See "How to Backpedal, Spin, and Doge [sic]—Justice Robert Young and the 'N' Word," on: http://www.attorneybutler.net/2010/10/page/2/. Last accessed: 09-19-11.

60. See: http://www.hiphopdx.com/index/news/id.7331/title.jesse-jackson-reportedly-used-n-word-in-tirade. Last accessed: 09-19-11.

61. Quoted in "Spike Lee: 'Jealousy' Behind Jackson Remark about Obama," July 12, 2008, at: http://www.hiphopdx.com/index/news/id.7300/title.spike-lee-jealousy-behind-jackson-remark-about-obama. Last accessed: 09-19-11.

62. See Danielle Harling's article, "Nas Reacts to Jesse Jackson's Comments," July 11, 2008, at: http://www.hiphopdx.com/index/news/id.7296/title.nas-reacts-to-jesse-jacksons-comments. Last accessed: 09-19-11.

63. Watch the video of Al Sharpton's comments at: http://www.mtv.com/videos/news/182827/rev-al-sharpton-says-nas-is-helping-out-the-racists.jhtml. Last accessed: 09-19-11.

64. See Shaheem Reid's article, "Nas Explains Controversial Album Title, Denies Reports of Label Opposition," on: http://www.mtv.com/news/articles/1572287/nas-explains-controversial-album-title.jhtml. Last accessed: 09-19-11.

65. Ibid.

66. Ibid.

67. Ibid.

68. See the video and read responses to "Jesse Jackson Wants to 'Cut Obama's Nuts Off?'" posted on July 11, 2008, at: http://www.youdecidepolitics.com/2008/07/11/video-jesse-jackson-wants-to-cut-obamas-nuts-off/. Last accessed: 09-19-11.

69. See Geneva Smitherman's *Talkin and Testifyin* (1977), page 60.

70. Check the video at: http://www.youtube.com/watch?v=zQ-hPNrKdZI. Last accessed: 09-19-11.

71. Not only does he repeat the refrain, "I'm the head of the muthafuckin State, nigga!" but this rap throws the "controversy" around Black Language's uncensored mode into high relief by using both *muthafuckin* and *nigga* frequently throughout. With ill lines like "See, Hillary, that's my *muthafuckin nigga* / I hang in DC wit them Senate House killas / Baracka Flocka Flame one hood-ass *nigga* / In the 6–4 bendin corners, my *nigga*..." and "See, Oprah, that's my *muthafuckin nigga* / We hang in the Chi wit them hit squad killas / Oprah Flocka Flame one hood-ass *nigga* / Ridin real slow, bendin corners, my *nigga*," it's clear that nothing and nobody is sacred in this parody, not Barack, not Michelle, not Hillary, not Oprah, not Waka Flocka, not politics, not Hip Hop! The Hillary line is especially poignant given her and Bill's attempts to use "Blackness" to box Barack out of the broader American public. And the Oprah lines instantly—and hilariously—reference the widespread opinion in Hip Hop circles that Orpah Winfrey hates on Hip Hop (in large part because of the "language").

72. From Arthur Spears, "African-American Language Use: Ideology and So-Called Obscenity," Mufwene, et al., eds., page 240. See note 3.

73. Tupac Shakur's full interview can be found in James G. Spady, H. Samy Alim, and Charles G. Lee's *Street Conscious Rap* (Philadelphia: Black History Museum, 1999 563 560).

74. Ibid., 563.

75. Ibid., 564.

76. Ibid., 565.

77. See Smitherman's "'A New Way of Talkin:' Language, Social Change and Political Theory," paper presented at the conference "Race and Class in the Twentieth Century," Oxford University, Oxford, UK, 28–31 January 1988. A revised version was published in Smitherman, *Talkin That Talk* (New York: Routledge, 2000).

78. From Arthur Spears, "African-American Language Use: Ideology and So-Called Obscenity," Mufwene, et al., eds., page 241. See note 3.

79. Ibid., 244.

80. Ibid.

81. See "The sacred art of giving dap," posted on June 4, 2008, at: http://www.ta-nehisi.com/category/entertainment/page/3. Last accessed: 09-19-11.

82. Tricia Rose makes this point exceptionally well in *Black Noise: Rap Music and Black Culture in Contemporary America* (Hanover, NH: Wesleyan University Press, 1994). See especially her breakdown of White rapper Vanilla Ice's straight up robbery of his Black "friend" and producer, Chocolate, pages 11–12. In this chapter, Rose busts up simple arguments of neutral cultural "borrowing" or "equally-owned" cultural forms by foregrounding "the racially discriminatory context within which cultural syncretism takes place," page 5.

5

"My President's Black, My Lambo's Blue"

Hip Hop, Race, and the Culture Wars

I think the potential [is there] for [Hip Hop] to deliver a message of extraordinary power, that gets people thinking—you know, the thing about Hip Hop today is it's smart. I mean, it's insightful...the way that they can communicate a complex message in a very short space is remarkable.[1]
—Barack Obama, 2008

This was a chance to go from centuries of invisibility to the most visible position in the entire world. He could, through sheer symbolism, regardless of any of his actual policies, change the lives of millions of black kids who now saw something different to aspire to....That's why I wanted Barack to win, so...kids could see themselves differently, could see their futures differently than I did when I was a kid in Brooklyn and my eyes were focused on a narrower set of possibilities....Since he's been elected there have been a lot of legitimate criticisms of Obama. But if he'd lost, it would've been an unbelievable tragedy—to feel so close to transformation and then to get sucked back in to the same old story and watch another generation grow up feeling like strangers in their own country, their culture maligned, their voices squashed. Instead, even with all the distance yet to go, for the first time I felt like we were at least moving in the right direction, away from the shadows.[2]
—Jay-Z, 2010

Some time before the most historic presidential election in the history of the United States, then-senator Barack Obama was captured on film talking to a crowd of mostly young Black people in his home turf of Chicago.

He was speaking at an event that, in part, celebrated Chicago's Hip Hop and R&B station, WGCI 107.5FM. From the screen of the cell phone camera, we see Obama with mic in hand: "So, my three year old, she especially loves GCI, that song, 'Drop—Drop It Like It's Hot.' [Laughter and cheers from audience]. She thinks it's 'Drop It Like A Sock'! [Laughter] So she's singin all in the back, 'Drop it like a sock, drop it like a sock,'" At this point, Obama starts dancing like his little girl and then continues: "And she loves GCI. I appreciate..." And before he can get any further, the DJ drops Snoop Dogg's hit song of the summer, "Drop It Like It's Hot," and Obama, not skipping a beat, starts dancing to it and says, "Drop it!" For the next 20 seconds, Obama entertains the audience, while the crowd cheers, "O-bama! O-bama! O-bama!" He keeps dancing, pointing his finger up in the air and bobbin his head to the beat.[3] As you could imagine, the crowd went bananas after witnessing a US senator gettin down to Snoop!

Later, in February 2008, the West Coast Hip Hop icon Snoop Dogg appeared on CNN's *Larry King Live* to discuss the presidential campaign. Larry King asked the question on everybody's mind that year: "Do you think America is *really* ready for a Black President? You see prejudice all the time." After acknowledging the continuing racial prejudice in America, Snoop responded:

> I think America *is* ready for a Black President. By him winning you know like he's winning so far, and even competing, to be in the talks right now—you know, I remember in the past when we had Presidential candidates like Jesse Jackson, it was a gimmick, it was like a joke because nobody really believed Jesse could win....Right now, people really feel like *this* man could really win. He's got the right thing goin for him; he's got the right conversation....You know, whether he wins or loses, I feel like he made a great step for Black America by even steppin to the table and pullin off something like this.[4]

Snoop Dogg's description of Barack Obama as having "the right conversation" was dead on point. With these three words, Snoop concisely captured Barack's ability to styleshift in linguistic terms (as discussed in detail in chapter 1), as well as his ability to navigate treacherous racially and politically charged terrain by reaching multiple constituencies at once. Speaking with National Public Radio (NPR) about Barack Obama's relationship to Hip Hop, Duke University professor Mark Anthony Neal suggested that many high profile Black artists understood this strategy because it is one that they use all the time. "There's a version of, for instance, Snoop Dogg that sells records, but that's a very different version of Snoop Dogg that's sitting with Larry King talking about the election."[5] This "multiple-versions" strategy is necessary because, as highly visible (and powerful) members of a maligned social group, both Barack Obama and Hip Hop are aware that dominant culture consistently frames them as "dangerous to America." When Snoop says, "Whether he wins or loses, I feel like he made a great step for Black America by even steppin to the table and *pullin off something like this* [our emphasis]," he implicitly acknowledges the racially discriminatory context of American politics. Obama—like Hip Hop has done over the years—stepped up to the table and pulled off what many assumed to be the impossible. As a high profile Black public voice, his having "the right conversation" was a prerequisite for his success in both Hip Hop communities and "mainstream" America. He went platinum in politics through his ability to use language to pass America's most treacherous racial test (would White Americans accept a Black man in the White House?). And he also went platinum in Hip Hop through his ability to linguistically navigate Hip Hop's unrelenting critique of government (would he really understand where the Hip Hop community was comin from?).

Hip Hop language and style were critically important symbols during the 2008 presidential campaign (and continue to be so). However, the question of Barack Obama being the first "Hip Hop president" is about more than just Barack's ability to kick it. This question is one that gets at the complicated relationships between Hip Hop music, race, and the culture wars in America. As Brown University professor of Africana Studies Tricia Rose argues in *The Hip Hop Wars*, even when it's not explicit, Hip Hop has become a primary means by which we talk about race in the United States.[6] As we will see below, a critical analysis of artists like Young Jeezy, Nas, Jay-Z, and Tupac (as well as the discourse of Hip Hop heads and haters, including Fox News)—demonstrates that the controversies that surround Barack Obama's relationship with Hip Hop have everything to do with issues of race, language, and cultural hegemony.

"Black Man Running and It Ain't from the Police": The First Hip Hop President

Let's take a trip down memory lane. In the early 1990s, Hip Hop icon Tupac Shakur spit a classic Hip Hop quotable in his record, "Changes": "And although it seems heaven sent, we ain't ready to see a Black president."[7] More than a decade and a half later, Hip Hop rode hard for Barack Obama, with most believing he could take the White House (talk about changes, huh, Pac?). West Coast legend Ice Cube, who rapped "Dream ticket: Ice Cube and Obama!" explained: "I think America, I hope it's smart enough to pick the best person. And right now it looks like nobody's better than Obama, you know...it seems like people are sick of the way it's goin, and nobody happy with the country, the way it's goin. People want a *real* change."[8] Artists all over California, from Oakland to Sac-Town, the Bay Area and back down, were also ridin for Obama, including San Francisco's JT the Bigga Figga, Oaklands' Mistah F.A.B, Vallejo's E-40, and East Los Angeles's Will.I.Am. Heads from "the Dirty Souf" were also stompin for Obama, including folks like New Orleans's Mia X, Houston's Scarface and Paul Wall, and Atlanta's T.I., Young Jeezy, Cee-Lo and Ludacris. T.I. agreed with Cube that the person who addresses—"and I mean really addresses"—the matters "that I think most affect this country's state right now, sincerely, passionately, is Obama."[9] Focusing in directly on the issues, he added: "Nothing against McCain, I just haven't really heard him talk about the things I'm concerned about, like getting out of the war and doing things for the ecosystem and conserving energy."[10]

The East Coast, too, rode hard for Obama, with big names like P. Diddy, Will Smith, Mos Def, Talib Kweli, Fat Joe, Lil Kim, Nas, and Jay-Z all comin out in strong support. These and other Hip Hop artists supported Obama in interviews or in their recordings. (Obama may very well be the most cited US president in Hip Hop Culture, rivaling the enormous amount of negative attention George W. Bush received from across the spectrum). Hip Hop artists also donated to the campaign, put on concerts and fundraisers, and designed T-shirts with catchy slogans ("Black Man Running and It Ain't from the Police!"). Some, like Jay-Z, donated their time to travel with Obama and even put out calls on his behalf. HipHopforObama.com posted Jay-Z's campaign call for Obama on their site the night before the election.[11]

Of course, the Midwest, especially The Chi, rode hard for Barack Obama, with artists like Kanye West and Kidz in the Hall representin. In 2007, long before Obama had even won the Democratic nomination, Chicago's Common released "The People," in which he rhymed, "My raps ignite the people like Obama!" On BlackTree.TV, Common spoke out at the height of the Reverend Wright controversy, fearing that Obama's candidacy was in jeopardy:

> Well, I mean, you know, the media's definitely tryna work him and tryna find something bad about him, because they lookin like, 'Man, this dude is just doin too much good.' You know, it's like, you see this guy talkin about unity for all people, talkin about helpin people that's poor...and people wanna go against that. You know, it's kinda crazy to hear the media tryna pull him down, especially you know, over a pastor....I go to that church,

Trinity....And since I was eight years old, and I ain't never left the church one Sunday ever feelin hatred towards anybody. So, you know, the media gotta find something, but the people know what's up.[12]

Hip Hop artists from around the world, including the Haitian-born Wyclef Jean and Senegal's Positive Black Soul, were vocal in their support of Barack Obama. While Hip Hop had Obama's back—even callin him "B-Rock"—Barack Obama was also showin Hip Hop some love.[13] In many high profile media outlets, he continually cited Hip Hop as one of his music interests. When Hip Hop critic and political journalist Jeff Chang asked him what he "got down to," he ran down his usual roster of Old School classics like Stevie Wonder, John Coltrane, Miles Davis, Aretha Franklin, and Earth Wind & Fire. But then he added: "So when the Fugees were together [the group included Lauryn Hill, Wyclef Jean, and Pras Michel], I loved listening to the Fugees. I think OutKast does a lot of interesting work. My fellow Chicagoan Common I think is outstanding. I really dig his stuff."[14] Later, in *Rolling Stone*, Obama explained: "Jay-Z used to be sort of what predominated, but now I've got a little Nas and a little Lil Wayne and some other stuff."[15] And in a widely circulated interview on Black Entertainment Television (BET), Obama was asked if he liked Hip Hop:

BET: Do you like Hip Hop?

OBAMA: Of course.

BET: Who do you like?

OBAMA: You know, I gotta admit, lately I've been listening to a lotta Jay-Z, you know, this new *American Gangster* album is tight.

BET: What do you like about it?

OBAMA: You know, it tells a story, and, you know, as Jay would say, he got flow. But Kanye, I like, you know, but I have to admit that I still am an old school guy. I'm still, you know, Stevie, Marvin, you know if you look at my iPod it's Earth Wind & Fire, Isley Brothers, Temptations, you know, I've got a lotta of that old school stuff. So, you know, I enjoy some of the newer stuff.[16]

In interview after interview, Obama kept it real by stating that he's "an old school guy," but he also continually mentions Hip Hop as being in regular rotation in his iPod. Will.I.Am's video "Yes We Can" became the Obama campaign's leading pop culture ad. DJ Green Lantern and Russell Simmon's mixtape took care of the streets (everybody from Busta Rhymes, Rhymefest,

Styles P, Wale, Joell Ortiz, Nas, Jay-Z, Twista, and Joe Budden was on that joint). And Chinese American rapper Jin's "Open Letter 2 Obama" burned up the Internet and was available as a free ringtone download on Obama's official campaign site.

Aside from harnessing the power of Hip Hop Culture for his campaign, Barack Obama also became a very powerful symbol for the Hip Hop community because he could "get with" Hip Hop like no other president before him. While often commenting on his politics, artists also picked up on Obama's style. Folks like Antonio "L.A." Reid, Chairman of Island Def Jam Music Group, commented on Barack's "swagger," while artists like Devin the Dude saw Barack as "intertwining culture just like Hip Hop does."[17] Rapper D.M.C. of Run-D.M.C. even likened Obama to "a dope MC."[18] A prime example of Barack's familiarity with Hip Hop came during one of his speeches in South Carolina where he responded to the negativity that was being hurled at him from the Clinton campaign. Barack calmly and coolly, and to resounding applause, looked over his shoulder and brushed it two or three times. While many in the crowd appreciated the gesture, those familiar with Hip Hop knew that Barack, by gettin that dirt off his shoulder, was sampling Jay-Z's hit from *The Black Album*.[19] The fact that a presidential candidate sampled a popular Hip Hop gesture in order to rebuff classic, textbook Washington politics was definitely not missed. As Common noted on CNN in summer 2007, "He's fresh, you know, he's got good style."[20] He later explained in an interview with BlackTree.TV: "I think he's a reflection of Hip Hop Culture in a way that he's in tune with it....And I know that the fact that he's in tune with it is a great example of what we need in the future cuz it's, to me...he's aware of what's goin on with the youth and we need that."[21]

Barack Obama also flexes his linguistic style, especially in his ability to use various features of Black Language. In the Chicago radio station event, we see and hear a Barack Obama who knows how to "drop it like it's hot" and, in linguistic jargon, monophthongize his diphthongs. In nontechnical terms, he pronounces *my* like *mah* and *CGI* like *C-G-ahh*, which is a salient feature of African American (and southern) pronunciation. He then not only lists Jay-Z's *American Gangster* album as something he likes but says that it's "tight," in part because Jay-Z "got flow." His familiarity with Black Language and Hip Hop's lexicon is not merely symbolic. It represents a presidential first. This is part of what prompts folks to refer to Barack Obama as the "first Hip Hop President" and also part of the reason why many political observers credit Hip Hop for bringin out the largest youth vote in presidential election history. Many Hip Hop artists, like KRS-One, B.G., Mike Jones, Plies, and others, explained in interviews that this was the first time that they were inspired to vote.[22] The Game even said he'd "vote twice" if he could. Meanwhile Fat Joe was busy packin people in his car to get them to register. After highlighting that Black and Latino communities were "getting hit the hardest by inadequate health care, fore-closures, and an unjust war," he stated: "I always been one of those who would say *Register to vote....* Now I've forced my wife to register. I drive my cousins, nephews, and friends to the library so they can register."[23] It was clear that Hip Hop heads wanted to "change the game in Washington," as Barack Obama wrote in his letter to *Vibe* magazine, again, capitalizing on Hip Hop's language.[24]

"I Can Only Pick a Nike or Adidas?": Hip Hop's Diverse and Sophisticated Political Views

As Hip Hop historian, critic, and journalist Davey D pointed out imme-diately after the inauguration, while race, culture, language, and age may have been important factors in Hip Hop's support of Barack Obama, it was his politics, first and foremost, that Hip Hop heads gravitated toward. Conservative columnists and pundits were quick to assume that Hip Hop voted for Obama either "just because he was Black" or "just because he speaks their language." However, as Davey D argued, these kinds of assumptions hinged on racist stereotypes of Black youth because they ignored the myriad sophisticated conversations and dialogues that occurred nationwide about the 2008 elections.[25] They also ignored the fact that Hip Hop did not offer unconditional support for Barack Obama. Rather, heads engaged the broader political issues more generally and pressed him on issues that directly impact many Black and Brown com-munities specifically.[26]

Davey D offers several examples of these kinds of Hip Hop political forums and conventions which addressed such key issues as "police bru-tality, education, poverty and crime" as well as global, environmental, and trade issues. He also highlighted the spirited political debate between Chicago rappers Lupe Fiasco and Rhymefest. Similar debates raged in Latino communities as well, like the highly publicized debate between Fat Joe and rapper/reggaetonero Daddy Yankee, who was one of the few supporters of John McCain.[27] Overall, these debates showed thoughtful, nuanced politi-cal views that demonstrated that many in Hip Hop "were not just blindly following a charismatic figure."[28] Importantly, these discussions "moved well beyond the 30 second soundbite, one size fits all mentality that this Obama and Hip Hop discussion is often reduced to."[29] They also reminded us that Hip Hop is, as Black historian, journalist, and Hip Hop critic James G. Spady has long argued, an "art form/forum."[30]

Many in Hip Hop also expressed a healthy skepticism toward Obama's, and government's, ability to fulfill promises of change. Some critical players urged folks to push Obama to make more difficult choices and to take more firm stances on progressive issues. Others urged youth to engage the political process, with or without Barack Obama, and to consider the Green Party's women of color ticket Cynthia McKinney and Hip Hop activist Rosa Clemente (who some argued was "the *real* Hip Hop" ticket).[31] Like D.M.C. noted, "You got the Republican Party and the Democratic Party. I'm neither. I'm Hip Hop."[32] Others, like the Pharcyde's Imani, lamented the two-party system through clever metaphors: "Are you telling me I get to pick, but I only get to pick out of two people? I can only pick a Nike or Adidas? My first pick was Reebok, my second pick was Puma. So now I'm left with Adidas and Nike? I'm going Adidas, man." And then he added jokingly, "I'm going with the black high-top Adidas. Hint, hint."[33] Others like the Afro-Peruvian Immortal Technique continually urged Hip Hop heads to think beyond Barack. In a blog post, he pushed folks to view political policies and processes as imbricated with global economic interests.[34] Stic.Man from dead prez kept it concise, "Even if Barack Obama wins, Uncle Sam still ain't our friend."[35]

While there were few public anti-Obama statements coming from Hip Hop communities, artists often found themselves in the difficult position of having to balance their usually uncompromising critiques of government with their support of Barack Obama. He was a candidate whom some viewed either as not progressive enough or as part of a hopelessly broken system in Washington. Still, they walked that fine line, often expressing opinions mixed with support and skepticism, with hope in Barack Obama and a lack of faith in Washington. Mississippi's David Banner reminded folks that Obama's election would not be "the end of anything," and while it "may be the most important election in history, it won't change things by itself. It's just the beginning." He added: "We're going to have to work hard. We're going to have to continue this process. Let's say if everyone in the South gets out to vote, Obama gets in, you know—will that trend continue? That is the important thing."[36]

"Art Can't Just Be a Rearview Mirror": Obama's Delicate Dance with Hip Hop Heads and Haters

The president has also had to walk a fine line in terms of how he represents his relationship to Hip Hop. Obama's delicate dance with Hip Hop heads and haters alike needed to show that he was willing to come down *on* Hip Hop, but at the same time, remain down *for* Hip Hop. While many used the phrase, "Hip Hop president" as a way to celebrate Obama's relative youth, hipness, and comfort and familiarity with Hip Hop Culture, others used the label as a means of fear mongering. Conservative critics, such as Craig Smith, for example, attempted to use "hip-hop" to scare White voters away from Obama, whom he described as "merely" a "hip-hop senator from Illinois."[37] In his racist, reductive rant against "the first hip-hop president," he suggested that the Obamas will use "ghetto slang" in the Oval Office and have "no sense of decorum." This lack of decorum would lead the "hip-hop president" to offer "bling-bling" to his guests instead of the customary cuff links and, even worse, to refer to his cabinet members as his "bitches." He then links Obama to a Hip Hop Culture that is not only dangerous and angry but has been "infiltrating every class and race in America for years" and "has led people to believe they deserve more" and that "things need to change" (the very reasons why Hip Hop supported Obama!). Smith goes on to frame both Barack Obama and Hip Hop as "dangerous for America." Returning to language one more time, he concludes condescendingly: "But hey, he will be dope. He will use all the cool language and slang. He will be a President who is able to hang with the homies."

While the Hip Hop community appreciates Obama's linguistic ability to styleshift, others read it as a threat to "standard English" and use it in racist, race-baiting rhetoric against the president. But language has also been a major part of President Obama's criticism of Hip Hop; he is often as critical of Hip Hop as he is celebratory. The previously cited BET interview is a case in point. In the interview, Barack states:

> [A]nd, you know, honestly, I love the art of Hip Hop, I don't always love the message of Hip Hop. There are times where even on the artists that I named, the artists that I love, you know, there's a message that is not only sometimes degrading to women, not only uses the N-word a little too frequently, but also—something I'm really concerned about—is always talkin about material things and always talkin about how I can get something, you know, how I've got more money, more, you know, cars, more.[38]

Here, Obama makes two very important points for two very different constituencies. First, for many members of the Hip Hop community, it was the first time that they had ever heard a presidential candidate (and now 44th president) refer to "the art of Hip Hop." While this point is obvious to many African Americans, the public discourse on Hip Hop Culture still remains woefully unsophisticated. (Outlets such as CNN, for example, still lead their Hip Hop stories with the headline: "Hip Hop: Art or Poison?" followed by menacing music.)[39] Obama, in this one interview, was seen as having the potential to reframe the conversation about Hip Hop music as really a conversation about art, poetry, and lyrical production. Hip Hop may not have needed to hear that because it already knew it, but it needed to hear those words in order to science out where Barack Obama stood vis-à-vis Hip Hop Culture. By using the word *art,* he demonstrated his respect for a culture that, despite its enormous commercial and global success, continues to be misunderstood and misinterpreted in the mainstream.

The second important point Barack Obama makes is that he is critical of "the message of Hip Hop." This was interpreted by some in the Hip Hop community as legitimate criticism and by others as Obama's need to support Hip Hop while not losing his broader base. As one young Black woman put it, "Can you imagine how quickly he would lose *all* of his White support—especially his White women supporters—if he *didn't* critique rap for its demeaning images of women?!"[40] When it came to the hot button issues of gender and race, Obama gave a little to both sides. He critiqued Hip Hop for messages that are "degrading to women" but prefaced that with "sometimes"; and he critiqued use of the N-word but followed that with "a little too frequently." In other words, his use of adverbs in these cases indicated that he wasn't just following the popular, reductionist scripts of "all Hip Hop is degrading to women" or "Hip Hop artists need to stop using the N-word altogether." His qualifiers here were a subtle yet important signal. When it came to something less controversial, though, Obama chose an adverb that gave the impression that he was *really* comin down hard on Hip Hop: "*always* talkin about material things." This is a critique that Hip Hop heads have heard many times before, and of course, while it could have been more nuanced, it was nothing new.

The BET interviewer continues by asking Obama if his administration would "explore how Hip Hop can be effectively used" to aid in issues such as education and incarceration. Obama, once again, walks the tightrope and achieves balance by embracing the Hip Hop community, though only conditionally, while appeasing constituents who were eager to hear him denounce "those Hip Hop people." In his response, Obama says that Hip Hop can "absolutely" be used in positive ways in his administration. He demonstrates his respect for Hip Hop by showing that he engages directly with the culture and that he appreciates it for its complexity and political potential (definitely a far cry from how any Republican president ever viewed Hip Hop, or even how President Clinton treated politically conscious Hip Hop artist Sista Souljah in the 1990s).[41] As Obama put it:

> You know, and I've met with Jay-Z and I've met with Kanye, and talked with other artists, about how potentially to bridge that gap and, you know, I think the potential for them to deliver a

message of extraordinary power, that gets people thinking—you know, the thing about Hip Hop today is it's smart. I mean, it's insightful. And, you know, the way that they can communicate a complex message in a very short space is remarkable.[42]

Again, referring to Hip Hop as smart, insightful, and complex art with the potential to produce thought-provoking music demonstrated to the Hip Hop Nation that Barack "gets" the culture. Yet again, Barack followed this praise with a critique of Hip Hop music that gave his Hip Hop–hating constituents something to cling to:

So, the question then is, what's the content? What's the message? I understand folks wanna be rooted in their community, they wanna be down. But what I always say is, is that, you know, Hip Hop is not just a mirror of what is, it should also be a reflection of what can be. And, you know, a lotta times folks say, 'I wanna keep it real,' and 'I wanna be down.' Then we're just trapped in what is....Art can't just be a rearview mirror, you know, it should have a headlight out there, you know, pointing to where we need to go.[43]

Hip Hop heads done heard this critique a thousand times and often in the form of internal critiques—recall the elongated debates between Ice Cube and Common in the 1990s or the more recent debates between Nas and Young Jeezy about the state of Hip Hop. Yet many of those outside of the Culture seem to be wholly unaware of Hip Hop's sharp, self-reflexive criticism. Obama's comments assuaged the worries of the Hip Hop haters by lending a presidential voice—and a Black one at that—to their concerns about Hip Hop's "message" and its "negative influence on young kids." At the same time, the critique rolled off of Hip Hop's back because: 1) Hip Hop is used to being thrown under the bus by politicians and scapegoated by society-at-large, 2) the community often delivers far more scathing self-critiques, and 3) again, while his critique could have been more nuanced, it was certainly nothing new.

Mark Anthony Neal describes Barack's delicate dance like this: "The challenge that Barack Obama had was really to be able to wink to the hip-hop community and say, 'I really can't acknowledge you in the mainstream, but understand that I'm hearing what your critique is...what your concerns are, and you now have a wide-open space in the so-called underground to talk about why my candidacy is important.'"[44] By the same token, as noted by Public Enemy frontman and global Hip Hop icon Chuck D, Hip Hop's challenge was to be ever alert so that "you don't drop the ball when Obama throws you a no-look pass."[45]

"My President Is Black, My Lambo's Blue": (Mis)Interpreting Barack Obama's Biggest Hip Hop "Controversy"

Given this general background and context, now we wanna get deep into what was perhaps Barack Obama's biggest Hip Hop "controversy"—the release and aftermath of Young Jeezy and Nas's "My President" (off of Jeezy's *The Recession* album, 2008, produced six months before Obama's victory) and Jay-Z's remix. "My President" was referred to by the *Washington Post's* Chris Richards as "the most compelling" Hip Hop record (there were dozens upon dozens) in support of Barack Obama's candidacy. It is, in his words, "a powerful confluence of pop hit, street anthem and rally cry...over a triumphant beat."[46] "My President" is not just compelling; it is perhaps one of the most "controversial" rap records and videos in recent memory. Though race is not the principal theme nor is Whiteness explicitly critiqued, the incredible amount of race talk generated by this record bears witness to its symbolic meanings. The response to "My President" and the remixes that followed underscored the deeply tense nature of contemporary race relations in America. The aftermath exposed the fact that Black and White Americans possessed radically differing ideologies of race and deeply contrasting views of who can talk about race, how, when, to whom, and for what purpose.

Some would say that Young Jeezy is everything that President Obama critiques and then some. Many Hip Hop heads and academics will realize that, relatively speaking, Jeezy is not by any stretch of the imagination one of Hip Hop's most complex lyricists. Nor does he fit neatly into acceptable paradigms of Blackness and masculinity espoused by many middle-class, university students at elite private institutions. Neither does he fit the "progressive" agendas of some Black bourgeois academics or, for that matter, the "radical" agendas of some working-class, anticapitalist, "socially-conscious" Hip Hop heads. As Mark Anthony Neal notes about Jeezy, in particular:

> Jeezy's a fascinating figure in this conversation because if we think about his rap persona, as a cat that's slinging dope on the corner, who's disaffected because the political process doesn't work...for a figure like that to come in from the cold and go into a voter booth and decide. 'This is going to be the first time that I'm going to cast a vote'—I think it speaks volumes to where the larger community is in terms of these kinds of marginalized figures, who've never been involved in the process.[47]

Jeezy has always viewed his music as inspirational, in part, because he knows that his fans understand that he's been through a lotta difficult shit. But in this case especially, he hopes that his fans will hear him "take a pause from all the normal rapper stuff" and say, "You know what, we got a problem and we got to address this. If you're out here, [a] hard-working American, and you can't even put food on your table, there's a problem with your system."[48]

When taken seriously as a cultural or literary text, "My President" is rich for its artistic and aesthetic qualities, its verbal wit and dexterity, its creative sociopolitical critique, and its attentiveness to multiple audiences. It is also notable for its ability to merge narratives of bleak, sociocultural, historic, and economic realities with the audacity to hope (to borrow a phrase from the homie) for a political change that's been a long time comin.[49]

The video opens up with a audiovisually dramatic scene right out of any Hollywood film. Over the loud roar of the engine and the screech of the tires, you hear and feel the built-up anticipation of a cheering crowd as a bright blue Lamborghini pulls up onto the scene. As the guards direct the driver to a parking space, the crowd continues to roar over a helicopter's propeller. It's the kind of grand entrance reserved for presidents. As the Lamborghini parks, its doors open upward and out comes, not the president dressed in a suit, but Young Jeezy, a Hip Hop artist dressed in a black hoodie, black baseball cap, and black stunna shades! Through the crowd and media cameras, you catch a glimpse of a guard whispering something into Jeezy's ear (some sort of intelligence perhaps). Under a political rally sign, a young White woman dances, filled with happiness. Young men, women, and children cheer even more loudly as Young Jeezy embraces two smiling, happy little kids.

The camera quickly cuts to a Hollywood film director's sign that reads, "Young Jeezy: My President Is Black," and underneath that the name of the director, "Gabriel Hart." As the arm of the sign swings down, the inspirational, anthemlike music begins. The camera scans the crowd, which is now clearly a political rally. Supporters hold (usually blue = Democratic) signs that bear the names of supporting groups ("Women for Obama," for example), various American cities and states (including Las Vegas, Brooklyn, Iowa, Colorado, Alabama, Arkansas, Hawai'i, Maryland, Maine, Missouri, etc.), other continents and countries outside the United States (from Jamaica, Japan and China to Haiti, Israel, and Africa), political revolutionaries and freedom fighters (from Che Guevara and Malcolm X to Gandhi and Sojourner Truth, and of course, Barack Obama), and importantly, fallen Hip Hop heroes and legends (including Tupac Shakur, Run DMC's Jam Master Jay, Soulja Slim, and the Notorious B.I.G.). The signs are a symbolic spatiotemporal collage that move across regional and national borders and travel centuries back to the American slavocracy and forward to the recent death of Black comedian and actor Bernie Mac. The crowd then becomes a swirl of ecstatic Black children smiling ear to ear, with an unfettered happiness and joy.

Over that image comes Jeezy's intro, where he boasts to other emcees and the Hip Hop community more generally: "Yeah, this be the realest shit I never wrote / I ain't write this shit by the way, nigga, some real shit right here, nigga / This'll be the realest shit you ever quote." Jeezy's introduction is important mainly because it highlights Hip Hop as a creative process, through which texts are written, circulated, reinterpreted, and put to various uses. While the politics of Hip Hop often lead to misinterpretation, the art and aesthetics of Hip Hop are often wholly misunderstood. In a cultural space where the aesthetic is political, these misreadings take on even greater importance. A listener must be in conversation with multiple discourses within and beyond the African American community in order to interpret these, as President Obama would have it, complex, multilayered texts.

In many cases, we can see how even the well intentioned and open minded can misread Hip Hop cultural texts, despite their professed love of and familiarity with the Culture. One interpreter, a young, White supporter of Barack Obama, writes passionately that the song is "nothing short of epic" because it "addresses the social, political, personal, historical, regional, religious, and literary just to name a few." After explaining how authenticity and "the real" are central to Hip Hop cultural production, he writes: "Most importantly, perhaps, in this regard are Jeezy's first few lines. He gleefully notes, 'I ain't [write] this [shit] by the way nigga, some real shit right here nigga.' Jeezy is willing to sacrifice that he is the writer behind the song to simply show that he is truthful. That he would undermine himself in his quest for the 'real' is most telling." What is most telling here is not Jeezy's relinquishing his authorship but, rather, this young man's gross misreading of even the first few lines of the text (despite being an avid listener of "underground" Hip Hop).

In these few lines, Young Jeezy is doing everything but giving up his authorship. Quite to the contrary, he's boasting about his ability to "write" rhymes without "writing" them. The oral production and memorization of rhymes is privileged in some emcee circles to the point that verbal artists such as Jay-Z and Beanie Sigel claim to write all of their rhymes in their heads. So, when Jeezy says, "I ain't write this shit," he's not speaking literally about authorship but, rather, the literacy practice of putting pen to pad. Not only is Jeezy placing himself in the most skilled circle of emcees who privilege orality as a means of lyrical production, but he is also placing himself in direct conversation, across time and text, with artists like Tupac Shakur. In 1996, Tupac opened up "Against All Odds" with the lines, "This be the realest shit I ever wrote…truest shit I ever spoke." Picked up by artists around the world since then, Tupac's text is loop-linked to the present. Artists like Atlanta's Young Jeezy and Oakland's Mistah F.A.B., among others, continue to signify on the lines by transposing *ever* and *never*. They reinterpret Pac's text in such a way as to highlight both its importance ("realness") as well as the oral means of its production. Recognizing the continuous life and intertextuality of rap lyrics, Jeezy not only boasts that he "never" wrote the shit but that it's so dope that he knows you gon quote it too.

Throughout the song, there is a conversation being had among members of the Hip Hop community. The song's full interpretation depends on one's familiarity with Hip Hop Nation Language, including an ever-evolving slang. But more importantly, it depends on one's familiarity with a range of Hip Hop texts and discourses, including all of the latest Hip Hop news and events. The artist often weaves this running conversation seamlessly into the rest of the text without detracting from the main thrust of the song. This is done by using double entendres, creative word play, and play on words. In addition to the preceding lines from Tupac Shakur, one critical interpreter, a 19-year-old from Botswana, notes that the opening of Jeezy's first verse cites and builds on one of Ice Cube's most famous refrains, "it was a good day," from the song by the same title (*Predator*, 1992). The interpreter refers to the start of the verse as "optimistic" because Jeezy's borrowing from Ice Cube "signifies the advent of a brighter future for Black people and the rest of the nation. He expresses that he hopes the good times continue by saying, 'hope I have me a great night.' From this, we can gather that he hopes that Obama will win the election."

Other Hip Hop internal references abound. Jeezy continues his first verse by voicing one of Hip Hop's major points of critique of the Bush presidency and the McCain candidacy—the motives behind the US government's involvement in the wars in Iraq and Afghanistan. He raps: "Mr. soul survivor, does that make me a convict? / Be all you can be, now don't that sound like some dumb shit? / When you die over crude oil as black as my nigga Boo / It's really a Desert Storm, that's word to my nigga Clue." In these lines, without being familiar with any of the references, one would hear a straightforward message describing: (1) a young Black male's struggle to "survive" (despite being cast as a convict), (2) a clear renunciation of the US Army's recruiting slogan ("Be All That You Can Be"), and (3) a questioning of the US government's motivation for the war in Iraq (i.e., the mercenary profits gained through control of Iraq's oil fields and production).

Aside from the direct political conversation, however, the artistry of Hip Hop often revels in its ability to encode messages to its listeners while maintaining the central meaning for those outside the critical circle. While this is often done for political purposes, there is also the pleasure involved in the poetic play. For example, in the first line, Jeezy's referencing his own hit "Soul Survivor" (2005, *Let's Get It: Thug Motivation 101*), which was a collaboration with Muslim Senegalese artist Akon. With some minor orthographic changes, the word *convict* becomes *Konvict,* a reference to Akon's record label, Konvict Muzik. Further, the critique of the war on Iraq as being motivated by a quest for "crude oil as black as my nigga Boo" (his homie who appears in the video) and labeled a "Desert Storm," suggests on one level that Bush Junior is merely completing the work of Bush Senior (George H. Bush's war on Iraq was labeled Operation Desert Storm). One White interpreter rightly notes that Jeezy's reference to Desert Storm points to the "echo it represents of the past Iraq War" and describes the verse as a critique of "the Iraq War recruitment which overly targets blacks." However, he misreads the following line ("word to my nigga Clue"), indicating that it's either a reference to "a friend that died or a nigga who needs a clue as to what is really going on." So, on another level, the hidden conversation that's being had here is that, in addition to critiquing the Bushes' military operations in Iraq, Jeezy is referencing Akon's Konvict Muzik and shouting out DJ Clue ("word to my nigga Clue"), who released a mixtape by the name of "Desert Storm."

Beyond these Hip Hop discourses, Jeezy weaves other discourses into his critiques of George W. Bush: "Bush robbed all of us, would that make him a criminal? / And then he cheated in Florida, would that make him a Seminole?" One Latina interpreter passionately described "My President" as a song that dually expressed the "hurt" of America's past as well as the "hope" of America's future. She writes eloquently, "When hurt and despair would otherwise rule those formerly treated, at best, like the step-children of America, we find in our less-affluent, in our 'poor,' the saving grace of America." Despite the depth of her reading, she and others critiqued Jeezy for "blatant racism" against Native Americans because it undermined his political activism on behalf of the Black community. While she appreciated the critique of former president Bush's "victory" in Florida ("And then he cheated in Florida, would that make him a Seminole?"), she did not appreciate that (in her interpretation) it came at the expense of Native Americans because "cheating is a stereotype of that ethnicity." These lines assume political knowledge of the 2004 US presidential voting scandal in Florida (where many perceived George W. Bush's victory in Florida as due, in part, to the fact that his brother Jeb Bush was governor). However, the discourse that is crucial to unlocking the meaning of this passage is that of college athletics. Rather than being a wrong-headed, racist attack on Native Americans, as some suggested, the line actually is a reference to the academic cheating scandal that rocked the Florida State Seminole football team in 2007.[50]

The point of this detailed explication is not to belittle these earnest efforts at textual analysis or simply to make the reader hyperaware of their own ignorance when critiquing rap music. Rather, it is to highlight the body of knowledge that listeners must possess in order to approach even the first few lines of what heads consider a straightforward rap record. It also underscores the fact that whether or not you agree with Obama's assessment of Hip Hop's remarkable ability "to communicate a complex message in a very short space" depends on your interpretive skills and familiarity level.[51] The average listener incorrectly assumes that their life experience—as far removed as it might be from the Hip Hop cultural world—has prepared them to unpack the various layers of these texts. It's this assumption of preparedness that often leads to and stokes the flames of some of the biggest "controversies" around Barack Obama's relationship to Hip Hop music.[52]

Inside the Mind of a Politicized "Snowman": Young Jeezy Speaks for "the Young and the Oppressed"

On its surface, "My President" is a celebration of the (not yet elected) nation's first Black president. The song is also a continuation of Hip Hop's relentless and uncompromising critiques of social inequality, poverty, government policies in relation to war, the "War on Drugs," and the criminalization and disenfranchisement of African Americans. What many readers might not know is that Young Jeezy has made his career around a persona (Snowman) known for selling "snow" or "white" (cocaine). Jeezy portrays himself in much of his music as a drug dealer turned rapper, not an unfamiliar storyline. In 2005, however, not only was his album flying off the shelves, so were his custom designed Snowman T-shirts, which featured a snowman with a scowl. Schools all over the country banned the T-shirts, youth refused to stop wearing them, parents bugged out, and the Snowman firestorm was on![53]

While some of Hip Hop's language is encoded in the relatively harmless and playful ways previously described, some of it is also encoded in contemporary street argot, especially the idiom of the informal economy. In the hook to Jeezy's "My President," he sings: "My President is Black, my Lambo's blue / And I'll be goddamned if my rims ain't too." Most folks only recognize these first few rhymes, but the rest of the hook is critical: "My momma ain't at home, and daddy's still in jail / Tryna make a plate, anybody seen the scale?...My money's light green and my Jordans light grey / And they love to see white, now how much you tryna pay?" Some earnest interpreters misread Jeezy's question, "anybody seen the scale?" as a reference to the scales of justice: "Clearly he wants to ask the audience to look at the breadth of history and the current inequality." However, in street slang, the scale refers to the equipment used by drug dealers to weigh their product. Further, the chorus ends with an apparent glorification of drug dealing: "And they love to see white [cocaine], now how much you tryna pay."

This hook has been described by some as just that same old "bling-bling" Hip Hop, where young Black men rap about all the material things "that all rappers talk about" like "cars, money, and shoes." Another commentator, after identifying as a "huge Obama supporter," one who "even paid 1500 dollars to fly to Washington to see him sworn in," asks: "[B]ut this song is talking about hoes and rims and lambos—how the hell does any of that pertain to Obama and what he's bringing to the table?" Many listeners were blinded by the bling of the blue Lambo and, surely, by the already well-established master narrative that explains the behavior of young Black men as unintelligent, empty, and nonsensical. As a result, they could only read the images as "classless," "ostentatious," or "showy" modes of wealth bereft of meaning ("This song is so stupid it's not even funny"). However, Jeezy offers a radically different perspective: "I'm putting meaning back into the music business. Everybody been thinking our music is about fancy cars and champagne. That ain't helping people get through their day."[54]

One critical interpreter, a 19-year old gay, South Asian male, responding to the hook, offers a much more insightful reading of these displays of Black wealth:

> The lambo remark seems to detract from the potency of this idea ("first Black president") because it is so materialistic and trivial in comparison. Yet, I would argue that by showing a Lambo, these black artists are able to question the low-income economic spheres that black people are socially and economically designated in our society.... By flaunting this wealth, the artists are able to portray African American people occupying new economic space just as Obama is able to demonstrate an African American person occupying a new political space.

And we would add, not just African American people but a particular type of "ghetto fabulous" hood aesthetic that prioritizes Black, working-class stylistic choices despite their broader social deprecation ("And I'll be goddamned if my rims ain't too!"). Further, Jeezy knows that it is and it ain't about a blue Lambo. As he speaks over the fading music in the outro, he says, "I'm important too though....I was, I was the first nigga to ride through my hood in a Lamborghini, yeah." Then he laughs knowingly, "Ha ha!" and concludes, "Nah, forreal though, we ready for change."

What remains problematic for some is that the means of achieving wealth in "My President" remains outside acceptable social norms. The hook, though, can be read as an internal dialogue about the complex decisions that some Black youth living in poverty have to make while growing up in dire socioeconomic circumstances. Here, Jeezy is not necessarily speaking for himself. Rather, he becomes the Everyman figure, speaking on behalf of all Black men in similar situations. Growing up in the projects of Atlanta in what he describes as a "dysfunctional family," with a mother "who had a lot goin on...personal problems, the streets"[55] might certainly have provided the firsthand experience necessary to speak on this issue. But that's not what's important. What's critical here is that Jeezy's so-called glorification of drug dealing can be read as a sociopolitical critique, one that points out that Black youth often only turn to the informal economy out of necessity. This is especially the case when their families are torn apart by the criminal justice system. As Jeezy raps, conveying the frustration of the struggling Black poor (those disproportionately affected by the worst recession since the Great Depression): "I said I woke up this morning, headache this big / Pay all these damn bills, feed all these damn kids / Buy all these school shoes, buy all these school clothes." With the continuing overrepresentation of Black men in prison cells and unemployment lines (hovering between 15–20 percent unemployment as this chapter is being written), selling drugs to put food on the table (to "make a plate") is viewed as a means of survival when the odds *been* stacked against you due to centuries of race- and class-based social inequality.[56]

As the Snowman, Jeezy often raps about the drug game as a "trap," where society offers you an existential dilemma with no way out. Like Nas rhymes on his verse to "My President," the "trap" has important political consequences: "Yeah, our history, Black history, no President ever did shit for me / Had to hit the streets, had to flip some ki's [kilograms of cocaine] so a nigga won't go broke / Then they put us in jail, now a nigga can't go vote." Nas continues Jeezy's narrative but highlights the fact that government failures to address centuries of inequality ("no President ever did shit for me") create desperate circumstances of poverty. Forced to make incredibly difficult choices (as Jeezy once said, "My aunt need a kidney, but she don't have no insurance"), some Black youth turn to the informal economy, which then leads to the "trap" of death or imprisonment. Nas makes it plain that these policies and "choices" conspire to take away folks' right to vote and lead to political disenfranchisement.

This perspective, where illegal or criminal behavior becomes framed as less of a moral question and more an issue of survival in the face of extreme poverty and structural racism, is a recurring theme in Hip Hop. It is also what makes many Americans extremely uncomfortable. As Tupac Shakur rapped in "Changes," highlighting the intersecting oppressions of young Black men, "I'm tired of bein poor, and even worse I'm Black / My stomach hurts, so I'm lookin for a purse to snatch." As Princeton University professor of African American Studies Imani Perry explains in her *Prophets of the Hood: The Politics and Poetics of Hip Hop*, this perspective must be understood within a Hip Hop interpretive framework. This view places narratives of "gangsterism, drug-dealing and other violence" within a large body of texts that provide a critique of "poverty, desperation, lack of educational opportunity." As a whole, these texts give us numerous examples of the "inconsistency between the constitutional and symbolic meanings of Americanness and the experiences of African Americans."[57] What is perhaps most troubling to many Americans, as Perry notes, is that Hip Hop continues the African American folk tradition of "embracing the outlaw," a literary, metaphorical, and sometimes personified figure that lives outside the bounds of dominant American social norms and "African American modes of social respectability."[58]

As with outlaw figures in diverse musical and oral cultures throughout the world—Mexican *corridos* and Egyptian *shaabi* music, for example—Hip Hop's irreverence toward dominant values and noncompliance with the status quo creates alternative, counterhegemonic spaces. In these spaces, artists personify and exploit America's worst nightmare—"young, Black, and holdin my nuts, *chyeah!*" (Jay-Z, "Young, Gifted, and Black")—in order to tell America about itself in a way that restores power to Black youth in the form of authorship. This is why Jeezy can be heard in the last few lines of the song—after recognizing the importance of the candidacy of Barack Obama—saying "I'm important, too, though." This verbal call for recognition is accompanied by visual signs of Hip Hop heroes right alongside the conventional icons of the Civil Rights Movement. These signs function as a testament to Hip Hop's importance as well as a corrective to Hip Hop's invisibility in contemporary historical narratives of the United States.

Far from nihilistic, Hip Hop has always been a major source of Black youth agency. The Hip Hop artist's pen allows the young and the oppressed to not just write rhymes but to right wrongs. In the process, youth write themselves into history in a way that restores their humanity. In this profound sense, the mic provides a sense of power to those who are often made acutely aware of their overwhelming sense of powerlessness. Hip Hop is not only, as Russell Simmons and many other supporters of Hip Hop say, "a sociological mirror of society." Hip Hop narratives do not merely reflect society; they reflect *on* society, providing critiques of the United States of America's most pressing social problems and broadcasting them to every corner of the globe. While some Americans would rather just pull the plug on Hip Hop or press the mute button, these texts serve an important function in that they consistently and relentlessly bring "the ghetto back into America's [and the world's] public consciousness."[59]

With this understanding, it's no wonder that Jeezy breathes new life into Tupac Shakur's verses. Jeezy's artistic practice of reinterpretation also creates a sociopolitical continuity between "The Trap Life" and "The Thug Life." When Tupac Shakur raised his shirt in front of television cameras and showed the world his new "THUG LIFE" tattoo across his midsection, his actions were immediately interpreted within the dominant master narrative that paints Black youth as angry, violent savages who are the cause of their own social problems. The media narratives continued nonstop, as they do today, depicting all Hip Hop artists as nihilistic and glorifying thuggish behavior. As a once 22-year-old Tupac explained in *Street Conscious Rap*, "THUG LIFE" was an acronym that stood for "The Hate U Gave Little Infants Fucked Everybody."[60] Imbedded in this acronym is a sociopolitical critique that insists on attributing society's problems to a sociostructural system of neglect and purposeful destruction. Tupac's social theory, for example, located the absence of a male figure in the lives of "thug niggas" within a framework that acknowledged American society's historical destruction of Black families, contemporary media portrayals of dysfunction, and in part, a government welfare system that provides incentives that destroy families—"And the government won't give my mama welfare money unless she tells them where my daddy is and says bad things against him and they put him in jail."[61]

Tupac and other outlaw figures in Hip Hop not only provide sociopolitical critiques and Hip Hop social theory, they also actively seek to restore the humanity of Black folks. Tupac's political agenda was not limited to political concerns; at its core, it was a human agenda that aimed to disrupt the overwhelming power of Whiteness in cultural and psychological terms. Tupac:

> I am a revolutionary in every sense of the word. I take care of anything that's mine and I'm handling my business every day. The fact that I can still sit here and look in people's faces and still be smiling, shows you that I am a human being. This is my agenda. I tackle some of these problems head on. My whole thing is to show young black men that you do not have to give up the essence of you to be successful in this country. You don't have to

do that. You can do whatever the fuck you want do to. You can curse how you want to, live how you want to, throw your finger in the air how you please and still make money. . . . So, I represent that thug life—all of the underdogs coming together and just uniting. Taking over. Instead of asking for any of they shit, just taking what we got and building on it.[62]

While not as overtly political and perhaps more flamboyant in his public performances than Tupac, Young Jeezy's private conversations often reveal a similar agenda. In 2005, he spoke to the authors of *Tha Global Cipha: Hip Hop Culture and Consciousness* and had this to say in response to the question about his writing process:

My music is like ghetto gospel. It comes from my heart. . . . It's heartfelt music. You know how when a preacher preaches and he gets into it and he really feels it and he'll do a hymn, stompin and movin like this [he demonstrates]. I feel music like that. . . . I'm basically telling them about our struggle. I'm speaking about a hard struggle, our struggle, our pain. And when I say our pain, it's the things we go through everyday, whether they be good or bad.[63]

Making a direct link between Tupac's thug life and thug ideology and Jeezy's "thug motivation" and "thug inspiration," he explains who he represents in his music:

It's basically this. I speak for the young and the oppressed. I speak for the people who ain't got it and who are trying to get it, dogg. I speak for those who do what they do. At the end of the day, I'm giving them hope. . . . I'm helping people get through their day cuz it's a real world out there. As bad as America try to hide me and make me look like the bad guy, they know just as well as I know that that is what really goes on in the streets.[64]

Jeezy continues:

They scared because they know if I can go do a stadium with 20,000 people and they recite me word for word, that's a problem. I can go to every city in America and do that. It ain't but two teams, theirs and ours. They don't wanna see that! They don't want nobody out here tellin people in the hood and in the ghetto, 'The Sky's the Limit.' They mad because the people in the suburbs, the White people, like the music, too, because they know it's real. And I think that's what's bothering them. I think that's why they're trying to ban my stuff, saying 'Snowman this,' 'Snowman that.' But at the end of the day, Snowman is a good dude. How you gonna knock a young brotha out here trying to mediate everything, trying to let everybody know, 'I understand y'all gangbangers, but are you gangbanging when you get some money and take care of your family? Why would you stay in the streets all of your life when you just saw your mans leave a situation and made a bad situation better?'[65]

As Jeezy's response shows, America's struggle with Hip Hop is often framed in racialized terms, with "White people" critiquing "Black artists" who view their role as mediators between Black youth and White society. It is Hip Hop's direct confrontation with Whiteness and power, its outright rejection of White norms and values, and its out-loud refusal to be silenced that often lead to some of the biggest "controversies" involving Hip Hop. In terms of Young Jeezy and Nas's "My President" and the various performances and remixes of that song, it was Hip Hop's open race talk that incited an overwhelmingly negative reaction from White listeners and overhearers. Even though most Black folks viewed this talk as benign and positive in its celebratory, unity-inspiring tone, online debates raged about Young Jeezy, Nas, and Jay-Z's "racist" and "divisive" discourse. Rather than viewing the celebratory video as capturing a moment of euphoria and joy for African Americans, many White Americans felt threatened and offended by the fact that Black Americans would actually be happy to see *one* president of Color after a string of 43 straight White presidents. As we noted earlier, while the song was entitled "My President," the song's hook was, "My president is Black"—and in the word *Black* lies the controversy.

"Who You Callin a Racist?!": "Sly Foxes," "Bad Niggas," and the Framing of Racist Discourse

While some Internet listeners referred to "My President" as "really good," "great," "amazing," "historic," "awesome," and "inspirational," the non-Black Internet audience described it as "controversial," "offensive," "bigoted," "racist," "demeaning," "ridiculous," "irrelevant," and "horrible." Despite the deep inquiry that Jeezy and Nas's text warrants, a large number of folks described the song as "some stupid random shit," "the most ignorant shit I've ever heard," and advised Jeezy to "think before he writes a song." The most common descriptors used to describe Jeezy (and Black people) were "stupid," "illiterate," and "uneducated." Some folks chimed in with exacerbation, using phrases like "grotesquely ignorant" and "mind-bogglingly stupid." Many posted about how Black people voted for Obama "just because he was black" or because they were "idiots" who "think that just because Obama is black he is going to do everything for you" and that "you won't have to work" and "you can just go on welfare." In some cases, respondents apologized for their grammar, acknowledging their "run-on" sentences but unapologetically referred to Blacks as "lazy" or "ignorant." The absurd number of overtly racist comments about this song, and Black people generally, most definitely revealed the ugly underbelly of anti-Black racism in the United States.

Rather than seeing the song and the video as a celebration of a multi-racial American society or the fact that America can one day elect anyone other than a White, heterosexual male as its leader, the very mention of the word *Black* agitated White listeners and pushed them to the point of rabid anti-Black rhetoric (the *N*-word "came out" repeatedly). While pointing out the overtly racist discourse is important, in some ways, it's the least interesting aspect of these online debates. What is fascinating is how some White people called the song "racist" and "bigoted" for the simple fact that it referred to the president's race: "The very fact that you're celebrating the election of a black man...is conflicting with the idea of racial equality."[66] The national television network Fox News, which Nas refers to as "Sly Fox" in his sustained critique of the network, fixated on this issue. Unfortunately, their analysts proved as unsophisticated as these online readers.

In January 2009, just days after the inauguration of President Barack Obama and the Martin Luther King, Jr. holiday, viewers watching Fox News heard the voice of a White woman anchor, Megyn Kelly, reporting about a cell phone video of Young Jeezy and Jay-Z's performance at the inauguration party celebrating Barack Obama's victory.[67]

MEGYN KELLY: Well, having an African American President in the Oval Office is certainly a watershed moment for America, but some very *visible* supporters of Barack Obama may have *tainted* the moment for some. This is rapper Jay-Z and rapper [pause, and then articulating with exaggerated head nods, as if struggling to pronounce the name] Young Jeezy celebrating the inauguration in Washington at a club on Monday night. And we warn you [dramatic pause], this is explicit. [The news feed at the bottom of the screen reads: "Some listeners call Jay-Z's rap, 'My President' racist." The program then cuts to a cell phone video of the celebration featuring Young Jeezy and Jay-Z.]

YOUNG JEEZY: [Speaking in front of a cheering audience] I wanna thank two people. I wanna thank the muthafucka [bleeped out by Fox with a loud tone] overseas that threw two shoes at George Bush. And I wanna thank [loud cheers]—wait, and listen, listen! And I wanna thank the muthafuckas [bleeped out again] who helped them move they shit [bleeped out] up out the White House! [loud cheers] Keep it movin, bitch, because my President is muthafuckin [bleeped out] Black, niggaaa [bleeped out] [Loud cheers].

JAY-Z: [Begins rappin the last few lines of his unreleased re-mix of "My President"] Never thought I'd say this shit [bleeped out] baby, I'm good / You can keep your puss [bleeped out], I don't want no more bush [Bush] / No more war, no more Iraq / No more white lies, my President is Black! [Crowd goes wild!]

YOUNG JEEZY: Yeahhhh!

At this point, a few things are worth noting, especially in relation to the pauses in this dialogue, which as we know, can be pregnant with meaning. From the beginning, the reporter frames rap and rappers as strange, with several online commentators noting that Kelly's exaggerated pause before mentioning Young Jeezy's name appears like an intentional attempt to undermine the rapper's legitimacy. ("I love how these Fox News folks try to pronounce rapper names like they don't speak English," as one critical interpreter pointed out. "She's acting like she's speaking Chinese or something.") After the awkward pause, there's a dramatic pause in between the words, "And we warn you...this is explicit." The language of these "rappers" is something to prepare yourself for, to fear. The broadcast continues with the introduction of Fox News conservative contributor of Color, Michelle Malkin.

MEGAN KELLY: [As if bewildered] Uhh, you know, this, this is *stunning*. Uh, this is the way they choose to celebrate the inauguration of our first Black President. Uh, so much for a *postracial America*, I guess.

MICHELLE MALKIN: Yeah, I posted the video on Monday night in the midst of the feel-good kumbaya leading up to the inauguration, and a lotta folks didn't want to pay attention to this very *ugly* underbelly that was going on in Washington, D.C., but it's not a shock to people who've been paying attention to these very high profile supporters of Barack Obama in the entertainment industry....[This performance] really gives lie to the concept that Barack Obama has ushered in this quote-unquote postracial era. In fact, the color-coded culture is alive and well, and it has been *stoked* by the rap industry, and unfortunately, you have heard no denunciations from the postracial president about this very vitriolic rhetoric, you know, that really is supposed to be something we've discarded and left behind.

MEGYN KELLY: Well, and it would be one thing if these were rappers who were sort of doing their own thing, on the outskirts, you know, what have you. That's been going on for a while, but *Jay-Z*, I, I believe he was in the VIP section watching the Inauguration. I mean, he was a *welcomed guest*, along with his wife *Beyonce*. This guy is well respected. I don't understand why he would participate in something like this. I think the Young Jeezy is the one who's been making these comments all along, but it's a little bit more controversial now that Jay-Z joins in and has no problem with these sorts of terms being thrown around. The N-word came out *repeatedly*, uhh, I mean, what kind of an example is this setting for, you know, young African Americans who would look to them for guidance on this?

MICHELLE MALKIN: A very poor and bigoted example, Megyn. And exactly the kind of example that Barack Obama said he had distanced himself from, from the campaign.... It's the same old Democratic mentality of treating people based on the color of their skin rather than the content of their character, or the content of their resumes. You know, not exactly the kind of legacy Martin Luther King was supposed to leave.

MEGYN KELLY: Well, I know Michelle that when you comment on these things, and when others comment on these things, some people come out and call *you* racist for even *commenting* on it, which seems a little bone-headed, to have the exact wrong message as a result of these...[68]

MICHELLE MALKIN: [Nodding very seriously]

MEGYN KELLY:...but we appreciate you blogging about it. We saw the tape. We were rather surprised by it, and we hope that we don't see more of it.

Fox News anchor Megyn Kelly finds it *"stunning"* that "they" [Black people, rappers, etc.] would celebrate the inauguration of the first Black president by pointing out that he was, well, Black. The perspective of one critical interpreter, a first-generation Black college student, conveys the feeling of joy (rather then racism) felt by many African Americans that night: "The gravity and magnitude of the song didn't hit me until election night after

Obama was elected. I felt intense happiness as I listened to the song all night in my room and reflected on there being a first Black President. Here I was during my first year in college, as a Black student, first-generation, and the first Black President was elected. The song captured the emotion of how inspirational it was." A White critical interpreter adds his perspective that, rather than hate and division, he liked "how the music video captures the pure joy and excitement that swept across the nation in November 2008 and shows smiling, happy people coming together for a collective celebration of change and renewal." Another reminds us that Young Jeezy raps "Obama for mankind," not "Obama for Black people."

Rather than reading Young Jeezy, Nas, and Jay-Z's work as racist, these interpreters read "My President," the video, and the performances of the song as a multiracial celebration of the diverse group of voters who helped elect Barack Obama. They further acknowledged the special significance this victory has for African Americans, with one saying:

> Many women, Democrat or Republican, would have been ecstatic if Hillary Clinton won, and many Latinos would have loved to see Bill Richardson as Obama's choice for Vice President. It just makes sense that people who belong to groups that have not yet achieved full equality can be happy that their group—it could be a gay man or woman next—is making progress, especially because it means that our country's making progress in terms of equality.

Interestingly, we see in the Fox News clip and Internet message boards that Black happiness somehow translates into hatred for Whites, as if expressing a deep-seated fear that Black Americans will somehow gain power and treat White Americans as poorly as Blacks themselves have been treated. In *Vibe* magazine's coverage of the campaign, Jeff Chang recalled Jon Stewart's satirical question to Obama, "Will you pull a bait-and-switch, sir, and enslave the white race? Is that your plan?"[69] While Stewart humorously captures irrational White fear, many Internet commentators' rants show that this scenario does not seem impossible and outlandish to some folks. Some writers actually feared that Black people would empower themselves and then wage some kind of "race war" against Whites. We warn you [dramatic pause], this is explicit:

> This song just goes to show how fucked up black people are in this country. I hate to be the racist one that lies in every white person but what I'm saying is true. And I'm no white supremisist [sic] either. . . . It seems like now that Obama has become

president of the U.S., african americans have become so ignorant to a point where it's just ridiculous. It seems like they think
they have won some kind of war over white people because
the president is now black. Trust me, there was/never will be
a war against black people...BLACK PEOPLE STOP BEING SO
FUCKING IGNORANT...just because we have a black president
doesn't mean you have any power over white people and don't
boast like you actually did something for this country because
there's a good chance you didn't do shit except complain that
white people have so much power. (sorry for the run-on)...I'm
sure 99% of black people in this country are in fact 'racists.'[70]

The video for "My President" probably had more non-Black people than most
other Hip Hop videos. Also, it was interpreted by many as a multiracial celebration by a diverse coalition of Obama supporters who made history by
proving that America was "ready for a Black President." Despite this, White
viewers more often than not framed it as "racist." Further, in this previous
example, the Internet commentator seemed to recognize the counterhegemonic possibilities that the song opens up for African Americans, ending
his racist rant by warning Black folks that this victory does not mean that
you have any real "power over white people." And that's what this "controversy" is really all about, isn't it?

Not only did the aftermath reveal anti-Black racist discourses, but it also
exposed the more subtle racist-classist workings of White hegemony. This
is especially evident in the different ways that Jay-Z and Young Jeezy were
framed. The anchorwoman is perfectly OK with Young Jeezy and other artists as long as they are unable to gain access to power or acceptance from
mainstream White America—as long as they remain invisible. But, Jay-Z,
she exclaims, is someone to worry about because he is a "very *visible*" and
"*welcomed guest*," for Christ's sake! The anchorwoman seems to be making
the case that, since the establishment let Jay-Z have a seat at the table—
instead of fighting for the crumbs with the likes of those other "dangerous" rappers "on the outskirts"—that he should now "behave properly." He
should act in a way that not only conforms to White linguistic and cultural
norms but that ultimately caters to White interests. As Imani Perry notes,
not all wealthy Blacks are, to use the anchor's words, "welcomed guests" at
the table of American power. In US society, as Perry writes, "Black wealth
is supposed to have a respectable face" and in order for Black folks to
succeed they are "supposed to fit into a White American comfort zone—
charismatic entertainers to be paid for, or Bill Cosby-style professionals,
or even better, actually meretricious Colin Powell-style achievers." If the
Black wealthy, like Jay-Z, who, as Kelly laments, was "in the VIP section

watching the Inauguration," do not neatly fit into any of these categories, "much speculation arises as to how this 'bad nigga' was 'let in.'"[71]

Jay-Z, Jeezy, and Nas are most definitely some bad-ass niggas. Jay-Z, in particular, was the strongest supporter of Obama's candidacy. In *The Source* magazine's politics issue, he speaks with a sense of urgency about the impact of this election: "If [Barack Obama] loses I really will feel sorry and sad for the state of America. The world is watching. And the world will judge us on that." Being in the public eye has made Jay-Z hyperaware of the intense level of scrutiny, monitoring, and policing that Black public figures receive. As if pre-empting the race-baiting question, he continues (taking a page out of Obama's book), "And I'm not voting for him simply because he's Black. The worst thing ever for Black people would be to put someone in who wasn't capable. I'm voting because he's capable." That said, Jay-Z does not deny the symbolism that this election could hold for young, poor Black children who, like him, grew up in the inner city's housing projects: "What he represents to a little kid in Marcy Projects right now is to make him feel like he's part of America. We never felt like we were part of the American Dream."[72] Jay-Z's comments underscore the irony that the hopeful narrative of Black inclusion was repeatedly read as a hateful narrative of White exclusion.

Before the election, Jay-Z expressed this hopefulness on the remix of "My President": "Hello Ms. America / Hey pretty lady / that red white and blue flag / wave for me baby." After the election, he explains this line in his book, *Decoded*:

> After Barack was elected, I realized that the same thing hip-hop had been doing for years with language and brands—that is, reinventing them to mean something different from what they originally meant—we could now do to American icons like the flag. Things that had once symbolized slavery, oppression, militarism, and hypocrisy might now begin to legitimately represent us. We're not there yet, but Barack's election offered a tantalizing hint of what that might look like, including things like having the American "first lady" be a beautiful Black woman who could trace her ancestry to American slaves.[73]

Sensing that some folks might be upset with his final line, "No more white lies, my President is BLACK," Jay-Z explains: "The point of the song is that we were progressing beyond simplistic talk about race and could start being honest about it so that we could, eventually, move on."[74] However, as the Fox News clip and the Internet message boards show, as a country, we have a *long* way to go before open, honest discourse about race can take place outside university classrooms, if it even takes place there. For now, it is clear that Hip Hop continues to challenge Whiteness by resisting simplistic discourses of "colorblindness" and "postraciality" and talking directly about race in an effort to take the conversation to the next level.

"I've Never Seen a Presidential Candidate Do That": Revisiting the First Hip Hop President

In exploring the question of Barack Obama as "the first Hip Hop president," our aim is not to link Barack Obama to Hip Hop by superficial characteristics, such as his race, age, or relative coolness, nor is it to draw a straight line "from Barack Obama directly to the hip-hop community."[75] It would be simplistic to do so. However, there are some final points to consider. "Rap music," as Tricia Rose wrote in 1994, "is a black cultural expression that prioritizes black voices from the margins of urban America" and continues to "articulate the shifting terms of marginality in contemporary American culture."[76] Just because we have seen the music go mainstream and global in the last decade, dominating record charts and the Internet, does not mean that Hip Hop is not Black American music. Not only does the language of Hip Hop Culture, "from Oakland to Auckland" (as Lupe Fiasco rhymes), draw inspiration from Black Language and Culture, but as Imani Perry notes, Hip Hop continues to occupy a "political location in society distinctly ascribed to black people, music, and cultural forms."[77]

Arguing from a distinctly Black *political* location, Hip Hop continues to broadcast a particular *physical* location into America's public consciousness and conscience: the ghetto. The very act of speaking up and out from this particular marginalized social location is to express a form of agency in and on the world. In Hip Hop, the lyrical is political for the very reason that its authors and narrators speak for folks who come from the bottom—or like Calle 13 put it—los de atrás y los de abajo. Further, as a self-reflexive community, many of these artists know that they are subject to disproportionate monitoring and uninformed critique. They know—as Barack Obama does—that before they even spit the first syllable outta they mouth, they are already framed as unintelligent, lazy, dangerous, or worse. In the face of, or perhaps because of, these potentially overwhelming discourses, Hip Hop remains one of the few, if not the only, musical genre in America that consistently talks openly, boldly and honestly about race.

Perhaps it is this political location that matters most in our conversation about Hip Hop and Obama. While others painted a caricature of Barack's relationship to Hip Hop (what you mean, growin up without a father and witnessing poverty ain't "Hip Hop"?), Hip Hop identified with Obama's experience as a community organizer in the hoods and churches of South Side Chicago, his commitment to buck the status quo in terms of health care and the economy, his radical position against the war in Iraq (forcefully and publicly calling it "a dumb war"), and his commitment to various social justice issues. But it wasn't just about issues. Perhaps most importantly was the strong, unflinching, smooth way he confronted the racial minefield of US politics as a Black man in an election cycle where the terms of racial reference constantly shifted from "Black" to "not Black enough" to "too Black" to "Arab" to "Muslim" to "nigger" and back again. In the midst of the racially charged Reverend Wright controversy, it was Barack's delivery of the "Race Speech" in Philadelphia that was perhaps the single most important event that captured the heart of Hip Hop. Because, as Mississippi's David Banner told *The Source* magazine, "Obama showed America that he wasn't no punk. He showed his strength by addressing what people viewed as his weaknesses. He didn't run from them. I've never seen a Presidential candidate do that."[78]

Hip Hop heads knew that Obama, as the first Black candidate for president with a serious chance of winning, would be subject to the kinds of critiques that they faced on the regular. During the contentious campaign, Hip Hop recognized Barack's political location and offered words of caution. Nas, in his verse on "My President," warned Obama: "Gotta stay true to who you are and where you came from / Cause at the top will be the same place you hang from." Nas and others knew that being the first Black editor of the *Harvard Law Review* or the only serving Black member of the US Senate— and even becoming president of the United States—would not necessarily mitigate the fact that he was Black. At the end of the day, even a president can get lynched from the political tree. Given the ever-present possibility of "lynching" and the extraordinary amount of pressure to "denounce" Reverend Wright, heads like David Banner, Common, and Jay-Z appreciated the fact that Barack, rather than backing down, stood up and said the very words that his detractors were hoping to hear: "I can no more disown him than I can disown the Black community."[79] As one, young Hip Hop head put it at the time, "Gotta respect the man's *gangsta* on that one!"

Despite the fact that we're talkin about politics, not pop culture, Barack occupied a version of that political location that Hip Hop had come to almost call home. After all, in a political world dominated by White men, Obama was the "OutKast." This was evidenced not only by the covert racist practices involved in the intense scrutiny of his every word but also—lest we forget—through threats of assassination. These last two points were not lost on rapper Big Boi of OutKast, who rhymed: "And who you votin for, Republican or Democratic? / Don't say it doesn't matter cuz that's how they stole the last one / Assassin's bullet might be waitin for Obama / Do you think they'll have a brotha before Billy's babymama? C'mon!"[80] Many Barack supporters, Blacks especially, recall praying silently when Hillary Clinton rather cavalierly compared Obama to Robert Kennedy, drumming up the specter of assassination.[81] Many others watched intently as his opponents tried desperately to paint him as overly concerned with race, being "one of those militant Blacks," or even worse, a "terrorist." Yet despite all this, Obama couldn't be faded.

Obama's ability to break barriers, defy odds, explode stereotypes, and exceed all expectations—his outright, Public Enemy–style "refuse to lose" mindset—is what, to many, makes him Hip Hop. As Hip Hop head and journalist Davey D wrote: "What makes Obama Hip Hop is that he's intelligent.... He defies all the nasty stereotypes that have been put out by corporate media that have left everyone around the world with a false impression of Black men." Then, as if comparing Barack Obama to the Trickster figure of Hip Hop and the African American Oral Tradition, he continues: "The fact that he was able to come seemingly out of nowhere and outsmart and outmaneuver the mighty Clinton machine when they appeared to have everything all sewn up.... The fact he was able to defy the odds by outlasting and overcoming all the racism heaped on him by his Republican opponents and full onslaught by Fox News and all their lies was incredible.... That's what makes him Hip Hop."[82]

NOTES

1. Check out the full interview by Jeff Johnson on the BET special *What's In It for Us?*, posted on February 3, 2008, on YouTube: http://www.youtube.com/user/hsamyalim?feature=mhee#p/a/12D691D04C9B36F5/0/pFSVG7jRp_g. Last accessed: 09-22-11.
2. From Jay-Z's (Shawn Carter's) highly recommended (dope-ass) book *Decoded* (New York: Spiegel & Grau, 2010, 168–171). Props to dream hampton.
3. Check the video, "Obama Dancing to Snoop Dogg," at: http://www.youtube.com/user/hsamyalim?feature=mhee#p/c/12D691D04C9B36F5. Last accessed: 09-22-11.
4. Check out the video of Snoop representin on CNN's *Larry King Live* at "Rapper Snoop Dogg Says Senator Barack Obama Can Win!": http://www.youtube.com/user/hsamyalim?feature=mhee#p/a/12D691D04C9B36F5/1/Od2tQyrf4vU. Last accessed: 09-22-11.
5. Quoted in "Obama Hip-Hop: From Mixtapes to Mainstream" at: http://www.npr.org/templates/story/story.php?storyId=96748462. Last accessed: 09-22-11.
6. Read Tricia Rose's *The Hip Hop Wars: What We Talk about When We Talk about Hip Hop—and Why It Matters* (New York: Basic Books, 2008).
7. Pac originally recorded "Changes" in 1992. The remix, which sampled Bruce Hornsby's "That's the Way It Is," became extremely popular in 1998 and hit number one around the world in places like Norway and the Netherlands. RIP 2PAC.
8. Check Cube's interview at: http://www.youtube.com/user/hsamyalim?feature=mhee#p/c/12D691D04C9B36F5/17/xz6TOLclg2U. Last accessed: 09-22-11.

9. Quoted in "Hip-Hop Stand Up!" in *The Source* magazine's politics issue, November 2008, Number 227, page 52.

10. Ibid.

11. This the transcript of Jay-Z's message: "Hey, this is Jay-Z callin on behalf of Senator Barack Obama's campaign urging you to vote tomorrow. Bring your friends and families. Make sure your voices are heard for change. It's time for change. It's time for Barack Obama. The polls are open from 6:30am to 7:30pm. Take your Ohio ID. If you don't have an ID, a utility bill, pay stub, bank statement or government document with your address is all you need to vote. Please call 1-866-675-2008. If you need a ride, need to find your polling location, or for *any* voting question, you can also visit ohio.barackobama.com. Vote for Barack Obama for President tomorrow. He is the change we can believe in. Paid for by Obama for America."

12. Quoted in: http://www.youtube.com/watch?v=FecQidSTTu0, posted March 29, 2008. Last accessed: 09-22-11.

13. See the November 2008 historic collector's edition of *Vibe* magazine.

14. From Hip Hop activist, cultural critic, and writer (and Executive Director of the Institute for Diversity in the Arts at Stanford University) Jeff Chang's, "Barack Obama—The *Vibe* Interview." Online at: www.thelavinagency.com/images/.../1212688601_chang-vibe.pdf. Last accessed: 09-22-11.

15. From Jann S. Wenner's September 28, 2010, article, "Obama in Command: The *Rolling Stone* Interview," at: http://www.rollingstone.com/politics/news/obama-in-command-br-the-rolling-stone-interview-20100928.

16. From Jeff Johnson's interview for BET. See note 1.

17. Check the November 2008 historic collector's edition of *Vibe* magazine for the article "It Takes a Nation of Millions: Here's What 99 Are Saying," page 100.

18. Ibid., 101.

19. "Dirt off Your Shoulder" was released in 2003 on *The Black Album* by Roc-A-Fella Records.

20. See Peter Hamby's CNN article "Obama Gets Name-Dropped in Hip Hop" posted August 17, 2007, at: http://articles.cnn.com/2007–08-17/politics/obama.hip.hop_1_hip-hop-appeal-obama-campaign-jen-psaki?_s=PM:POLITICS. Last accessed: 09-22-11.

21. See the BlackTreeTV interview in note 12.

22. See *Vibe*'s "It Takes a Nation of Millions: Here's What 99 Are Saying," pages 98–105. See note 17.

23. Ibid., 101.

24. Barack Obama's September 9, 2008, letter to *Vibe* magazine appeared in the November 2008 issue, page 91.

25. See Davey D's January 30, 2009, blog post, "Is Obama a Hip Hop President and Does It Really Matter?" at: http://trggradio.org/2009/01/30/is-obama-a-hip-hop-president-does-it-really-matter/. Last accessed: 09-23-11.

26. For example, as Davey D wrote in "Is Obama a Hip Hop President and Does It Really Matter?": "In June of 2007 a number of artists including Saigon, Rebel Diaz, Sess 4–5 and Mia X out of New Orleans teamed up with the Washington DC based Hip Hop Caucus and the ACLU to do a concert and fundraiser." The event "brought attention to the elimination of Habeas Corpus and to the rampant torture that was going on at Guantanimo Bay [and] the plight of New Orleans residents who still found themselves unable to return home two years in the aftermath of Hurricane Katrina." Highlighting the fact that the event wasn't merely a "show," he added, "Each performance was preceded by artists taking the stage and talking to the audience about specific policy recommendations and action steps." In addition, Bakari Kitwana's Rap Sessions national tour on Obama and Hip Hop serve as a treasure trove of information and provide numerous examples of in-depth, political conversation and critique. See both www.daveyd.com and http://rapsessions.org/ for Hip Hop news, politics, and cultural analysis.

27. Daddy Yankee endorsed John McCain and even performed at concerts to raise funds for his campaign, stating: "He has been a fighter for the Hispanic community, and I

know that for me personally, I chose him as the best candidate because he has been a fighter for the immigration issue." (*The Source*'s November 2008 issue, 53, see note 9). Responding in the same issue, Fat Joe asks: "How could you want John McCain in office when George Bush and the Republicans already have half a million people losing their homes to foreclosure? We're fighting an unjust war. It's the Latinos and Black kids up in the frontlines, fighting that war." He then urged Daddy Yankee, who seemed to be a "one issue voter," to get "educated on politics." (54).

28. Davey D, January 30, 2009. See note 26.

29. Ibid.

30. See James G. Spady's chapter, "Password: Nation Conscious Rap," in the pioneering Hip Hop volume, *Nation Conscious Rap: The Hip Hop Vision* (Philadelphia: Black History Museum, 1991, 401–415). This wordplay highlights both the aesthetic ("art form") and the political ("art forum") in Hip Hop and takes as a given the community's diverse and sophisticated political views.

31. See Rosa Clemente's article commissioned by the Green Institute, "Why President-Elect Barack Obama Is Not the First Hip Hop President," at: http://www.greeninstitute.net/clemente_obama. Last accessed: 09-23-11.

32. Quoted in the November 2008 issue of *Vibe* magazine, page 101.

33. Ibid., 102.

34. See Immortal's July 23, 2009, blog post on *The Revolutionary Hip-Hop Report*, "America's Great Hope (Obama Was Necessary)" at: http://rhhr.wordpress.com/2009/07/23/is-obama-a-hip-hop-president-the-debate-continues/. Last accessed: 09-23-11.

35. Quoted in the November 2008 issue of *Vibe* magazine, page 105.

36. Quoted in a conversation with Jeff Chang, posted on November 2, 2008, at: http://cantstopwontstop.com/blog/qa-david-banner-on-what-tuesday-means/. Last accessed: 09-23-11.

37. See Craig R. Smith's August 25, 2008, article, "The Hip Hop President," on WorldNetDaily at: http://www.wnd.com/index.php?pageId=73276. Last accessed: 09-23-11.

38. Quoted in Jeff Johnson's BET special, *What's In It for Us?* See note 1.

39. Read the transcript of the 2007 show with Paula Zahn (minus the menacing music) at: http://transcripts.cnn.com/TRANSCRIPTS/0702/21/pzn.01.html. Last accessed: 09-23-11.

40. Personal communication (February 4, 2008) with education scholar and cultural analyst Donielle A. Prince.

41. In 1992, former president Bill Clinton attacked the raptivist Sister Souljah for "racist" lyrics on her album *360 Degrees of Power* and comments she made in the national press. Sister Souljah also happens to be a fiction writer, a graduate of Rutgers University, and has visited and lectured in several countries, including the former Soviet Union, England, France, Portugal, Finland, Holland, and South Africa. When she referred to a "war zone" in her comments about the Los Angeles insurrection (riots), she was referring to the depressed state of many urban communities in America when, at the time, statistics reported that it was actually safer to have been a soldier in Vietnam than to be a Black male between 14 and 24 living in America. For more on this, see H. Samy Alim's *Roc the Mic Right: The Language of Hip Hop Culture* (New York: Routledge, 2006, 28–29). See also Mattias Gardell's *In the Name of Elijah Muhammad: Louis Farrakhan and the Nation of Islam* (Durham, NC: Duke University Press, 1996, 299).

42. Quoted in Jeff Johnson's BET special, *What's In It for Us?* See note 1.

43. Ibid.

44. Quoted in "Obama Hip-Hop: From Mixtapes to Mainstream." See note 5.

45. Chuck D spoke at, "Global Flows: The Globalization of Hip Hop Art, Culture, and Politics," hosted by Stanford University's Institute for Diversity in the Arts and the Center for Comparative Studies in Race & Ethnicity on April 28, 2011. Also featured on the panel were Gaye Johnson (UCSB), Dawn-Elissa Fischer (SF State), Samir Meghelli (Columbia), DJ Emacipacion, and Jeff Chang (Stanford). Davey D, Omar Offendum,

Blitz the Ambassador, Ragtop, and Mark Gonzales also participated. Check out Davey D's Hip Hop Corner for OpenLine Media's coverage of the event at: http://hiphopand-politics.wordpress.com/2011/05/23/our-coverage-of-the-global-hip-hop-conference-at-stanford/. Last accessed: 09-23-11.

46. See Richards's April 25, 2010, article at: http://www.washingtonpost.com/wp-dyn/content/article/2010/04/23/AR2010042300046.html. Last accessed: 09-23-11.

47. Quoted in "Obama Hip-Hop: From Mixtapes to Mainstream." See note 5.

48. Ibid.

49. Our critical analysis of "My President" represents our own reading of the text, but importantly, it draws from a racially and ethnically diverse group of critical interpreters of the culture, ranging from 17 to 24 years old. Participants were enrolled in a Hip Hop course at Stanford University, one of dozens now across the world from Harvard to Hong Kong University. These students, as a critical circle of interpreters and a cipher, applied the theoretical and methodological approaches of cultural and literary studies to Hip Hop texts. Our analysis also draws from media discourses, numerous Internet message boards and online conversations about Hip Hop.

50. Approximately 25 of their players were accused of unethical behavior. See Mark Schlabach's December 19, 2007, article on: http://sports.espn.go.com/ncf/news/story?id=3159534. Last accessed: 09-23-11.

51. This point is made brilliantly by Imani Perry throughout her book *Prophets of the Hood: Politics and Poetics in Hip Hop* (Durham, NC: Duke University Press, 2004). Close readers will make a link to Hip Hop's ability to draw on multiple texts through the coded use of language to Obama's coded references to Malcolm X in South Carolina. Through the use of *hoodwinked* and *bamboozled*—among other examples, as we discussed in chapter 1—he communicated subtle messages to his Black electorate.

52. As Michael Eric Dyson has cautioned all would-be critics of Hip Hop: "It would be outlandish to comment on, say, metaphysical poetry without interacting critically with its most inspired poets. At least *read* Dante. And if one were to make hay over the virtues of deficits of nineteenth-century British poetry, or, twentieth-century Irish poetry, then one should encounter the full range of Tennyson's or Yeat's work before jumping, or slouching, to conclusions." See Dyson's foreword to Murray Forman and Mark Anthony Neal's (eds.) *That's the Joint!: The Hip-Hop Studies Reader* (New York: Routledge, 2004, xiii).

53. See Jonathan Martin's November 28, 2005, article, "Snowman Shirts Causing Controversy in Schools," at: http://www.wrdw.com/home/headlines/2024407.html. Last accessed: 09-23-11.

54. Quoted in a revealing 11-page interview in James G. Spady, H. Samy Alim, and Samir Meghelli's *Tha Global Cipha: Hip Hop Culture and Consciousness* (Philadelphia: Black History Museum, 2006, 98).

55. Ibid., 102.

56. See Annalyn Censky's September 2, 2011, article, "Black Unemployment Rate: Highest Since 1984," on CNNMoney: http://money.cnn.com/2011/09/02/news/economy/black_unemployment_rate/index.htm. Last accessed: 09-23-11. Censky writes: "Overall, black men have it the worst, with joblessness at a staggeringly high 19.1 percent, compared to 14.5 percent for black women.... Black unemployment has now remained above 10 percent for four straight years, and given current economic sluggishness, some experts say it's safe to predict the rate will remain above 10 percent for four more years."

57. Check Imani Perry (2004), page 107. See note 51.

58. Ibid., 107.

59. Check Tricia Rose's foundational book, *Black Noise: Rap Music and Black Culture in Contemporary America* (Hanover, NH: Wesleyan University Press, 1994, 11).

60. Read the full interview with Tupac in James G. Spady, H. Samy Alim, and Charles G. Lee's *Street Conscious Rap* (Philadelphia: Black History Museum, 1999, 566). Pac breaks it down in there, forreal, but his interview is not without its contradictions.

61. Ibid., 565.
62. Ibid., 567.
63. Quoted in James G. Spady, H. Samy Alim, and Samir Meghelli's *Tha Global Cipha: Hip Hop Culture and Consciousness*, page 101. See note 54.
64. Ibid., 98.
65. Ibid., 98.
66. This is a sad fallout of the simple logic that upholds "colorblind" racial ideologies. Many White people claim that they are not racist because they don't see color. Therefore, the very act of seeing color becomes an act of racism. Go figure.
67. Check the video posted on January 22, 2009, "Fox News on Jay-Z and Young Jeezy's Inaugural Anti Bush Rap," on: http://www.youtube.com/watch?v=kuE4WDFaibA. Last accessed: 09-23-11.
68. If only Megyn Kelly had read Eduardo Bonilla-Silva's chapter, "The Style of Color-blindness: How to Talk Nasty about Minorities without Sounding Racist," in *Racism without Racists: Color-Blind Racism & Racial Inequality in Contemporary America* (Plymouth, UK: Rowman & Littlefield, 2010, 3rd edition, 53–74), she would know that her rhetorical strategies have been well studied. Her use of "projection as a rhetorical tool" ("They are the racist ones," for example) is a well-documented strategy of those who would like to "escape from guilt and responsibility and affix blame elsewhere" (63–64). Michelle Malkin is incredibly adept at projection, which often goes hand in hand with co-optation. We see this first in her insistence that Obama has ushered in a "postracial" era followed by a co-optation of the progressive rhetoric that racism is alive and well: "[This performance] really gives lie to the concept that Barack Obama has ushered in this quote-unquote postracial era. In fact, the color-coded culture is alive and well, and it has been *stoked* by the rap industry, and unfortunately, you have heard no denunciations from the postracial president about this very vitriolic rhetoric." Then she takes another well-documented approach, co-opting Martin Luther King's discourse to project racism onto Black Americans: "It's the same old Democratic mentality of treating people based on the color of their skin rather than the content of their character, or the content of their resumes. You know, not exactly the kind of legacy Martin Luther King was supposed to leave." Yawn. Read a book.
69. See Jeff Chang's November 2008 article, "The Tipping Point," in *Vibe* magazine, pages 92–97.
70. Read "romodavid's" January 26, 2009, post at: http://www.songmeanings.net/songs/view/3530822107858743658/. Last accessed: 09-25-11. While you're at it, read all the comments, if you got the stomach for it. The advent of the Internet has definitely made it easier for folks to spit anti-Black racism.
71. From Perry (2004), page 113. See note 51.
72. Quoted in *The Source* magazine's politics issue, November 2008, page 52.
73. From Jay-Z's (Shawn Carter's) in-depth and insightful (deep and dope-ass) book *Decoded* (New York: Spiegel & Grau, 2010, 231).
74. Ibid., 231.
75. Kiese Laymon makes this point well in the June 16, 2010, article, "Is Obama the First Hip-Hop President?" at: http://www.thegrio.com/specials/hip-hop-politics-from-the-beat-to-the-ballot/is-barack-obama-the-next-hip-hop-president.php. Last accessed: 09-25-11.
76. Check out Rose (1994), pages 2–3. See note 59.
77. Check out Perry (2004), page 10. See note 51.
78. Quoted in *The Source* magazine's politics issue, November 2008, page 52.
79. For a full transcript of the speech, see T. Denean Sharpley-Whiting (ed.) *The Speech: Race and Barack Obama's "A More Perfect Union"* (New York: Bloomsbury, 2009, 237–251). It was delivered on March 18, 2008, in Philadelphia and is known as the "Race Speech" or just "The Speech." You can also catch it on YouTube: http://www.youtube.com/watch?v=zrp-v2tHaDo. Last accessed: 09-25-11. When Barack eventually distanced himself from Reverend Wright, it wasn't seen as a backing down—by many

folks' standards, Reverend Wright's hunger for the spotlight was detracting from Obama's campaign. This feeling was expressed by Nas, who rhymed, "You ain't right, Jeremiah Wrong pastor" ("Black President"). Despite distancing himself from Wright, Obama made it clear that he was not about to distance himself from "the Black community." As we enter 2012, however, certain segments of the Black community may be the ones distancing themselves from Barack Obama as an increasing number of vocal Black critics continue to feel that Obama has neglected the concerns of African Americans.

80. From his song "Daddy Fat Sax" on one of the best Hip Hop albums of 2010, *Sir Lucious Left Foot: The Son of Chico Dusty* (Purple Ribbon Records and Def Jam Recordings).

81. If you don't recall this, check the video at: http://www.youtube.com/watch?v=E0QAewVrR28. Last accessed: 09-25-11. Hillary Clinton, at the time (May 2008), was not willing to back out of the race. Further, the presumptive nominee, Barack Obama, had already received multiple death threats. While many in her party were pushing her to quit for the sake of "party unity," she pushed on, saying, "You know, my husband did not wrap up the nomination in 1992 until he won the California primary somewhere in the middle of June, right? We all remember Bobby Kennedy was assassinated in June in California." While her campaign brushed off accusations of "dirty politics" as ludicrous, others couldn't help but think of the move as calculated.

82. Davey D, January 30, 2009. See note 26. While this captured the sentiment of Davey D and many in Hip Hop, Davey D has become a very vocal critic of Barack Obama and what he sees as his lack of concern for Black communities. Some have even repeated Kanye West's famous comments about George W. Bush ("George Bush does not care about Black people.") and replaced his name with Obama's. In the Black tradition, the Trickster figure uses his guile and intelligence to defeat the White power structure. Obama, on the other hand, ran one helluva campaign, in which he apparently "tricked" much of both White *and* Black America (as well as progressives of all stripes, many who are now embarrassed and/or embittered because they were among the "believers"). Despite everything that they knew about politics—namely, that "change" almost never happens from the top-down, that politicians do what they do best (i.e., get elected), and so on—they somehow believed Obama would be different. Those in Hip Hop who expressed a healthy skepticism toward Obama's ability—or any president's ability, for that matter—to fulfill sweeping promises of change were ahead of the curve. Take this excerpt from an open letter to the president penned by Brooklyn MC Talib Kweli: "If someone asked me, I would explain why I didn't vote. It was pageantry and I wasn't with it. This was all before Barack Obama threw his hat in the ring. My criticism of the political system is that it siphons all rational thought because you have to be all things to all people. You can stand for anything doing that... I am not delusional about what the office of the president represents..." (quoted in William Jelani Cobb's *Barack Obama and the Paradox of Progress*, New York: Walker, 2010, 110). Or as Stic.Man from dead prez put it earlier in this chapter— even more strongly—"Even if Barack Obama wins, Uncle Sam still ain't our friend." As we ramp up for the 2012 presidential election, it'll be interesting to watch Hip Hop's evolving stance towards Barack Obama and the role Hip Hop will or will not play this time around.

6

Change the Game

Language, Education, and the Cruel Fallout of Racism

None of us—black, white, Latino, or Asian—is immune to the stereotypes that our culture continues to feed us, especially stereotypes about black criminality, black intelligence, or the black work ethic. In general, members of every minority group continue to be measured largely by the degree of our assimilation—how closely speech patterns, dress, or demeanor conform to the dominant white culture—and the more that a minority strays from these external markers, the more he or she is subject to negative assumptions.[1]
—Barack Obama

The language, only the language....It is the thing that black people love so much—the saying of words, holding them on the tongue, experimenting with them, playing with them. It's a love, a passion. Its function is like a preacher's: to make you stand up out of your seat, make you lose yourself and hear yourself. The worst of all possible things that could happen would be to lose that language....It's terrible to think that a child with five different present tenses comes to school to be faced with books that are less than his own language. And then to be told things about his language, which is him, that are sometimes permanently damaging....This is a really cruel fallout of racism.[2]
—Toni Morrison

Over the last few years, we have been contacted by journalists seeking "expert" linguistic opinions on President Obama's speech. Early into Obama's first term, a writer for one of the more progressive Internet news websites asked us if we would comment on the "growing trend" of Black parents wanting their children not to "be like Mike" but rather to "talk like Barack." Or in her words, "to speak standard English." After speaking with her for only a few minutes, we agreed on two facts: One, Barack Obama was indeed a skilled speaker; two, schools continued to fail in their teaching of "standard English" to Black students. Eventually, though, it became clear that she held some pretty strong biases against "African American English." After a little more probing, she finally recognized that what she was secretly hoping for was that "Barack Obama's public speaking abilities [would] influence African Americans to move away from African American English," since this "incorrect" and "unacceptable" way of speaking was "holding them back." When we asked her to consider that it was a helluva thing to have your language thought of as a handicap, she insisted that she didn't necessarily agree with that view, but that she was genuinely concerned about the educational plight of African American students. This well-intentioned insistence on the part of White folks (and many middle-class Black folks) that working-class Black people *need* to change the way they talk so that White America can accept them is troublesome for many reasons, not the least of which are its racist and classist overtones.

First, it is questionable whether or not it was even a "growing trend" that Black parents wanted their children "to speak standard English." Far as we know, Black parents have always wanted their kids to speak "standard English," at least for instrumental purposes like doing well in school or getting a job. Second, it's more complicated than her one-way push toward "standard English" would suggest. In our own work we have found that many parents want their children to be fluent in multiple language varieties, including Black Language and "standard English."[3] Rather than seeking a linguist to endorse her own views, we suggested that she might consider talking to members of the Black communities that we study and participate in. Folks certainly respect President Obama for his mastery of "standard English," but he is more often admired as a linguistic role model for his ability to shift in and out of different ways of speaking.

Third, while this journalist wanted Black Americans to abandon Black Language in an effort to "talk like Barack," the irony is that Barack Obama himself was employing Black Language in an effort to "talk like the people." In other words, unlike this journalist, he recognized Black ways of speaking as valued symbols of identity and solidarity for members of the Black community. From the basketball courts to the campaign trail to the pews of Trinity United Church of Christ and the barbershops of South Side Chicago, Barack regularly switched back and forth between multiple ways of speaking—*without devaluing any of them*. It is in this sense that he serves as a linguistic role model not just for Black Americans but for all Americans.

Y'all Don't Hear Us Though: Recognizing the Complexity and Richness of Black Language

One of our major goals in this book has been to show how we need to *language* race—to think about the linguistic dimensions of race—in order to move the national conversation on race forward. From our analysis of the way Americans describe Barack Obama's language to the *articulate* controversy to the complexities of the "Race Speech" and the "fist bump" fiasco, we have shown throughout this book how Black Language continues to be monitored and maligned in the American public sphere. In this chapter, we shall see how the complexity and richness of Black Language often goes completely unnoticed and is regularly censored in American society. In particular, we see how Black folks' use of Black Language can often lead to misinterpretation and conflict in America's schools and White public spaces. Importantly, we also argue that the critical linguistic perspective that we adopt in this book can and should be taught in schools in order to bring about social change.

While differing rules of language use certainly play a role in Black-White communicative conflicts, that's only half the story. These conflicts often occur in sociopolitical contexts where communities are at odds, not for linguistic reasons but for economic, political, and social ones.[4] Any honest look at Black-White communicative conflicts must take into account the persistent racial tension that exists between communities in the United States and the White cultural hegemony that undergirds it. It's no secret that many White and other Americans still view Black Language through the ideological lens of Black intellectual and moral inferiority—the overtly racist message boards following every single online news story about Black Language can testify to that. Although little acknowledged in these public discussions, what usually lies behind comments like "Black Language is nothing but a lazy, ignorant way of speaking" are racist beliefs about Black people themselves as "lazy" and "ignorant." (Hatin on a particular language is linked to hating its speakers, straight up.)[5]

The sad and twisted irony for linguists, of course, is that those who refer to Black Language as "ignorant" are only revealing their own ignorance of basic linguistic principles. As we stated in chapter 1, Black Language is a linguistic system born out of a Creolization process that merged African and European languages and ways of using them. As the linguistic legacy of the African slave trade, it is oftentimes more complex grammatically and functionally than any other form of American English. This is one of the reasons—aside from America's obsession with anything Black folks say or do—why it's the most studied language variety in the United States. Of course, any sociolinguist coulda told you that, but y'all don't hear us though.

Despite linguists' best efforts to reach the public, most folks reading this book right now are unaware that Black Language is a complex system of structure and use that is distinct from White Mainstream English in the US. While it is true that Black Language shares much of its structure with White Mainstream English, there are many aspects of Black Language syntactic (grammar) and phonological (pronunciation) systems that mark it as distinct from that variety. If we examine syntax alone, sociolinguists have described numerous features of Black Language, such as copula absence (as we saw in Barack Obama's use of "Nah, we Ø straight" for "Nah, we are straight" in chapter 1), invariant *be* for habitual aspect ("He *be* talkin a lot in class," meaning "He usually/regularly/sometimes talks a lot in class") and equatives ("We *be* them Bay boys" for "We are them Bay boys"), *steady* as an intensified continuative ("She *steady* prayin her son come back from Iraq," meaning "She is intensely, consistently and continuously praying her son comes back from Iraq"), stressed *been* to mark remote past ("I *been* told you not to trust them," meaning "I told you a long time ago not to trust them"), *be done* to mark the future or conditional perfect ("By the end of the day, I *be done* collected $600!" meaning "By the end of the day, I will have collected $600!"), aspectual *stay* ("She *stay* up in my business," meaning "She is always getting into my business"), 3rd person singular present tense—*s* absence ("I know who *run* **this** household!" for "I know who *runs* **this** household!"), and possessive—*s* absence ("I'm braidin *Talesha* hair" for "I'm braidin Talesha's hair"). These next features of BL syntax come from Obama's book, *Dreams from My Father*, where he represents the voices of various people in his life: *multiple negation* ("You can't help folks that ain't gonna make it nohow" for "You can't help folks that ain't gonna make it anyhow"), *negative inversion* ("Ain't nothing gonna change" for "Nothing is gonna change"), and generalization of *was* to use with plural and second person subjects ("Tell me we wouldn't be treated different if we was white" for "if we were white"), among several other features.[6]

While most sociolinguists have focused on grammatical and pronunciation patterns of Black Language, many also know that it cannot be defined as merely a checklist of features that are distinct from White Mainstream English.[7] Black Language is not just a set of "deviations" from "the standard"; it is a system in its own right and has been analyzed on its own terms, not just in relation to some "idealized" form of White speech. Aside from having an ever-evolving lexicon, speakers of Black Language may participate in numerous linguistic practices and cultural modes of discourse such as *signifyin* (and *bustin, crackin, cappin* and *dissin*), *playin the dozens, call and response, tonal semantics, battlin* and *entering the cipher*, and the artful use of direct and indirect speech, among others.[8] Black Language, then, refers both to a set of grammatical rules as well as to the way Black folks use language on a day-to-day basis.

While Black Language is not controversial to linguists, racially charged national firestorms over Black Language occur about once every 20 years (with, of course, local fires burnin in between). Who can forget the madness that broke out after "the *King* case" in Ann Arbor, Michigan in 1977, when the lawsuit was filed, to the time of the trial in 1979? Or more recently, during "the Oakland Ebonics controversy" in 1997?[9] As the saying goes, if we don't learn from our history we're destined (and in this case, doomed) to repeat it.

"Inconvenient Truths": Disrupting White Linguistic Hegemony (No Matter How Well-Meaning)

To begin with, we must acknowledge certain inconvenient truths (shout-out to Al Gore) about American society. For us, there is no skirting the fact that American society remains one in which, as Barack Obama put it, "members of every minority group continue to be measured largely by the degree of [their] assimilation—how closely their speech patterns, dress, or demeanor conform to the dominant white culture." The cultural dominance of Whiteness—the fact that White people consider themselves the "standard" by which "Others" are measured—has real and tangible effects on the lives of people of Color.

As folks who study Whiteness argue, Whites can exercise power through overt (obvious) and covert (hidden) racist practices. Covert practices—the focus of this chapter—are of special interest because they often reveal racist ideologies that even the racist may not be aware of. The fact that it is the language and communicative norms of those in power, in any society, that tend to be labeled as "standard," "official," "normal," "appropriate," "respectful," and so on, often goes unrecognized, particularly by the members of the dominating group. In our case, White Mainstream English and White ways of speaking become the invisible—or better, inaudible—norms of what educators and uncritical scholars like to call academic English, the language of school, the language of power, or communicating in academic settings.

The following conversation with a well-meaning high school teacher in the San Francisco Bay Area serves as a good starting point for our discussion of how Black Language (and its speakers) are viewed in America's schools. Below, the teacher is describing the communication goals of the school and the language and communication behavior of her Black students.

As you read, check the key words and phrases that reveal this teacher's language attitudes:

> TEACHER: [We] have a lot of presentation standards, so like this list of, you know, what you *should* be doing when you're having like an oral presentation—like you should speak slowly, speak loudly, speak clearly, make eye contact, use body language, those kinds of things, and it's all written out into a rubric, so when the kids have a presentation, you grade on each element. And so, I mean, in that sense, they've worked with developing communication. I mean, I think the thing that teachers work with, or <u>combat</u> the most...is definitely like issues with <u>standard</u> English versus <u>vernacular</u> English. Um, like, if there was like one of the *few* goals I had this year was to get kids to stop sayin, um, "he was, she was."
>
> ALIM: They was?
>
> T: "They was. We be." Like, those kinds of things and so we spent a lot of time working with that and like recognizing, "Okay, when you're with your friends you can say *whatever you want* but...<u>this is the way it is. I'm sorry, but that's just the way</u>." And they're like, "Well, you know, it doesn't make sense to me. This sounds right." "She was." Like, and that's just what they've been used to and it's just...
>
> A: Well, "she was" is right, right? You mean, like, "They was"?
>
> T: "They was."
>
> A: And "we was" and that kinda thing.
>
> T: Yeah, "we was." Everything is just "was."
>
> A: [Laughter]
>
> T: And like, just trying to help them to be able to differentiate between what's <u>acceptable.</u>....There's a lot of "ain't", "they was," "we ain't not."
>
> A: [Laughter]
>
> T: And <u>they can't codeswitch</u> that well.
>
> A: Uh-huh.
>
> T: Um, and I have to say it's kind of <u>disheartening</u> because like despite *all* <u>that time that's been spent focusing on grammar</u>, like, I don't really see it having helped enormously. Like, if I stop them in class and they're like, you know, "The Europeans, they was really blah-de-blah." and I'd be like, "Oh, they *was*?" And they'd be like, "they were," like they'll correct themselves, but it's not to the point where it's <u>natural.</u>...They're like, "Why does it matter?"

A: "You knew what I said, right?"

T: Yeah...I'm not sure they understand *why* it's necessary.

A: Do you have any other ideas about language at the school, like maybe the way the kids speak to themselves versus they way they speak in class, or do you notice...

T: Well, I mean, of course, they're not gonna be as <u>free</u> as when they're speaking to each other when they're speaking to me. I mean, I guess the only thing is not so much spoken language as it's like unspoken language, like tone, like a lot of attention is paid to like tone and body language, in terms of <u>respect- ful attitudes</u>....For a lot of kids, they don't see the difference. They're like [loud voice and direct speech] "Yeah, I just asked you to give me my grade. Like, what's the big deal?" And I'm like, "You just ordered me. I mean, you talked to me like that." Like, it's like, [loud again] "You didn't give me a grade!" like that, it's very <u>abrasive</u>, but they don't realize that it's abrasive. And so, I mean, it's just like, I guess, teaching them like the nuances of like when you're talking with people, what's <u>appro- priate</u>? Should you be sitting up, or should you be kinda lean- ing over [and she leans in her chair].

A: [Laughter]

T: Like that your body language and your facial features like speak just as loudly if not *more* loudly than what you *actu- ally* say.[10]...I mean, just even bringing awareness to that, like, it's upsetting to them and it's like shocking to them that we'll comment on that, like, <u>maybe their parents let them get away with that and speak to them that way</u> and having to be like, "Hey, you know what, like, maybe your parents let you, but here that's never acceptable."[11] Like, there's just so many—I mean, thinking about it, it's just, it's asking a lot of them to do, not only to speak standard English but to know all these other like smaller nuances that they've never experienced before and never had to think about. Like, it's probably on some level pretty overwhelming to them to have to deal with all of these things at once. Because, I mean, their parents say "they was."

A: Yeah, is there any talk about what they're being expected to do, and what they do ordinarily, in the community, in the home, or anything?

T: Um, I mean, not officially or regularly, but I'll always be like, "I know you might speak this way at home, but in an academic setting, or if you're interviewing for a job, or if you're applying to college, and you talk to someone like that, they will like not even give you the time of day."

A: Do they ever ask why?

T: Yeah, they're just like, you know, "Why?" and I'm like, "I don't know!" [Laughter!] "You know, that's just the way that it is! You have to learn how to play the game guys! I'm sorry."

A: Right, and I can see that being such an inadequate answer for a student who doesn't care about "they was" or "they were," being like, "What's the difference? What's the big deal? Like what's the overall picture?"

T: Right, and I don't know how to provide that.

A: Yeah.

"We Ain't Not": Hearing What's Not Said and Missing What Is

Despite its grammatical complexity, the language of the Black child has consistently been viewed as something to eradicate, even by the most well-meaning teachers. In fact, this particular teacher is genuine about her commitment to seeing as many of her students attend four-year colleges as possible. And when she states, "I have to say it's kind of disheartening because like despite *all* that time that's been spent focusing on grammar, like, I don't really see it having helped enormously," one gets the sense that she is actually disheartened and saddened by her lack of results.

What teachers like this one are probably not aware of is how their attitudes and approaches to Black Language uphold White cultural and linguistic hegemony. Let's take a minute to break it down. One, it is revealing that the teacher describes the language of her Black students as the thing that teachers "*combat* the most." Her attempt to stamp out the language patterns of her Black students has been "one of the *few goals*" she has had throughout that academic year. Two, the teacher not only works to eradicate the language patterns of her Black students but responds negatively to what she calls "unspoken language," or the students' "tone." Black students and their ways of speaking are described with adjectives like *abrasive* and not *respectful*.[12]

Three, as many of you probably noticed, the teacher points out her students' failure to speak "standard English," while failing to realize that her own speech variety—which some would label as White California Valley Girl Talk—is not exactly what you would call "standard."[13] The teacher also fails to make several linguistic distinctions in the speech of the students, implying that Black Language has a random system of negation ("we ain't not" is actually not found in Black Language or any other language variety in the United States) and erroneously pointing out "he was" and "she was" as use of incorrect Black Language. Further, she's also not aware of the stylistic sensitivity in the use of *was* and *were*. When the teacher says, rather exasperatedly, "Everything is just 'was,'" she is not hearing the subtle stylistic alternation of *was* and *were* that Black Language speakers employ as they move through different contexts and situations.

Somehow, despite the vitality of Black Language, teachers continue hearing what's not said and missing what is. After years of workin on the frontlines of education, as teachers and as teacher-researchers from Detroit to Philly to the San Francisco Bay Area, there's "one thing that we know for sure" (word to Oprah): Teachers' language attitudes have remained remarkably consistent over the last several decades, particularly in terms of the language of their Black students. By no means is this teacher alone in her biases.

"Cuz We Like It!": Black Linguistic Flexibility and Creativity

Contrary to the teacher's comments that her Black students could not "codeswitch" (we use the term *styleshift*)—that is, shift in and out of different ways of speaking—our sociolinguistic research with youth at this same school demonstrates clearly that Black youth possess a wide range of linguistic styles. These results are outlined in great detail in Alim's *You Know My Steez: An Ethnographic and Sociolinguistic Study of Styleshifting in a Black American Speech Community*.[14] Like all speakers, Black youth vary their speech style based on factors like topic, age, situation, and so on. But they also vary their speech based on who they're speaking to, particularly in terms of the person's race, gender, and their cultural knowledge (familiarity with Hip Hop, in particular).

Furthermore, while many youth can learn "standard English" grammar, they resist the constant and unrelenting imposition of White linguistic norms by their teachers. It's one thing to learn grammar rules but quite another to be rewarded for "sounding White" (as if there's something inherently wrong with "sounding Black"). These youth grew up in speech communities where folks are, as Toni Morrison put it, in love with "the saying of words, holding them on the tongue, experimenting with them, playing with them." So, rather than take their teachers and other White folks for their linguistic role models, they choose folks who they see as more linguistically creative. They select speakers who, rather than follow a fixed set of rules, know the rules well enough to bend them in ways that are pleasing to them. Take this example from three youth at the well-meaning teacher's school:

> LATASHA: Yeah, like the way I talk to my teacher ain't the same
> way I talk with the 3L Click.
> ALIM: 3L Click? What's that?
> L: All of our names begin with "L," so we named our click after
> that, the 3L Click. It's me, LaToya, and Lamar.
> A: And how is the way y'all talk different from the way you talk
> to the teacher?
> L: Well, it's like, you know that rapper, Nelly?
> A: Yeah, yeah.
> L: How he say everything like "urrrr," like for "here" he'll be like
> "hurrrr"?
> A: Yeah! [Laughing] "I ain't from round hurrrr!"
> L: [Laughing] That's how we try to talk!
> A: Why, though?!
> L: Cuz we like it!

When Latasha's linguistic role models, Nelly and the St. Lunatics, bust onto the Hip Hop scene, their language was a major part of their popularity. They often emphasized words that rhymed with "urrrr" to highlight a well-known (and sometimes stigmatized) aspect of southern/south midland pronunciation. As we see from Latasha's comments, she and her northern California-based 3L Click borrow this phonological feature of Black Language to play with different regional and linguistic identities. Although teachers may not recognize it, Black youth are often more interested in exploiting differences between "standard English" and "Black Language"—as well as interregional differences in Black Language styles—than they are with simply mimicking White ways of speaking.

In addition to preferring a more fluid, flexible approach to linguistic structure, youth who grow up in Black speech communities also appreciate the verbal art that's involved in numerous language games. Language is not just merely a means of communication; its use is meant to "make you stand up out of your seat, make you lose yourself and hear yourself." Students at the well-meaning teacher's school often engage in various verbal games, such as *battlin* and *hush mode*. *Battlin* is a form of Black verbal dueling associated with Hip Hop Culture and the verbal art of improvisational rhyming. *Hush mode* is a game associated mostly closely with Black girls' interaction, argumentation, and play. In battlin, the object is to outsmart your opponent through linguistic wit and creativity, while in hush mode the goal is to leave your opponent dumbfounded and speechless. Both games highlight the value placed on verbal creativity and competition in the Black speech community.[15]

Unfortunately, teachers who are not familiar with Black Culture and Language often misunderstand these linguistic practices. For example, while Black youth place extreme value on the verbal inventiveness and competition involved in battlin, teachers broke up the biggest rhyme battle in the school because, as one student relayed, "Whenever they see a group of Black folks they automatically think it's a fight!" One teacher described the event in these words, "Whatever they were doing, it wasn't appropriate on school grounds." Rather than capitalizing on the skills displayed in these improvisational verbal exchanges, the teachers viewed these Black linguistic competitions as *violence*. This misinterpretation is particularly poignant when one considers that the youth themselves define battlin as "taking the place of actual fights." Rather than a physical fight, students gain status in their peer group by exchanging blows in a game of verbal oneupsmanship.

The stylistic flexibility of Black youth, their various verbal art genres, and the pleasure some derive from pushing the envelope of the English language could fill—have filled—volumes. Rather than interpreting Black language behavior through the lens of Black inferiority, ignorance, or violence, these creative language practices should be utilized for educational purposes. There is a growing community of language and literacy scholars working to connect the verbal skills that Black youth display outside the classroom with the verbal skills required inside the classroom.[16] Yet, it's not only that well-meaning teachers are unaware of these Black linguistic practices. They also have no way to critically engage them (and much of the scholarship is unhelpful on that point). This places teachers in a tough situation. In the case of our teacher, despite loving her students and genuinely wanting the best for them, she continues to feel as if she has failed them. Or as one teacher put it, capturing the frustration shared by many, "I feel like I'm banging my head against the wall with this standard English thing." When faced with difficult questions, they are left with unsatisfying retorts like, "I know you talk this way at home, but in an academic setting, or if you're interviewing for a job, or if you're applying to college, and you talk to someone like that, they will like not even give you the time of day."

Sensing that this might be an inadequate answer for her more critical students, we asked if her students ever push her to explain why particular varieties are associated with power, prestige, and upward mobility while their variety is not. The teacher's answer to them is a frustrated and apologetic "I don't know! You know, that's just the way it is! You have to learn how to play the game guys! I'm sorry." Unfortunately, we've been stuck in that same sorry place for decades (at least since the push in the 1960s for racial integration when Black Language began to be seen as a "problem"). Unless we come up with better answers, students will continue to resist the imposition of what are essentially White ways of speaking. Teachers' traditional focus on grammar—without a critical examination of the social, cultural, and political forces at play in language use—will continue to fall short of the mark. In terms of helping her students think more critically about language, she concludes by admitting that she honestly does not know "how to provide that."

So, how can we help teachers provide answers to youths' critical questions about language? How can we help teachers move away from eradicating their students' language to recognizing, maintaining, and building on the skills that they bring with them to the classroom? In the remainder of this chapter, we outline one example of a critical linguistic approach to language education. This approach addresses the difficult race and class tensions around language by confronting them head on. Rather than checking students' language at the door, we view it as a rich and complex linguistic system, one that should be part of any approach to critical language education.

Studying What Gets "Checked at the Door": A Critical Linguistic Approach to Language Education

Rather then rejecting the language of students' families and communities, a critical linguistic approach connects meaningfully with youth by viewing local cultures and language practices as powerful resources for learning. In the case of this particular high school, the dominant youth culture was heavily influenced by Hip Hop Culture, music, and language, as might be the case in other majority-minority communities around the United States. Of course, if critical approaches are gonna be effective and relevant, they must be continuously adapted to reflect youths' social worlds (Hip Hop or not).

DEVELOPING AN AWARENESS OF SOCIOLINGUISTIC VARIATION

"Real Talk," in the language of Hip Hop, is an expression that builds on what generations of Black Americans have referred to as "straight talk." This approach borrows the phrase "Real Talk" to create a new way of thinking about language in educational contexts. It utilizes "Real Talk" (naturally occurring conversations) to teach youth explicitly about the sociolinguistic variation that they manipulate on a regular basis. The project begins with the sociolinguistic analysis of a conversation with one of the local area's best known street Hip Hop artists, JT the Bigga Figga. The class exercise begins by listening to an audiotaped interview, and copies of the tape are then distributed to the students, each of whom has his or her own tape recorder. They are instructed to transcribe the first small portion of the tape *exactly* as they hear it. What they then find out as a class is that they have each produced a unique transcript of the same speech sample. Invariably, some youth will "standardize" the speech samples, and others will "vernacularize" them. As we search for differences between our transcriptions, they begin to notice sociolinguistic patterns in the rapper's speech (e.g., "In the first sentence he said, 'He run everything,' and then later he said, 'He runs everything.'"). We take this one feature of the rapper's speech (third-person singular—*s* variability) and conduct a sociolinguistic analysis of his language, which leads to a larger understanding of the structure and systematicity of spoken language.

LANGUAGE LEARNING THROUGH REFLEXIVE, ETHNOGRAPHIC ANALYSES

After learning about the systematicity of spoken speech and that sociolinguistic variation refers to the variable frequencies of certain features within a linguistic system, we introduce the concept of variation in terms of language use, or ways of speaking. The "Language in My Life" project begins by introducing youth to Dell Hymes's theory[17] of the ethnography of speaking and ends with student-conducted, reflexive, ethnographic analyses of their own speech behavior. The goal is for them to answer the question: How do I use language in my life? They are given an ethnography of speaking reference sheet that outlines basic concepts in this area, such as speech situation, speech event, and speech act, as levels of analysis in a communicative encounter.

ETHNOGRAPHY OF COMMUNICATION

The ethnography of communication is the scientific study of a culture and their communication patterns. Ethnographers of communication seek to understand a culture through a detailed study and description of their language and communication behavior.

- *SPEECH SITUATION*—The largest level of analysis. The social occasion in which speech may occur (for example, lunchtime in the cafeteria; group work in class; birthday party; Hip Hop concert)

- *SPEECH EVENT*—During a speech situation, you will see/hear many speech events (for example; a Hip Hop concert is a speech situation, and a backstage interview with the artist—Jay-Z or Kanye West or Nicki Minaj—is a speech event). The speech event is a smaller layer of analysis that occurs inside the speech situation.
- *SPEECH ACT*—Each action of speech inside of a speech event. This is the smallest layer of analysis (for example, during the backstage interview with Lil Wayne, we might start off by greeting each other—"Wassup, Weezy?"—that greeting is a speech act). In the middle of the interview, he might tell me a joke. That joke is also a speech act (greetings, commands, questions, jokes, etc.).

Students are then presented with another sample of Real Talk—this time with New Orleans rapper Juvenile (in order to use a speaker who is not from their local community)—and are guided through an ethnography of speaking analysis of an interview, which they learn is a speech event. A small sample from the interview is used to create a worksheet:

Interview with Juvenile
J = Juvenile
A = Alim

A: Wassup, Juve?
J: Wassup, woadie?
A: What's goin on?
J: Chillin, you know me. I'm chillin.
A: How would you describe the last year, year and half for you?
J: Spectacular, man! I've been blessed, you know.
A: It's a blessing, ha?
J: Workin real hard, you know. Just a lot of things. A lot of things have been goin on and so far everything's been goin right. I've been makin the right moves.

They are encouraged to notate the transcript in detail. Youth are usually adept at identifying a certain level of informality (through the use of "slang" like "wassup," "chillin," "you know what I'm saying?") as well as regionalisms in the New Orleans–based rapper's speech (such as "woadie," which can mean, "man," "homie," etc.; "It's all gravy!" for the commonly used "It's all good"), and Alim's use of "ha?" as an attempt to build rapport with (or "be cool with") the rapper by using one of his most famous expressions.

Table 6.1 **Ethnogography of Communication**

S	Setting/scene	Physical circumstances; your definition of an occasion
P	Participants	Speaker/sender/addressor/hearer/receiver/ audience/addressee
E	Ends	Purposes and goals; outcomes
A	Act sequence	Message form and content
K	Key	Tone, manner
I	Instrumentalities	Channel (verbal, nonverbal); forms of speech drawn from communicative repertoire
N	Norms of interaction and interpretation	Specific properties attached to speaking; interpretation of norms within a culture
G	Genre	Textual categories

But, of course, they are told, you can only gather so much information by reading a transcript—you have to "go out into the field." After introducing the theory and doing a hands-on ethnography of speaking analysis, we wanted them to be able to analyze their own communication behavior in their everyday environments, from their actual lived experiences. After challenging them and asking if they thought that they could do an ethnography of speaking with their own language data, we introduced the "Language in My Life" project. The students were instructed to analyze their own communication behavior as it shifted across contexts and situations. As ethnographers, they were charged with carrying an ethnography notebook and documenting their communicative encounters. The notebook consisted of grids that were to be filled in throughout the day. An example from an eighth grader follows.

Language in My Life

Immediately, this project validates the language practices that youth engage in outside the classroom—for example, rappin or battlin—by allowing them to see their speech behavior taken as a subject of analysis. Further, after collecting data on their own speech, they gain a much higher level of metalinguistic awareness (speaking of themselves as style-shifters possessing multiple languages and a range of speech styles). This allows them to not only better understand the abstract theory of speaking but also to better understand the linguistic landscape of their social worlds. Again, these worlds are not marginalized inside the classroom or

Table 6.2 **Language in My Life**

Date:	Time:
November 22	Early in the morning, like, 7 am

Mode of Language (reading, speaking, writing, listening, etc.):

Speaking, listening, rappin

Name of Language:

Mostly in slang, or Ebonics, but sometimes in standard English because my aunt was there and she talks like that.

Context (who's involved, where is it happening, what's happening):

I was sitting in the kitchen with my dad, eating cereal before I had to go to school. Before that, I was reading this rap I had wrote over and over again in my room, so I wanted to rap it for my dad. I did, and he was feelin it! He said the he could do a better one, so he tried, but it wasn't better. He called my mom and aunt over from the other room and told me to rap for them and I did. My mom was like, "Wow, Lamar! You bad!" I said, "I know." (Being cocky, as I am!) And my aunt said, "What a talented young man." My dad said he was gonna battle me after school.

Comments on the style(s) of language used:

The language with me and my dad was mostly in slang, or Ebonics, as I like to call it. Nah, I mostly say slang. And my mom, too. But my aunt, she talks standard English. I don't know, maybe because she's older.

left outside the door, but they are seen as valuable cultural and linguistic spaces for learning.

THE ETHNOGRAPHY OF CULTURE AND COMMUNICATION

After the students have learned about and conducted sociolinguistic and ethnographic analyses of their own speech behavior, we encourage them to "go back into the field" and expand their focus. This time, they are to investigate their social worlds through an analysis of their peer group and peer culture. One of the primary ways to accomplish this is through the study of localized lexical usage (or local words, phrases, and slang). We begin by raising youths' awareness of the variety of lexical innovations within Hip Hop Culture (of course, most are already aware of this, since they actively participate in these innovations). To pique their interest as well as to localize the dialogue by focusing on the Bay Area, we provide a specific example of a research interview about the language of Hip Hop Culture with JT the Bigga Figga. In the following short excerpt, JT provides what ethnographers call an emic (insider's) view of Hip Hop's evolving lexicon.

J = JT the Bigga Figga

A = ALIM

A: What does it mean to be certified with game?

J: **Certified** mean you official....How it got incorporated into our language in the streets, from my first experience with the word in the streets, was from **mobb** cars. And the mobb cars is Caprice Classics or Chevy Impalas '87 to '90. Them three years right there. And if you get a mobb car and it don't have a certain seal on it, it's not certified. So when dudes buy the car, it have to have that seal. You want yo car to be certified, you know what I'm saying? And that's just like if you into the collector's cars and if it don't have the same steering wheel or if you change something it's not certified no more. So it's original, you know what I'm saying? *And another meaning for certified meaning that you **official**....*If I say, "Man, Alim's gon handle it. If he said he gon handle it, he certified, man. He gon handle it." So somebody who word is good.

Upon reading the transcript aloud as a class, students immediately respond by critiquing phrases, calling some out of date, providing new or similar phrases, comparing with other regional phrases, and so on. This excitement is channeled into further training in ethnographic methods. For this particular case, we borrow from the introduction to linguist Geneva Smitherman's *Black Talk: Words and Phrases from the Hood to the Amen Corner.*[10] The following worksheet translates academic language into a familiar Hip Hop–stylized way of writing (again, validating multiple forms of language).

ETHNOGRAPHIC METHODS USED BY GENEVA SMITHERMAN TO WRITE *Black Talk: Words and Phrases from the Hood to the Amen Corner.* We should use all of these methods in writing our own book (by the way, we need a title—what's up?)

(1) Written language surveys and word lists completed by Black people. She made up surveys and gave them to some folks that she knew and many that she didn't and asked them to fill out the surveys. What would a survey look like?

(2) Songs and hit recordings. Basically, she blocked out 30 minutes or so in her daily schedule to play some of her CDs and tapes. As the songs played, she listened really closely for any unique words and phrases. Most of us listen to music way more than 30 minutes a day, right? I know I do.

(3) Radio shows. My radio stay locked on KMEL, so this one should be easy. Whether you listen to Chuy in the morning or Big Von in the evening for the 7 O'Clock Drop, you'll hear tons of slang words and phrases.

(4) Movies and television. You can block out 30 minutes to watch your favorite TV show (*106th and Park, Rap City,* BET, whatever) and catch all the slang that's being used. If you happen to be watching a movie that day or that week, pay extra attention to the slang. You can probably get hecka words from one movie.

(5) Collecting words from community bulletins, leaflets, magazines, announcements, or other written material. Can you think of any that you might use?

(6) Face-to-face interviews. You can ask people if they know any slang words or phrases that you can include for your slang dictionary. Sometimes we can't think of all of these terms by ourselves, right, so we need some help from our people. How would you ask somebody to help you? Who would you ask?

(7) Eavesdropping. I ain't gotta tell y'all about that one. Mmm-hmmmm...

(8) Participant observation. Participant observation means that you are not only observing the event or the scene, but you are also actively participating in it. In what events or scenes do you hear lots of slang talk? I bet you the talk at lunchtime is full of slang words and phrases, huh? This is your first official ethnographic assignment. You are to be a participant observer at lunch tomorrow (Thursday) and at least one other day before we meet again next Wednesday. Keep your lil notebooks handy so you can jot words down as you hear them. I know some of you are dying to ask, so yeah, you can combine this with eavesdropping, but if you get popped in the eye, I'ma be like Silkk the Shokker and say, "OOOOOH, it ain't my fault!"

The students are given further training in these methods as we move through the unit. They are charged with the immense responsibility of archiving Black Culture—in this case, Hip Hop Culture—through words. Going above and beyond what is often expected of them, they contribute to a body of scholarly literature on their own speech variety (an object of study that has historically been dominated by White researchers).[19]

MOVING FROM INDIVIDUAL TO STRUCTURAL UNDERSTANDINGS OF LINGUISTIC RACISM

Our goal is to develop an approach that does more than provide students with the tools to analyze language and to theorize its use in their local, social worlds. Beyond this, a critical approach helps youth think about complex issues of language and power. Many of our youth, particularly those who speak marginalized language varieties, are already acutely aware of the fact that people can use language to discriminate against "Others"; they and their families are often those "Others." To begin with, students (and teachers) can learn directly about the relationship between language and discrimination in American society. A critical approach should begin with teaching about the diverse range of language varieties spoken in the United States so as to combat linguistic prejudices as well as internalized feelings of linguistic shame. For example, linguists have helped produce documentary films that can serve as excellent resources for youth who are developing ideas about the concept of linguistic discrimination. Students can share their opinions about the diverse issues and perspectives raised in the film. For instance, one class was given this handout during a viewing of the film *American Tongues* (1986), an effort by sociolinguists to communicate the fundamental principles of language to a wider audience:

AMERICAN TONGUES

Learning all about American English language varieties

Opening Exercise:

Define these unique words from around the country:
Cabinet, Gumband, Pau hana, Jambalaya, Antigogglin, Snicklefritz, Schlep

Opening Questions:

What did you get out of this video?
What was the most interesting thing you learned?
What was the funniest part of the movie?
How would you relate this video to your life and the way that you talk?

Discuss these quotes from the movie with a partner. What's *your* opinion about the issues that these people bring up?

"It's easy to figure out which dialects are more desirable and which dialects are less desirable—just look at which *groups* are more desirable and which groups are less desirable. We tend to think of urban as better than rural. We tend to think of middle class as better than working class. We tend to think of White as better than Black. So if you're a member of one of those stigmatized groups, then the way you talk will also be stigmatized. This goes on *all* over the United States—in every community."

"[The way we talk] it's ignorant. It *sounds* ignorant. Oh, come on, these people hear this stuff they're gonna say, 'What the heck is that garbage coming out of their mouth?!' That's gonna happen. And they're gonna say, 'Look at them two beautiful girls. If they'd shut their mouths they'd be great.'"

"I think that the majority of White America, you know, does not accept Black English. But not because of the language itself, because of the people who speak it, which is racism."

"Even though Black English is mocked and looked down upon by many White people, a lot of Black Americans use it to relate to one another every day. And those who don't use it in their home communities run the risk of becoming outsiders."

"I have two sons, one's 12 and one's 15. And when I hear them talk, I say, 'God, am I raising two White boys here?' And I don't mean that to be negative in respect to White males, but I don't want my boys sounding like White males!"

"Black or White, Texas or New York, few people talk the same way all the time. There's one way of talking with friends and family, and another way for business or school. We switch back and forth because we know there's no one way that works in every situation."

"There's a feeling that anybody who talks like that can't be very smart. And if I don't talk like that I must be smarter than you, and I don't want anybody who's not very smart representing my company. And those kinds of folks tend to have a hard time getting a job. So their speech is very, very important."

Once students have shared their opinions and stories, the goal should be to focus on how these examples of *individual prejudice* (which students can easily point out) lead to *structural discrimination* (which is a little more difficult but embedded in the responses that relate to "representing a company" or "getting a job," etc.). While most American sociolinguists and teacher educators do a good job showing America's linguistic diversity, they often fail to show how this diversity is linked to America's social inequalities. In other words, most of our suggestions about pedagogy on language attitudes and awareness tend to discuss linguistic stigmatization in terms of individual prejudices rather than as discrimination that is part and parcel of the sociostructural fabric of society. This limited understanding is suspect because it serves the needs of those who currently benefit the most from language discrimination while ignoring the needs of those who suffer from it.

To serve the needs of our youth, we need to incorporate the full range of what linguists know about the relationship between language, power, and discrimination. A great way to do this is to introduce the sociolinguistic research that addresses *linguistic profiling*, which has been described by linguist John Baugh as the auditory equivalent of racial profiling.[20] This type of profiling, usually occurring over the phone, can prevent potential home owners from moving into certain neighborhoods, for example. Students are introduced to this compelling research by watching a video of ABC cable news coverage of the Linguistic Profiling Project. The research findings, which show that the majority of Americans can make correct racial inferences based on the pronunciation of the single word *hello*, inspire a whole unit of activities designed to investigate this phenomenon. Youth are also encouraged to collect data about linguistic profiling in their communities. The following worksheet accompanies the video and includes various short assignments:

LINGUISTIC PROFILING WORKSHEET

What is *linguistic profiling*? What is the relationship between linguistic profiling and racial profiling? Do you think you can tell whether somebody "sounds White" or "sounds Mexican" or "sounds Black" or "sounds Indian" or "sounds Arab" or any other race or ethnic group? Today we are going to talk about the relationship between race, language, profiling, and discrimination. We are about to watch a news story that ran on ABC News with Peter Jennings. This news segment is a case of what we call, "Applied Linguistics"—i.e. an area of research where linguists apply their scientific knowledge about language to real-life situations that affect everyday people—like you and me.

FREEWRITE First impressions. What do *you* think?

OUTLINE OF NEWS STORY

8:52—Language as a criterion for discrimination. Linguistic profiling → racial profiling.

9:32—James Johnson's housing application, his experience and his experiment. Fair housing agency experiment.

10:32—John Baugh, Stanford University professor—one simple word, "Hello." Linguistics and the law.

11:24—Linguistic Profiling experiment at Stanford in Alim's Hip Hop class. Percentages of correct answers. Is this reality?

SUMMARY PARAGRAPH

[Open space for students' summary of the research presented in the news story]

ASSIGNMENT

Let's design a series of interview questions. In the coming week, interview 3 or 4 people (or more, if you choose)—they can be

> family or friends—about linguistic profiling and record or take
> notes about their responses. Compile your responses and sub-
> mit for next week.

It is at this point in the developmental progression of the unit that youth
begin to explore the relationships between language and structural discrimination. They also begin to see how the struggles of their particular
groups relate to the struggles of other groups. For example, while one
Black American student interviewed his aunt and discovered that she had
a very painful experience of discrimination in the housing market (she
would often be told that units were "still open" only to be turned away
upon arrival), a Latina student shared a narrative from her father in which
he was fired from his truck-driving job because of "phony" charges of tar-
diness. In the first case, the Black American aunt spoke "proper" on the
phone, but she was still often denied access to housing based on the visual
representation of her race ("when they saw I was a Black person"). And in
the second case, the Latino father spoke English as a second language and
believed that he was fired not because of his job performance (or his race)
but his "problem with English," as he put it.

These narratives offer opportunities for our youth to explore and critically
interrogate the links between language, discrimination, and power. Further,
after being made aware of how linguistic profiling affects their communities, they are motivated to engage in community activism around issues of
linguistic discrimination. Youth are not only thinking critically about language, but they are also putting their knowledge to work for their communities by developing consciousness-raising campaigns. These campaigns help
provide resources for community members to engage in the transformation of their neighborhoods. From a critical perspective, dissatisfaction and
awareness aren't enough; action is needed to bring about social change.

At this point, it should be obvious that critical approaches take students
well beyond the elementary skills required for the memorization and production of certain grammatical rules in the traditional language classroom. These
traditional approaches expect very little from Black youth. Teachers continue
to read Black students' resistance to White linguistic norming as a sign of their
inability to grasp "standard English." As our well-meaning teacher reflected:

> I mean, thinking about it, it's just, it's asking a lot of them to do,
> not only to speak standard English but to know all these other
> like smaller nuances that they've never experienced before and
> never had to think about. Like, it's probably on some level pretty
> overwhelming to them to have to deal with all of these things
> at once.

While the blame game is not a useful strategy, teachers often use these infantilizing discourses to shift blame from themselves onto their students. But as we've seen, Black youth manipulate language in a number of inventive ways, engage in creative exploitation of linguistic differences, and participate in complex verbal games that require high-level improvisational skills. A critical approach expects much more from students, going beyond traditional grammar lessons to teach students how to analyze and manipulate language in their social worlds (why reserve this knowledge for privileged university students?). Finally, it teaches students that we must do more than study the relationships between language, racism, and power—we must do what we can to alter them.

"That's Just the Way the World Works": Exposing the Covert Racism of Cultural Scripts

Undoubtedly, some readers of this chapter are still stuck on the "standard English" question. Others are still trying to make sense of the conversations with the well-meaning teacher and the well-meaning journalist (the one who asked about Obama's speech). While these folks are obviously not dressed in white hoods, foaming at the mouth, and shouting out racial slurs (a limited depiction of racists, to be sure), a critical examination of their beliefs gets at the subtle workings of racism through language. At the same time, we can't stop there. To be honest, we must turn this critical examination inward on sociolinguistics and teacher education to figure out how we may be complicit in this type of covert racism.

To focus on the teacher, how did she arrive at the belief that her students absolutely needed to learn "standard English" in order to succeed in society? First, while teachers are some of the most hardworking members of society and often seem to have supernatural stores of energy, they do not have superhuman abilities. Teachers, like the rest of us, are not immune to the stereotypical language beliefs that are at the core of what Americans "know" about language (rather than poking fun at the teacher, we need to look at ourselves in the mirror to see our own language prejudices—Real Talk). Still, it is imperative to ask how she might have arrived at the following conclusion:

> I know you might speak this way at home, but in an academic setting, or if you're interviewing for a job, or if you're applying to college, and you talk to someone like that, they will like not even give you the time of day...that's just the way that it is! You have to learn how to play the game guys! I'm sorry.

Let's begin by taking a closer look at the teacher's training. This teacher was enrolled in a teacher education program at the elite, private university located within a few miles of her high school. In one three-week course, she learned about Black Language, linguistic diversity, language attitudes, and teaching strategies for linguistically and culturally diverse students. The course clearly didn't have a lasting impact in this particular case. In fact, we believe that the course may have been at least partly responsible for perpetuating the discriminatory language attitudes that it was meant to counter. In the course, the instructor uncritically used the documentary film *American Tongues* (recall the worksheet included in this chapter) as a central text.[21] The film, although somewhat outdated, is ideal for exposing teachers to linguistic diversity in the United States. It not only introduces viewers to the concept of language variation, but it also provides several examples of linguistic, racial, and regional discrimination. After discussing Black Language at length, the film cuts to an interview with one of the foremost sociolinguists in the field, who concludes, somewhat apologetically:

> Let's face it. There are certain consequences for not speaking a standard dialect. For example...you may have certain limitations in terms of the job market. If you don't wanna deal with the negatives, it may be very helpful to learn a standard dialect for certain situations. It may not be fair, but that's the way it is. (Walt Wolfram, principal advisor to the film)

While this film was intended to communicate some of sociolinguistics's fundamental principles to a wider audience, it also communicated some of the field's fundamental biases (check out how this well-meaning sociolinguist's comments map almost word-for-word onto the well-meaning teacher's comments). It is clear from this example that the American sociolinguistic establishment, by and large, has been complicit in speaking from a position of privilege. This position incorrectly depicts speaking a "standard dialect" as a simple question of individual choice. But as we know, White America doesn't just ask Black people to learn a few grammatical rules. Rather it demands that they act, talk, and sound like Whites if they are to enter the "mainstream." Sociolinguists, like teachers, it turns out, are clearly not immune to discriminatory language attitudes nor do we always recognize our own subtle forms of racism.[22]

Rather than insisting on the need for working-class Blacks (and other groups pushed to the margins of American society) to speak "standard English," we need to expose widely repeated American cultural scripts for the myths that they are. We also need to call out approaches that merely pay lip service to the "systematic" and "highly verbal" linguistic practices of Blacks, while turning around and telling Black people to they face that Black ways of speaking ain't good enough for any important or intellectual business. The scripts that claim that "certain languages are appropriate for certain contexts" or "of course, all languages are equal, but we need to teach Black students the 'discourses of power'" don't change a damn thing. Actually they do a terrific job of maintaining the status quo. These approaches keep the position of the dominant culture intact, not because Blacks believe in its superiority, but because Blacks—and Whites—tacitly accept the notion that the White middle class either cannot or will not accept Black Language.

How many countless White folks have you heard say, "Well, fair or unfair, that's just the way the world works"? Black folks got their version of this too: "It's their world and we're just in it—so as long as they're in charge, we gotta play by their rules." Rather than viewing these statements as an end point, we take them as the starting point for the critical discussion that we need to be having. Instead of agreeing for one reason or another that we "absolutely have" to provide "these students" with "standard English," we might ask: How are we all involved in perpetuating the myth of a "standard" and that it is somehow better, more intelligent, more appropriate, more important, and so on than other varieties? Why do we elevate one particular variety over all others, even when all of our linguistic knowledge tells us that "all languages are equal in linguistic terms"? Why does the "standard" continue to be imposed despite the fact that what we have for a "standard English" in the United States is nothing short of the imposition of White, middle-class language norms? How and why do we continue to measure the worth of People of Color largely by their level of assimilation into dominant White culture? (See Barack Obama's quote at the opening of this chapter.) These questions are especially important since this hegemonic move is used to grant opportunities to Whites while denying opportunities to as many others as possible (including poor, marginal Whites).

Challenging Hegemony: Moving from "Playing the Game" to "Changing the Game"

Asking different kinds of questions and developing different kinds of approaches, we can stop apologizing for "the way things are" and begin helping our students imagine the way things can be. By asking different kinds of questions, we can begin to think differently—that is critically—about the relationships between language, racism, education, and power in society. By asking different kinds of questions, we can stop silently legitimizing "standard English" and tacitly standardizing "Whiteness."[23] In leaving out critical issues of race and class, students inevitably begin to view their culture and language as unfit for school or any other context linked to status and prestige. If we continue to uncritically present "standard English" as somehow better than other varieties of English, we are implicitly devaluing these varieties and the people who speak them. As a result, many students not only come to see their *language* as having a lesser role in places like schools, but more dangerously, they start to see *themselves* in that light too.[24] This logical conclusion would be, in Morrison's words, the "really cruel fallout of racism."

Rather than falling back on uncritical conformist and assimilationist models of schooling, perhaps we can learn from other models of language education from multilingual democracies around the world. What might the research in Sweden, Norway, and other countries which shows that "recognizing the legitimacy of other varieties of a language" improves "standard" language learning have to offer us here in the United States? What about South Africa's policy of 11 official languages, enshrined in its Constitution, which elevates its African languages to the status of English and Afrikaans? What can Americans learn from Perú's innovative new multilingual law that calls for the preservation and use of its indigenous languages? In this so-called developing democracy, bilingual, intercultural education is now the law of the land: All children who speak an indigenous language as their first language have the right to be educated in Spanish and in their first language at all levels of the education system. There are other more egalitarian, democratic models out there.[25] Withholding opportunities from all folks who don't talk like you ain't "the way the world works"—it's the way hegemony works.

Our students and teachers need to be made aware of the different ways that the game's being played. Rather than creating cultural and linguistic clones, schooling should be about the serious business of educating young minds to deal with (and, when necessary, on) a society of power politics and incredible complexity. Schooling should not be about convincing students to play the game but, rather, about helping them understand how the game's been rigged and, more importantly, how they can work to change it. Real Talk.

NOTES

1. See Barack Obama's *Audacity of Hope: Thoughts on Reclaiming the American Dream* (New York: Crown Publishers, 2006, 235).
2. Check out the full interview with Toni Morrison (by Thomas LeClaire) in *The New Republic*, March 21, 1981, pages 25–29. Shoutout to John R. Rickford and Russell J. Rickford for bringing this to our attention in your book, *Spoken Soul: The Story of Black English* (New York: John Wiley & Sons, 2000).

3. As one middle-class Black father famously put it in the 1986 documentary film *American Tongues*, "And I don't mean that to be negative in respect to White males, but I don't want my boys sounding like White males!" For him and others, it's important that their children keep their cultural and linguistic heritage intact even as they master other ways of speaking and being in the world.

4. Linguist Rosina Lippi-Green makes this point forcefully in her book, *English with an Accent: Language, Ideology, and Discrimination in the United States* (New York: Routledge, 1997). This now classic work has just been updated and republished in 2012.

5. As linguist and anthropologist Arthur Spears wrote in the introduction to *Race and Ideology: Language, Symbolism, and Popular Culture* (Detroit: Wayne State University Press, 1999, 12–13): "The more recent neoracism is subtler, in most cases claiming a cultural basis for what is seen as low achievement by people of color....Neoracism is still racism, in that it functions to maintain racial hierarchies of oppression. Its new ideological focus on culture has the same function, and provides a vast new field to mine for supposed causes of lower achievement of groups of color based on dysfunctional attitudes, values, and orientations." In our case, folks claim that their attacks on Black Culture through its language are not racist because they don't hate "all Black people." So, what, you only hate the ones that don't conform to your norms? You're neo, baby. Check yourself.

6. We wasn't playin (that's generalization of *was* to plural subjects) when we said that Black Language was *the* most studied variety by sociolinguists. These linguistic features and more can be found in William Labov's "Contraction, Deletion, and Inherent Variability of the English Copula," *Language* 45(1969): 715–762; William Labov's *Language in the Inner City: Studies in the Black English Vernacular*, Philadelphia: University of Pennsylvania Press, 1972; Ralph Fasold's *Tense Marking in Black English: A Linguistic and Social Analysis*, Washington, DC: Center for Applied Linguistics, 1972; H. Samy Alim's *You Know My Steez: An Ethnographic and Sociolinguistic Study of Styleshifting in a Black American Speech Community*, Durham, NC: Duke University Press, 2004; John Baugh's *Black Street Speech: Its History, Structure, and Survival*, Austin: University of Texas Press, 1983; Peter Sells, John Rickford, and Thomas Wasow's "Negative Inversion in African American Vernacular English," *Natural Language and Linguistic Theory* 14(3): 591–627; and for two excellent books that bring a lot of these sources together with comprehensive overview and analysis: Lisa Green's *African American English: A Linguistic Introduction* (Cambridge, UK: Cambridge University Press, 2002) and John R. Rickford's *African American Vernacular English: Features and Use, Evolution, and Educational Implications* (Oxford, UK: Blackwell, 1999).

   As mentioned, the last several examples of BL come from Barack Obama. He not only uses BL when speaking (as we outlined in detail in chapter 1), but his writings offer plenty of examples. The example of *multiple negation* ("You can't help folks that ain't gonna make it nohow") is from *Dreams from My Father*, page 136. The example of *negative inversion* ("Ain't nothing gonna change") is from page 248. And the generalization of *was* to use with plural and second person subjects ("Tell me we wouldn't be treated different if we was white") comes from page 74. While Obama usually presents his own speech without any distinctive features of BL, he uses the features generously while reporting other people's speech (these three features, and especially copula absence, seem to be his favorites).

7. A must read on this is Marcyliena Morgan's "The African American Speech Community: Reality and Sociolinguistics" in her edited book *Language and the Social Construction of Identity in Creole Situations*, (Los Angeles: Center for Afro-American Studies, UCLA, 1994, 121–148).

8. Black lexicon (words and phrases) goes way back, both in terms of scholarship and in terms of its African roots. Definitely check out Lorenzo Dow Turner's 1949 game-changing classic, *Africanisms in the Gullah Dialect* (Chicago: University of Chicago Press); Clarence Major's two collections of African American slang, the first from 1970 and his more recent update, *From Juba to Jive: A Dictionary of African-American*

Slang (New York & London: Penguin, 1994); Joey L. Dillard's *Lexicon of Black English* (New York: Seabury, 1977); Edith Folb's *Runnin' Down Some Lines: The Language and Culture of Black Teenagers* (Cambridge, MA: Harvard University Press, 1980); Joseph Holloway and W. Vass's *The African Heritage of American English* (Bloomington: University of Indiana Press, 1997); and Geneva Smitherman's more contemporary perspective in *Black Talk: Words and Phrases from the Hood to the Amen Corner* (Boston/New York: Houghton Mifflin, 1994 [2000]).

Check out the work that's been done on *signifyin* since the 1960s. It came out of folklore, intercultural communication, linguistic anthropology, and related fields: Roger Abraham's *Deep Down in the Jungle: Negro Narrative Folklore from the Streets of Philadelphia* (Chicago: Aldine, 1964)—you gotta wonder what Schoolly D, Beanie Sigel, and Freeway would say about this now, almost 50 years later! And this one, Thomas Kochman's "'Rapping' in the Black Ghetto," *Trans-Action*, February, 1969, pages 26–34; and this one by a sista scholar, Claudia Mitchell-Kernan's *Language Behavior in a Black Urban Community* (Berkeley: University of California, Language Behavior Research Laboratory, 1971); William Labov's *Language in the Inner City: Studies in the Black English Vernacular* (Philadelphia: University of Pennsylvania Press, 1972); Geneva Smitherman's "The Power of the Rap: The Black Idiom and the New Black Poetry" in *Twentieth Century Literature: A Scholarly and Critical Journal* (1973, 259–274) and *Talkin and Testifyin: The Language of Black America* (Houghton Mifflin, 1977; reissued, with revisions, Detroit: Wayne State University Press,1986); another sista scholar, Marcyliena Morgan's "Conversational Signifying: Grammar and Indirectness among African American Women" in Elinor Ochs, Emmanuel Schegloff, and Sandra Thompson's (eds.) *Grammar and Interaction* (Cambridge, UK: Cambridge University Press, 1996).

For two classic works on *playin the dozens*, a must-read is H. Rap Brown's "Street Talk" in Thomas Kochman's edited volume *Rappin' and Stylin' Out: Communication in Urban Black America* (Urbana: University of Illinois Press, 1972, 205–207); also, Roger Abraham's "Rapping and Capping: Black Talk as Art" in John Swzed's edited volume *Black America* (New York: Basic Books, 1970).

For classic *call and response* work, check out Jack Daniel and Geneva Smitherman's "How I Got Over: Communication Dynamics in the Black Community" in *Quarterly Journal of Speech 62*, February 1976; Geneva Smitherman's *Talkin and Testifyin: The Language of Black America* (Houghton Mifflin; reissued, with revisions, Detroit: Wayne State University Press, 1977[1986]); For an updated Hip Hop version of call and response, check out Imani Perry's *Prophets of the Hood: The Politics and Poetics of Hip Hop* (Durham, NC: Duke University Press, 2004) and H. Samy Alim's *Roc the Mic Right: The Language of Hip Hop Culture* (New York: Routledge, 2006).

In addition to Geneva Smitherman's *Talkin and Tesftifyin*, check out Cheryl Keyes's classic article, "Verbal Art Performance in Rap Music: The Conversation of the 80s" in *Folklore Forum 17(2)*, Fall 1984, pages 143–152.

These Hip Hop practices extend the Black Oral Tradition and have gone global so kids thousands of miles apart are adopting and adapting them in their local social worlds. Check out Dawn Norfleet's *Hip-Hop Culture in New York City: The Role of Verbal Music Performance in Defining a Community* (PhD dissertation, Columbia University, 1997); Michael Newman's "'Not dogmatically / It's all about me': Ideological Conflict in a High School Rap Crew" in *Taboo: A Journal of Culture and Education*, 2001; H. Samy Alim's *Roc the Mic Right: The Language of Hip Hop culture* (New York: Routledge, 2006) and H. Samy Alim, Awad Ibrahim and Alastair Pennycook's edited volume, *Global Linguistic Flows: Hip Hop Cultures, Youth Identities, and the Politics of Language* (New York/London: Routledge, 2009).

See Arthur Spears's "African-American Language Use: Ideology and So-Called Obscenity" in Salikoko Mufwene, John R. Rickford, Guy Bailey, and John Baugh (eds.) *African American English: Structure, History, and Usage* (New York: Routledge, 1998, 226–250) and Marcyliena Morgan's "More Than a Mood or an Attitude: Discourse and Verbal Genres in African-American Culture" in the same book, pages 251–281.

9. The word *Ebonics* was thrust back into the spotlight in 2010 when the Drug Enforcement Administration posted a job announcement for linguists fluent in "Ebonics." Check out this article by H. Samy Alim and Imani Perry at: http://www.thegrio.com/opinion/why-the-deas-embrace-of-ebonics-is-lost-in-translation.php. The term *Ebonics* was coined by psychologist Robert Williams during a private meeting of Black linguists, educators and other scholars attending a 1973 conference on language and the urban child. Williams details the circumstances of this meeting and his and these other Black scholars' rationale for preferring the term *Ebonics* in his 1975 edited publication of the conference papers, *Ebonics: The True Language of Black Folks* (St. Louis: Institute of Black Studies). The term made its national debut in 1997 when the Oakland School Board passed a resolution that teachers take the language of their students (those for whom Black Language was their primary language) into account when teaching "standard English." While the rest of the world went apeshit—to be blunt about it—linguists were like, "Here we go again." The Linguistic Society of America tried to quell the madness with their own resolution, which stated: "The systematic and expressive nature of the grammar and pronunciation patterns of the African American vernacular has been established by numerous scientific studies over the past thirty years. Characterizations of Ebonics as 'slang,' 'mutant,' 'lazy,' 'defective,' 'ungrammatical,' or 'broken English' are incorrect and demeaning....There is evidence from Sweden, the U.S., and other countries that speakers of other varieties can be aided in their learning of the standard variety by pedagogical approaches which recognize the legitimacy of the other varieties of a language. From this perspective, the Oakland School Board's decision to recognize the vernacular of African American students in teaching them Standard English is *linguistically and pedagogically sound.*" [our emphasis]. For an excellent breakdown of Oakland's and the Linguistic Society of America's resolutions, read John Baugh's *Beyond Ebonics: Linguistic Pride and Racial Prejudice* (New York: Oxford University Press, 2000). And for the best, comprehensive discussion of what Oakland was *actually* trying to do—from scholars and the teachers and school board members themselves—a must-read is Theresa Perry and Lisa Delpit's *The Real Ebonics Debate: Power, Language, and the Education of African-American Children* (Boston: Beacon Press, 1998).

   Linguists were used to the racist vitriol that accompanies any effort on the part of educators to recognize Black Language as a legitimate variety. Two decades earlier in Ann Arbor, Michigan, what became known as the "Black English case" (*Martin Luther King Jr. Elementary School Children v. Ann Arbor School District Board*) was the talk of the nation. Geneva Smitherman served as chief consultant and expert witness for more than two years of litigation on behalf of 15 Black, economically deprived children residing in a low-income housing project. Instead of incorrectly placing children in learning disability and speech pathology classes, Smitherman and others argued that teachers should take the language variety of their students into account and use it to help students acquire "the standard." Though "Black English" was not found to be a barrier to students' leaning per se, the uninformed and racist institutional response to it was. The full story is too long for an endnote. For a full breakdown of the case with expert linguists, lawyers, and literary figures, definitely check out Geneva Smitherman's edited volume *Black English and the Education of Black Children and Youth: Proceedings of the National Invitational Symposium on the King Decision* (Detroit: Wayne State University, Center for Black Studies, 1981) and also her "What Go Round Come Round: *King* in Perspective," *Harvard Educational Review*, February 1981, pages 40–56.

   One reason we wrote this current book is to help prevent the next 20-year firestorm and to be about the serious business of educating Black and other linguistically marginalized youth.

10. Freudian slip? Nah, surely she meant facial *expressions*.

11. Notice how Black ways of speaking are subtly framed as something to "get away with." Note also the troubling view of Black parenting that creeps into many of these conversations.

The fact that her students' ways of speaking are linked to a different culture of communication altogether (one that values certain ways of speaking that may be at odds with White, upper-middle-class ways of speaking) is never considered.

12. Of course, White America's mapping of negative characteristics onto the language of socially marginalized groups is not unique. Studies have shown that dominant cultures around the world do the same thing, puttin other people's language down in order to lift theirs up. This attribution of negative characteristics due to cultural differences has been noted frequently in studies of intercultural communication. For pioneering work on this, see John Gumperz's *Discourse Strategies* and his *Language and Social Identity* (Cambridge, UK: Cambridge University Press, 1982, for both books).

13. We don't mean to have fun at the teacher's expense. Valley Girl Talk has actually been studied by sociolinguists. If you're not familiar with this kind of talk, you should check out Robert MacNeil and William Cran's *Do You Speak American? A Companion to the PBS Television Series* (New York: Nan A. Talese/Doubleday, 2005). In the case of this particular teacher, I mean, like, how many times can you, like, say the word *like* in like the same sentence, riiight? In all seriousness, though, the American public has made teachers out to be monsters in recent years. Our goal here is not to contribute to that but to see ourselves in that teacher—hope you're lookin in the mirror as you read this.

14. For the technical linguistic and ethnographic details, check H. Samy Alim's *You Know My Steez: An Ethnographic and Sociolinguistic Study of Styleshifting in a Black American Speech Community* (Durham, NC: Duke University Press, 2004).

15. Nobody really puts this better than John Wideman: "There is no single register [style] of African American speech. And it's not words and intonations, it's a whole attitude about speech that has historical rooting. It's not a phenomenon that you can isolate and reduce to linguistic characteristics. It has to do with the way a culture conceives of the people inside of that culture. It has to do with a whole complicated protocol of silences and speech, and how you use speech in ways other than directly to communicate information. And it has to do with, certainly, the experiences that the people in the speech situation bring into the encounter. What's fascinating to me about African American speech is its spontaneity, the requirement that you not only have a repertoire of vocabulary or syntactic devices/constructions, but you come prepared to do something in an attempt to meet the person on a level that both uses the language, mocks the language, and recreates the language." That's from his piece, "Frame and Dialect: The Evolution of the Black Voice in American Literature" in *American Poetry Review* 5.5 (Sept.–Oct. 1976), pages 34–37.

16. See especially the work of Carol D. Lee, Shirley Brice Heath, Keith Gilyard, Elaine Richardson, Ernest Morrell, and Maisha T. Winn. They have produced some of the most critical work. Most recently, check Gilyard's *True to the Language Game: African American Discourse, Cultural Politics, and Pedagogy* (Routledge, 2011), which contains a chapter that examines the political discourse surrounding the rise of Barack Obama. A valuable resource for those teaching students in high school and first-year college courses is Geneva Smitherman and Victor Villanueva's *Language Diversity in the Classroom: From Intention to Practice* (Carbondale: Southern Illinois University Press, 2003). The work offers a historical perspective on the "Students' Right to Their Own Language" policy of the National Council of Teachers of English (NCTE) and the Conference on College Composition and Communication (CCCC) and advocates language and literacy teaching practices that promote linguistic diversity. The collection was motivated by the dismal results of a national survey of teacher language attitudes conducted by the CCCC Language Policy Committee, chaired by Smitherman.

17. Dell Hymes was one of the most influential linguists and anthropologists of the twentieth century. Check this source for his early theoretical work on ethnographic approaches to language and culture: *Foundations in Sociolinguistics: An Ethnographic Approach* (Philadelphia: University of Pennsylvania Press, 1974). The handouts borrow generously from his work.

18. Geneva Smitherman's *Black Talk: Words and Phrases from the Hood to the Amen Corner* (Boston/New York: Houghton Mifflin) was released in 1994 and 2000. The next handout borrows heavily from her work and down-to-earth explanation of complicated methods.

19. In terms of lexicon and its relation to local cultures, for example, the students documented the use of the term *rogue*. The term is a localized example of *semantic inversion* that highlights a very specific regionality, as it is used only within their 2.5-square-mile city. Folks use it to describe those who possess a nonconformist, street ethic, but it's also used more broadly to refer to friends and associates (like the terms, *homie*, *potna*, etc.). Semantic inversion involves flippin a bad meaning into a good one. So, rather than follow conventional meanings of *rogue* (for example, in the way that US foreign policy under George W. Bush defined states that did not conform to the will of the United States as rogue states), they create new ones, used for those who don't bow down to the demands of unjust authorities, those who make a way outta no way when the cards are stacked against em.

20. See John Baugh's piece, "Linguistic Profiling," in Sinfree Makoni, Geneva Smitherman, Arnetha F. Ball, and Arthur K. Spears (eds.) *Black Linguistics: Language, Politics and Society in Africa and the Americas* (London: Routledge, 2003, 155–168).

21. *American Tongues* was produced and directed by Louis Alvarez and Andrew Kolker (New York: Center for New American Media, 1986). The film is one of the best documentaries ever produced about language in the United States and remains one of the best teaching tools in the game. While its attempts to address linguistic prejudice are laudatory, a more critical approach is needed in order to serve the needs of marginalized communities.

22. Walt Wolfram has been on the cutting edge of research on marginalized language varieties for the better part of five decades. It should be noted that his well-meaning comments here were not at all controversial to the majority of sociolinguists when *American Tongues* was produced; with some notable exceptions, such as Geneva Smitherman, James Sledd, and a few others, his comments were par for the sociolinguistics course.

23. Norman Fairclough, a leader in the critical language approach, refers to traditional approaches as merely "dressing up inequality as diversity." Check out the intro to his classic edited volume in this arena, simply titled *Critical Language Awareness* (London & New York: Longman, 1992). Also check out the chapter by Hilary Janks and R. Ivanic, "Critical Language Awareness and Emancipatory Discourse" in the same book. These works have been useful in the formulation of our approach here in the United States. Also, Alastair Pennycook's work has been invaluable—begin with his already classic text, *Critical Applied Linguistics: A Critical Introduction* (Mahwah, NJ: Lawrence Erlbaum Associates, 2001).

24. David Corson's overview of the critical approach out of Britain is extremely useful in this sense. Check it out: *Language Policy in Schools: A Resource for Teachers and Administrators* (Mahwah, NJ/London: Lawrence Erlbaum Associates, 1999).

25. Shoutout to Ana Celia Zentella, Laura Graham, and other members of the Society for Linguistic Anthropology's Task Force/Committee on Language and Social Justice for bangin on these issues. Shoutout to John R. Rickford and the Linguistic Society of America on Sweden and Norway. Thanks to Luis O. Reyes for bringing the news of Perú's new multilingual law. Also, if you wanna see what other models look like, check out Nancy Hornberger's edited volume, *Continua of Biliteracy: An Ecological Framework for Educational Policy, Research, and Practice in Multilingual Settings* (Cleveland: Multilingual Matters, 2003). It's got leading scholars from around the world offering multilingual, democratic approaches to language and education.

Index

Information in figures, tables, and notes is indicated by *f, t,* and *n*.

A

Abernathy, Ralph, 74
acoustic identity, 61n27
African American Language. *See* Black
    Language
African Holocaust, 104, 127n32
Ahlin, Elizabeth, 105
Akon, 145
"aks," 37–38
Alexander, Michelle, 89n23
Alim, H. Samy, 9, 26n9, 28n15, 28n16, 56,
    61n27, 110, 128n41, 128n50, 128n51,
    129n71, 163n41, 164n54, 164n60,
    165n63, 175, 193n6, 194n8, 195n9,
    196n14
American Dream, 81
American Tongues (film), 185–186, 190, 193n3
anaphora, 29n27
Ann Arbor, Michigan, 195n9
Arrested Development, 113
articulate
    bi- and multilingualism and, 45–48
    as exceptionalism, 32–34, 41–44
    as gatekeeping mechanism, 52–56
    Obama as, 34–39
    paternalism and, 48–52
    policing and language and, 34–39
    use of, 39–40
Asante, Molefi Kete, 83
Ashton Filmer, Alice, 61n27
Asian Americans, 46, 61n28
"ask," 37–38
assimilation, 167
Audacity of Hope, The (Obama), 57, 75
audience
    copula and, 9
    styleshifting and, 13

B

Baia, Ashley, 18
Bailey, Guy, 26n7
"Ballot or the Bullet, The" (Malcolm X), 82
Banner, David, 137, 160
"Baracka Flacka Flame," 121, 129n71
battlin, 176–177
Baugh, John, 26n7, 56, 62n40, 186, 195n9
"becoming Black," 14, 28n23
"been," stressed, 170
benign neglect, 72, 89n22
Ben's Chili Bowl, 7–10
Bercovitch, Sacvan, 77, 91n36
*Between Barack and a Hard Place: Racism and
    White Denial in the Age of Obama* (Wise),
    33
Biden, Joseph, 31, 34, 59n1, 59n8, 61n24
Big Boi, 160–161, 166n180
bilinguals, 45–48
Birther movement, 22
Black folk theory, 48–52
Black Freedom Struggle, 73, 90n27
Black Language
    Africanisms, 127n23
    in Ann Arbor case, 195n9
    ask vs. aks, 37–38
    as "baby talk," 49
    "becoming controversial," 121–122, 125
    complexity of, 169–171
    copula absence in, 8–9, 170
    creativity in, 175–178
    early scholarship on, 49
    in education, 171–174
    flexibility in, 175–178
    as inferior, 169
    lexicon, 193n8, 197n19
    in Oakland case, 171, 195n9